The South Pacific Narratives
of Robert Louis Stevenson
and Jack London

Also available from Bloomsbury

Contemporary Caribbean Writing and Deleuze, Lorna Burns
Sexuality and the Erotic in the Fiction of Joseph Conrad, Jeremy Hawthorn

The South Pacific Narratives of Robert Louis Stevenson and Jack London

Race, Class, Imperialism

Lawrence Phillips

Bloomsbury Literary Studies

B L O O M S B U R Y
LONDON • NEW DELHI • NEW YORK • SYDNEY

Bloomsbury Academic

An imprint of Bloomsbury Publishing Plc

50 Bedford Square
London
WC1B 3DP
UK

1385 Broadway
New York
NY 10018
USA

www.bloomsbury.com

Bloomsbury is a registered trade mark of Bloomsbury Publishing Plc

First published 2012
Paperback edition first published 2013

British Library Cataloguing-in-Publication Data
A catalogue record for this book is available from the British Library.

ISBN: HB: 978-1-4411-9956-0
PB: 978-1-4411-9956-0
ePDF: 978-1-4411-9928-7
ePUB: 978-1-4411-7338-6

Library of Congress Cataloging-in-Publication Data
Phillips, Lawrence (Lawrence Alfred), 1966–
The South Pacific narratives of Robert Louis Stevenson and Jack London: race, class, imperialism/Lawrence Phillips.
p. cm. – (Continuum literary studies)
Includes bibliographical references and index.
ISBN 978-1-4411-9956-0 (hardcover: alk. paper) –
ISBN 978-1-4411-9928-7 (ebookpdf: alk. paper) –
ISBN 978-1-4411-7338-6 (ebookepub: alk. paper)
1. Stevenson, Robert Louis, 1850–1894–Criticism and interpretation.
2. London, Jack, 1876–1916–Criticism and interpretation.
3. Islands of the Pacific–In literature.
4. Oceania–In literature. 5. Imperialism in literature. I. Title.

PR5496.P48 2012
823´.809–dc23

2012005163

Typeset by Newgen Imaging Systems Pvt Ltd, Chennai, India
Printed and bound by CPI Group (UK) Ltd, Croydon, CR0 4YY

MIX
Paper from
responsible sources
FSC® C013604

Contents

Acknowledgements   vi

1   Introduction   1
2   'Race', Class and Imperialism in Stevenson's *The Amateur Emigrant*   19
3   Jack London's *The People of the Abyss*: Socialism, Imperialism
    and the Bourgeois Ethnographer   45
4   Death, Disease and Paradise: A Parable of Imperial Expansion   67
5   The Inequities of Trade: Adventure Narratives, Ethics
    and Imperial Commerce in Robert Louis Stevenson's *The Wrecker*   93
6   The Indignity of Labour: Jack London's *Adventure*
    and Plantation Labour in the Solomon Islands   133
7   Fragments of Empire, Fractured Identities   159

Afterword   193
Bibliography   197
Index   209

Acknowledgements

This book has had a long gestation and like all long projects it has accumulated a number of key intellectual debts. I would like to thank everyone who was good and patient enough to let me bend their ear on the subject of the colonial South Pacific, Robert Louis Stevenson and Jack London. More substantial debts are owed to Laura Chrisman, Marcus Wood, Stephen Fender, Rod Edmond, David Richards, David Rose and, especially, Helen Carr. More personal support has been provided without reservation from my family, Laila, Justin and Edward.

During the course of writing this book I published numerous articles some of which drew upon the preliminary results of my research. Those which feature in this book are listed below. I would like to thank the editors and publishers for permission to reproduce elements of those works here.

'The Canker of Empire: Colonialism, Autobiography and the Representation of Illness—Jack London and Robert Louis Stevenson in the Marquesas', in *English Association Annual Series of Essays & Studies, 1999: Postcolonial Criticism and Theory*, Laura Chrisman and Benita Parry (eds), Cambridge: Brewer, 2000, 115–32.

'The Indignity of Labour: Jack London's *Adventure* and Plantation Labour in the Solomon Islands', *Jack London Journal*, No. 6, 1999, 175–205.

'The Bourgeois Artist as Social Critic: Discourses of Class, "Race" and Colonialism in Robert Louis Stevenson's *The Amateur Emigrant*' in *Race & Class*, 46.3 (January – March 2005), 39–54.

'Jack London and the East End: Socialism, Imperialism, and the Bourgeois Ethnographer', in Lawrence Phillips (ed.) *A Mighty Mass of Brick and Smoke: Victorian and Edwardian Representations of London*, Amsterdam and New York: Rodopi, 2007, 213–34.

'Colonial Culture in the Pacific in Robert Louis Stevenson and Jack London', *Race & Class*, 48.3 (January – March 2007), 63–82.

Introduction

Robert Louis Stevenson and Jack London

The South Pacific writing of Robert Louis Stevenson and Jack London is a remarkable body of work through which one can explore the ambivalences of class, gender and nationality during the apogee of the imperial era at the end of the nineteenth and the beginning of the twentieth centuries. It is a body of writing in which attitudes and beliefs formed at home are brought face to face with the extremes of colonial practice as the West completed its foreclosure of what remained of the 'blank spaces of the earth' to use Joseph Conrad's memorable phrase from *Heart of Darkness*. Their work highlights the historical distinctiveness of colonial practices in the South Pacific and the cultural intersection between imperial discourses, the *fin de siècle* and the emergence of modernism.

Both authors were major public figures in their day, but are now strangely sidelined in most literary canons. Stevenson, a bourgeois author acutely sensitized to the suffering of others was a victim of the backlash against Victorian culture in the 1920s, not least because of the excessive hagiography his memory was subjected to following his premature death; London, an early – if ultimately ambivalent – class warrior best remembered for his work on the Yukon gold rush apparently of too narrow a range to be taken seriously as a literary artist. Of course, that both enjoyed huge commercial success in their lifetimes might also have served to discourage serious study; an ambivalence anticipated by contemporary jealousies and a sometimes equivocal critical reception. A further peculiarity lies in the critical neglect specifically of their South Pacific writing. Not all of it might be said to be aesthetically important – a particular issue for readers of some of London's primarily commercial efforts – but as chroniclers of a new American imperialism that would ultimately eclipse the older European empires, their cultural and historical significance in relation to the development of the relationship between the United States and Europe in the twentieth century is beyond question. How often is the phrase 'white man's burden' from Rudyard Kipling's jingoistic poem of the same title taken as the quintessential expression of European imperialism, when it was addressed to and concerned the emergence of the United States as an imperial power after the European model following the dubious war with Spain in 1898? Then there is the interstitial nature of the period itself. The work by Stevenson and London that this study concerns itself with was written and published between 1880 and 1916; a period dominated in most cultural histories by the *fin de siècle* and the emergence of Modernism and in social histories by the somnolent sigh of the late Victorian/Edwardian Indian summer giving way to the horror and social upheaval presaged by the First World War. The period itself is conceived as transitory and is no doubt contributory to the marginal significance afforded to two authors who were literary lions of their day. This neglect perhaps stems from the difficulty of fitting either into this neat script. They are neither easily related to the popular discourses of *fin de siècle* decadence nor ostensibly to the experimentation of some early Modernist writers. They are of their moment and suffer from the historical squeeze afforded by conflicted, thence complex, periods. As David Trotter writes of the Edwardian period but with equal relevance to the longer period from the 1880s as the roots of Modernism are dug ever deeper into the Victorian era:

> The Edwardian period would seem to have quite a lot going for it, as a period. However it is defined, it is short, and not lacking in political and socio-economic excitements: National Insurance, Suffragettes, an armaments race, the strange death of liberal England. What more could one possible want? And yet the feeling persists that, as far as the evolution of British culture is concerned, the Edwardian period was something of an interregnum, or a pause for breath. Historiographically, a bypass that connects the theme park of *fin de siècle* decadence and renovation to the Modernist metropolis, and few commentators spare as much as a glance for the unprepossessing market town that carries them around. (Trotter 2001 12)

Despite the fact that Stevenson, dying in 1894, wrote all his work in the nineteenth century, and London, dying in 1916, wrote much of his work in the twentieth century, they both experienced and participated in an interrelated historical, geographical and social milieu. In outline, this milieu includes political and cultural rapprochement between the United States and Great Britain; the USA's rapid industrial growth and colonial influence; the emergence of a particular variant of Social Darwinist-inspired racial nationalism which – for want of a better phrase – I will dub pan Anglo-Saxonism; and, of course, a shared experience of what amounted to a 'scramble' for the Pacific islands between the USA, Britain, France and Germany analogous to the 'scramble for Africa' between the latter three powers. It is no coincidence that these countries would find themselves in devastating conflict just a few decades later in the First World War.

Much as both Stevenson and London and their respective nations were drawn into and caught up in these issues, marked differences in national perspective must not be underestimated. While they often use a similar vocabulary in relation to class, 'race' and colonialism, their intent can be deceptively at variance and particularly revealing. 'For although two nations use the same words and read the same books,' observed Stevenson, 'intercourse is not conducted by the dictionary. The business of life is not carried on by words, but in set phrases, each with a special and almost slang signification' (*Scotland to Silverado* 113). Stevenson's observation gestures towards the complexities that such semantic disruption implies, revealing a deeper cultural and, thence, experiential disjunction. Nor can one simply ignore the chronological distance between the two writers. While this is not wide historically as I noted above, in personal terms they are certainly of different generations. In many ways, Stevenson, whose writing I shall discuss from his departure for the United States in 1879, experienced residual and emergent historical and cultural processes – to employ Raymond Williams' terminology – that had undergone some realignment by the time of London's sojourn in the East End during 1902. I do not intend to create some arbitrary teleology here, but part of the value of the Stevenson/London comparison is to reveal such disjunctions, developments and, most importantly, continuities that reflect differing cultural and national outlooks. By doing so it becomes possible to begin to trace those realignments in relation to class, colonialism and ethnicity that are in emergent form in Stevenson's writing, yet highly developed by the time London made his comparable physical and textual journey some 20 years later.

America and Britain

One overriding issue that spans the entire period of Stevenson's and London's writing is the emergence of the United States as a major economic and military power. The younger nation had moved further away from the Old Country and the ways of Europe than many contemporary commentators of either nation were perhaps willing to concede. Yet as this industrial and political expansion proceeded it increasingly brought the United States into close ideological and practical alignment with the empires of the Old World, even if this is expressed in terms of commercial and political competition. In many ways the old models and frictions still prevailed: for Americans, their particular form of constitutional republicanism was seen as a considerable advance in personal and political freedom over that enjoyed under Britain's antiquated system of constitutional monarchy and traditions. The economic and political aspirations of the vast majority of its people that were so well met in their own country were, Americans argued, in Britain fatally constrained by conservative traditions. Yet as Leonard Reissman observes: 'Americans have been especially predisposed to social, economic, and political conservatism' (Reissman 22). A particular point of contrast being the overt class stratification in Britain contrasted with the American belief in social equality. Arguably this is more a matter of a lack of consciousness rather than a realized achievement, as Reissman continues: 'This anti-radical spirit and philosophy, then, also worked to keep Americans from becoming conscious of class. Class was an alien category that most Americans did not want to recognize or use' (Reissman 22). That this belief perhaps conceals a closer similarity than contrast can be inferred from American respect for the cultural accomplishments of the Old World and the prestige of the European – particularly the British – empires remained. As the historian Milton Plesuer argues: 'The Old World was at one and the same time alluring and repulsive to Americans' (Plesuer 126). Even as late as 1913, Ezra Pound asserted that he felt compelled to move to London because 'it was the cultural capital of the United States, moving from the periphery to the centre' (Carr 213). For Britons, America was often portrayed as an immature offspring, impetuous and naive from the perspective of the condescending sophistication of its parent as can be seen from Kipling's laudatory poem celebrating American acquisition of the Philippine Islands from Spain, 'The White Man's Burden' (1899) mentioned earlier, in which the United States is welcomed to a new maturity worthy of 'The judgement of your peers.' Americans were highly sensitized to such condescension. 'One American newspaper,' observes Plesuer, 'felt that England regarded the United States as an uncouth upstart' (Pleseur 126).

This is, of course, to deal in contemporary generalizations and stereotyping to some extent, although it is best not to overlook the power of such views at any time. Moreover, there was little to choose between the great metropolitan centres of the United States and Europe in term of complexity, industrialization or, indeed, the misery of the urban working classes and the destitute. This was also evident in terms of cultural sophistication evidenced by the import of talent from Europe to supply American tastes, even if it awaited the emergence of

Modernism focused on New York and Chicago before America could be said to have been a major contributor to an international cultural movement of significance. Indeed, one might note that the rise of the great industrial cities following in the wake of the Industrial Revolution was little more than a century old as a phenomenon, so transatlantic comparisons in fact imply less of a historical disjunction than might at first glance appear to be the case. Stevenson certainly had little to say on the score of relative development as he passed through the economic and transportation hubs of New York and Chicago other than the unsettling contradiction between the rudeness and kindness of their inhabitants. Indeed, even after going 'out upon the New York streets, spying for things foreign' he compares the city with another industrial and transportation hub, Liverpool (*Scotland to Silverado* 95). London also saw little to distinguish the East Coast conurbations from their European counterparts. For him they held an equal horror, as his daughter and biographer Joan London recalled: 'He hated and feared New York. When he had become a successful author he went there only when it was absolutely necessary and, acutely aware of what the city meant in term of suffering and deprivation, he never stayed longer than business demanded' (Joan London 83). The comparison is underlined when, while crossing the Atlantic in 1902 on the way to the East End, he wrote to Anna Strunsky: 'A week from To-day [sic] I shall be in London. I shall then have two days in which to make my arrangements and sink down out of sight in order to view the Coronation [of Edward VII] from the standpoint of the London beasts. That's all they are – beasts – if they are anything like the slum people of New York – beasts shot through with stray flashes of divinity' (*Letters* 303–4).

If the East Coast cities were nothing other than absolutely modern in their relative sophistication and potential for human misery, American feelings of cultural insecurity and European condescension might appear to be founded on little more than the stereotyping already mentioned. Yet even stereotypes have some connection to cultural actuality, however perverse or abstracted that connection may have become. Sander Gilman suggests that stereotypes are 'part of our way of dealing with the instabilities of our perception of the world' (Gilman 18), so European condescension might be said to betray an uneasiness at the United States' rapid accumulation of economic and political power, while American insecurity might betray a sense of not having distinguished themselves as far in cultural terms as they had in more material accomplishments. Such popularly held attitudes represent varying degrees of historical distortion and are related to another rather amorphous concept – the frontier, a culturally significant national 'idea' for both Americans and Britons.

The Significance of the Frontier in British and American History

For Americans, the frontier was (and is) a powerful enabling national myth, but its crudities and lawlessness have also been a source of cultural embarrassment. A vestige of this persisted even as late as the early 1900s. Indeed, for the early leaders of the new republic, the 'frontier' and the people who settled there represented an essentially uncivilized zone, virtually ungovernable with, ironically, the potential for insurrection, even revolution. It is no accident that the plot of many popular Westerns pivots on the extension of the federal government's writ to newly settled regions. As the historian Gregory H. Nobles observes: 'Anglo-American writers had commonly described frontier folk as the dregs of [an] otherwise decent society, a deviant and dangerous element hardly worthy of tolerance' (Nobles 103). But increasingly through the nineteenth century the idea of the frontier had also come to shape American attitudes towards class. As Reissman argues: 'The frontier . . . as a social value fitted neatly into the dominant tones of individualism, self-achievement, and social equality that were so characteristic of the American value system. Like the value of anti-aristocracy, the frontier belief served to delay the recognition of class differences' (Reissman 16). By the turn of the nineteenth century congruent with the emergence of the United States as an Old World imperial power following the war with Spain; this belief in a classless individualism existed side by side with a xenophobic class consciousness in response to mass immigration. Like the early elite of the republic this can be discerned among the educated WASP elite of the Eastern states at the end of the nineteenth century in response to anxieties towards mass immigration of decidedly non-Anglo-Saxon origins. As Helen Carr observes: 'The United States was, after all, territorially, demographically, and economically a different country from a hundred years earlier, and many of the East-Coast intelligentsia were not at all sure they liked it, particularly not the influx of supposedly ill-educated and culturally dubious immigrants' (Carr 214). Such anxieties reflect a powerful class discourse that is related to contemporary fears of the urban poor on both sides of the Atlantic in which class could masquerade as race and race as class. While the frontier could represent pioneering vigour and – in popularized Social Darwinist terms – racial triumph and virility, it could also signify violence, ignorance and an element of anarchy to Americans of the longer-settled regions as well as Europeans who could easily be displaced onto the culturally alien slums of the most modern of cities. As John Marriott argues: 'Within the orbit of modernity, poverty, slavery and colonial expansion came to be perceived as aberrant; the poor, slaves and colonial subjects as defiant. Progress thus acted as an antithetical articulating principle, as a result of which distinctly dystopian visions of degeneration, decline, failure and evil gained currency' as we shall see from Stevenson's and London's Pacific writing (Marriott 12). Upton Sinclair's novel depicting the squalor and exploitation of the immigrant working classes of Chicago *The Jungle* (1906) is a powerful example of a how a different type of uncivilized zone could be imagined within an otherwise 'civilized' context – the jungle projected onto an urban setting. The jungle suggests an absence of civilization, of the dominance of nature, whereas the frontier conjures ideas of a vast, open and empty space eminently ripe for taming and settlement, the jungle conveys ideas of density, darkness, horror and anxiety, which Conrad exploits to the full in the analogy he draws between the view of urban London from the Thames and the jungle from the river Congo in *Heart of Darkness* (1899). The jungle is readily associated with an overseas, explicitly colonial, frontier and the presumption of racial difference. The jungle is after all not 'native' geography to Europe or North America, but an exotic alien environment. Yet, just as the burden of blame for the dangers of the frontier in American were displaced onto the 'savage' Indians rather than settlers, so responsibility of the appalling conditions of the urban slums was shifted from rack-renting landlords, exploitative employers and government neglect to the assumed racial and cultural degeneration of the poor.

The frontier in North America also continued to resonate as a popular idea in Britain and in a similar way it was presumed to have energized American culture. Certainly, even before the publication of F. J. Turner's seminal essay of 1893 'The Significance of the Frontier in American History', a more positive conception of the frontier as constitutive of the strength and values inherent in the 'American character' had long been in the ascendancy as a national mission and cultural rebirth (Turner 271–9). For example, the slogan 'Go west, young man, go west and grow up with the country' was given currency through Horace Greeley's *New York Tribune* from 1841. Yet it was also a conceptualization in which the British saw themselves sharing; the frontier *topos* in this instance reinforcing a sense of racial and cultural continuation. Richard Heindel in his 1968 study, *The American Impact on Great Britain, 1898–1914*, emphasizes this sense of shared cultural imaginary:

> The United States had been a frontier to Great Britain, and just one significance
> of the frontier in America had been a fertile clue, *mutatis mutandis*, one may

reflect that meditations on the hypothesis may well wander eastward, beyond the seaboard states, on across the Atlantic Ocean, and, in point of time, on beyond the first century and a half of plantations in America, perhaps, the more obvious period of European repercussions. (Heindel 3)

Stevenson's fascination with this energetic, pioneering image is significant in this respect: 'For many years America was to me a sort of promised land. "Westward the march of empire holds its way;" the race for the moment young; what has been and what is we imperfectly know; what is to be yet lies beyond the flight of our imaginations' (*Scotland to Silverado* 89). The play on the 'youth' of the United States nicely demonstrates the cultural condescension noted earlier, but the misquotation from Berkeley's 'On the Prospect of Planting Arts and Learning in America', which in fact reads 'Westward the course of empire takes its way' is significant. Berkeley's 'Takes its way' implies *British* expansion with its American 'colonies' acting as its proxy in the expansion of the empire across the continent – an ambition taken up later by the internal colonial discourse of the United States with some vigour. Stevenson's 'holds its way', however, is rather more ambivalent. While hold could of course mean direct physical influence, seen from the context of late-nineteenth-century Anglo-American relations it more likely implies cultural hegemony, especially from the pen of a British author. Yet Stevenson's evocation of a sense of 'racial family' and echoes of 'manifest destiny' favoured by cultural and racial theorists on both sides of the Atlantic is so in keeping with the contemporary context of this sentiment that it seems likely that the misquotation was either deliberate or subconsciously altered. Stevenson's use of this discursive register – 'the race is still young' – stresses a cultural kinship which transcends national boundaries for Stevenson as a Briton – 'America was to me a sort of promised land' – even to the extent of implying that there exists a single Anglo-American cultural empire of which the United States is the youngest offshoot. At the turn of the nineteenth century, such shared mythologies were invariably expressed in racial terms. Thence for him American had been a 'promised land' and 'our imaginations' clearly encompasses both 'Anglo-Saxon' Americans and Britons.

'Race' in the century between 1850 and the beginnings of systematic decolonization following the end of the Second World War was a widely used and very influential analytical concept in the West with a number of possible connotations. It could designate an organic species or subspecies or variety, as in the subtitle of Darwin's *On the Origins of Species by means of Natural Selection, or the Preservation of favoured races in the Struggle for Life* (1859), or a human group, usually regionalized, such as the 'European race'. Equally, in a formulation influenced by theories of cultural development that collapsed national traits and institutions into 'racial' characteristics, it could designate a single nation, such as the 'English race'. Closer to the modern – and bitterly contested – meaning is the 'scientific' categorization based ostensibly on superficial physical characteristics such as 'Negroid' and 'Caucasoid'. Each of these perspectives is at work in Stevenson's sentence, but uppermost is a particularly subjective deployment of racial congruence: the call to broad racial categories that had been derived from the categorizations of philology such as 'Celtic' or rather more broadly 'Aryan', but here especially 'Anglo-Saxon'. As Mike Hawkins observes, such notions were also 'hierarchically arranged according to a scale of physical, mental or moral value' (Hawkins 5) closely aligned with class. This sense of shared cultural and racial heritage could prove an irresistible allure to Americans drawing them eastward, quite as much as the frontier mythos attracted the imaginations of the British. Alternatively, perceptions of the British Empire could simultaneously conjure visions of the despotic oppressor of the Revolution and the war of 1812, a great power and competitor to be feared and resisted, but also in some sense reflecting racial glory on Americans as well as Britons an emblem of an intensely intimate and mutually supportive tie between the two nations. London, writing to his friend Cloudesley Johns towards the end of 1899 about the Boer War, strenuously insists on the overwhelming importance of this cultural, economic and racial – 'blood' – interdependence: 'The day England goes under, that day sees sealed the doom of the United States. It's the Anglo-Saxon people against the world, and economics at the foundation of the whole business; but said economics [are] only a manifestation of the blood differentiations which have come down from the hoary past' (*London 1* 123). Even more than Stevenson who merely implied that Americans and Britons were culturally and racially one, London directly creates an image of an embattled single people, the 'Anglo-Saxon people', suggests an intensification of the sentiment in the late 1890s compared with Stevenson's observation in the late 1880s in the face of the stiff economic competition that would contribute to the causes of the First World War a few decades later. However, the sentiment can be found throughout the second half of the nineteenth century even when contemplating the grimmest urban poverty as in Thomas Beames' *The Rookeries of London* (1850):

> True, thoughts of Rookeries recall, if not old Saxon times, yet times when we Anglo-Saxons were one people, ere the First and Second Charles had driven out the stern Republicanism destined to bear such fruit in the next century, ere

the traveller's gig broke down in a Cheshire village, and a night's lodging at the hospitable home of a stranger gave him a bride, and that bride gave the world George Washington, – ere in a word, the Anglo-Saxon name, language and string manly spirit had become common to vast nations in both hemispheres. (Beames 3–4)

For both authors, the direct experience of the other's country revealed the strain that lay beneath such abstractions, which materially affected their personal and literary response to the South Pacific.

The Pacific and Colonialism

The colonial history of the Pacific Islands begins with the early explorers and the published accounts of their voyages, particularly Cook's and Bougainville's expeditions and Joseph Banks' account of Cook's first voyage (Rennie 83–108). Such accounts were replete with favourable reports of the climate and picturesque geography of the high islands, and of the attractiveness and apparent sexual freedom of Polynesian women and society. This in turn inaugurated in the 1760s and the 1770s a fascination among Europeans who represented the islands of the South Pacific as not only inhabited by 'noble savages' in a state of prelapsarian sexual innocence, but also something darker. It was these voyages that also introduced the innovation of including professional naturalists to augment the cartographic record with scientific observation. Joseph Banks, Fellow of the Royal Society and later founder of Kew Gardens (a significant imperial institution in itself as it developed throughout the nineteenth century on Banks' foundation), accompanied Cook on his first voyage. His journal demonstrates the emergent dichotomy in Western approaches to South Pacific Island customs that would persist throughout the nineteenth century and beyond – an Edenic paradise or something uniquely perverse. The following two passages from Banks' Journal recording observations on Tahiti illustrate how in a single narrative the Western observer may travel between desire and what can only be called cultural horror:

> Three [pieces of cloth] were first laid. The foremost of women, who seemed to be the principal, then stepped upon them and quickly unveiling all her charms gave me a most convenient opportunity of admiring them by turning herself gradually around: 3 pieces more were laid and she repeated her part of the ceremony: the other three were then laid which made a treble covering of the

ground between her and me, she then once more displayed her naked beauties and immediately marched up to me. (Banks 275)

This passage suggests something of the titillation of the formal disrobing, a graceful and arousing act performed for the European male observer. By contrast, the following passage is significantly not performed for the pleasure of the European male strikes a rather different note:

One amusement more I must mention tho I confess I hardly touch upon it as founded upon a custom so devilish, inhuman, and contrary to the first principles of human nature that tho the native have repeatedly told it to me, far from concealing it rather looking upon it as a branch on which they valued themselves. I can hardly bring myself to believe it much less expect anybody else shall. It is this that more than half of the better sort of the inhabitants of the Island have like Comus in Milton entered into a resolution of enjoying free liberty in love without possibility of being troubled or disturbed by its consequences; these mix together with utmost freedom seldom cohabiting together for more than one or two days by which means they have fewer children than they would otherwise have, but those who are so unfortunate as to be begot are smothered at the moment of birth. (Banks 351)

The actions in the second passage are condemned as 'contrary to the first principles of human nature' when promiscuity and its consequences occur among the 'natives' whereas the first seems to accept the promise of promiscuity directed towards the European male. The sense of duality of, on the one hand, admiring Polynesian people and culture as something natural and desirable and, on the other, uncovering a savage and unnatural way of life sets the basic template of writings on the South Pacific for subsequent European visitors.

Yet both Cook and Bougainville recognized that their own sailors brought several viral serpents into this paradise but, above all, syphilis. Cook who visited Tahiti after the Bougainville expedition noted in his journal that 'the venereal distemper [is] now as common as in any part of the world' (Cook 98–9). During his third voyage when making landfall on the Hawaiian island of Maui it became apparent that Cook's previous measures to control the spread of venereal diseases had failed since two of the islanders who boarded the ship 'had a clap'. Consequently, Neil Rennie observes: 'Perhaps because the damage had been done, Cook lifted the ban on women' (Rennie 133). Cook himself had been repelled by the sexual licentiousness he had witnessed on Tahiti and certainly saw this as a flaw in Polynesian culture, but his recognition that the sexual desires of his own crew posed the threat of infection is interesting in light of the later history of the colonial Pacific over which European and American ships spread both alien diseases and trade good with near equal levels of devastation for indigenous communities.

The missionaries who followed Bougainville and Cook to the South Pacific in the nineteenth century vigorously suppressed not only local religious practices but also anything that hinted at the erotic, which sounded the death knell for the culturally central expressive dances widespread throughout the Polynesian islands. As one of the last major explorers of the South Pacific, the Russian Otto von Kotzebue was to observe, the new regime was total: 'By order of the Missionaries, the flute, which once awakened pleasure, is heard no more. No music but that of the psalms is suffered in Tahiti: dancing, mock-fights and dramatic representations are no longer permitted. Every pleasure is punished as a sin, among a people whom Nature destined to the most cheerful enjoyment' (Kotzebue 172). Moreover, the different groups were divided both by doctrine and by nationality and competed among themselves to gain a foothold for their sect or doctrine closely mirrored the imperial interests of their home nations. It scarcely needs stressing that the agenda of these later colonists differed fundamentally from the eighteenth-century explorers conditioned by the 'noble savage' tradition of Montaigne and Rousseau. If direct colonial exploitation and occupation tempered the view of the Pacific Islanders, the eighteenth-century valorization of the Pacific Island as both natural paradises and a space of sexual adventure persists to this day, thanks, in no small part, to popular American authors such as James A. Michener and the Hollywood film industry. Michener's *Tales of the South Pacific* (1947) – winner of the Pulitzer prize for the same year – provided the raw material for the Rodgers and Hammerstein musical *South Pacific,* which was filmed in 1958, reflecting the revival of American popular interest in the region among American servicemen who were stationed there during the Second World War.

Despite the persistence of this paradisal image, the movement from explorers to direct colonization heralded a distinct alteration in attitudes towards the Pacific Islanders; less innocent children of nature they came to be seen as recalcitrant savages with appalling customs in dire need of the benevolent helping hand of the 'civilized' West, a view which typically existed alongside the stereotypical image that such 'savages' were biologically degenerate and naturally dependent on and subservient to the white man. Underlying this self-justifying discourse lie the economic and political imperatives of empire. As Ania Loomba suggests 'representations of the "other" vary according to the exigencies of colonial rule'

(Loomba 113), and certainly one of the most important of these factors was the change in status from anthropological/philosophical curiosity to potentially lucrative work force and consumer supported by the missionary homily that saved souls were usefully employed hands. In fact, missionaries had early been engaged in trading activities to fund their work in the Pacific and were, quite often literally, supported by the labour of their converts. It is unsurprising, therefore, that William Ellis, who had been dispatched to the South Pacific by the London Missionary Society in 1817, was to publish a strongly worded refutation of Kotzebue's claims:

> No one can have read the accounts of the most transient of early voyagers without the disgust at the manners they describe . . . deeds, in broad open day, so gross and horrid, that the slightest notice of them would be to outrage every feeling of delicacy and propriety implanted by nature, or cherished by religion . . . Now what is the fact? In 1815, 16, and 17 the people embraced Christianity . . . The virtue of chastity was inoculated and maintained; Christian marriage was instituted soon after . . . and whatever deviations may have arisen, the great principle is uniformly maintained to this day. (Ellis 78–9)

Note how the local culture is 'gross and horrid' in a way that encompasses not only the public displays of eroticism and indigenous ritual that offends nature itself, thence pointedly naturalizing both Christianity and Western moral ideals in one rhetorical flourish. Indeed, missionaries soon sought legitimization as healers representing success – often exaggerated – as evidence for the superiority of Christianity by taking advantage of the Islanders' belief in the supernatural causes of illness. Yet as Western-imported diseases reached epidemic proportions in the Pacific, many Islanders soon learnt that Westerners were more typically bearers of disease rather than supernatural healers and soon comprehended such ideas as infection. Indeed, local diseases were practically forgotten faced by this onslaught as Frederick Bennett reported when he visited Tahiti in the 1830s. The Islanders had become,

> . . . staunch ultra-contagonists: they consider that all diseases are infectious, and should they so far overcome their prejudice as to attend upon a sick relative, they will on no account use domestic utensils in common with him. Upon the same principle, also, they find an exotic origin for nearly all their disorders, leaving us no doubt (if their traditions of imputed disease are to be believed), how the aborigines terminated their existence, unless by violent death or extreme old age. (Bennett 93)

The subtle mockery of the fastidious Tahitians seems misplaced since their precautions are nothing but sensible given their susceptibility to these new diseases, so why the humour? Bennett mocks the Tahitians for suggesting that all diseases derive from an 'exotic' cause, from beyond Tahitian culture. In short, from the white man. Their quite logical precautions towards imported disease betray, to Bennett, the incompleteness of their comprehension and adaptation of Western medical methodology, which blinds them to the local origin of any disease. This is not surprising, given that familiar distempers have an indigenous cultural interpretation that dictates both cause and treatment. Alien disease is treated using the methodology of those who brought it to the Pacific. What Bennett fails to recognize is that the Tahitians do recognize indigenous diseases; it is he who cannot see how it is encoded into Polynesian culture. The Tahitian practice represents a far more accomplished and culturally sophisticated negotiation in that they manage to give meaning to both signifying systems. Indeed, it is Bennett's position that is potentially undermined here on two key levels. First, there is the tacit recognition that it is the Western explorers, traders, missionaries and colonists who have infected the indigenous population with new diseases. Second, his mockery of Tahitian adaptation of Western medical methodology betrays his uneasiness that the Islanders can also interrogate his culture and appropriate what they need reversing the observers presumption of superiority.

Homi Bhabha's notions of hybridity and mimicry are useful for understanding such colonial encounters:

> It is precisely in that ambivalent use of 'different' – to be different from those that are different makes you the same – that the Unconscious speaks of the form of Otherness, the tethered shadow of deferral and displacement. It is not the Colonialist Self of the Colonised Other, but the disturbing distance in between that constitutes the figure of colonial otherness – the white man's artifice inscribed on the black man's body. It is the relation to this impossible object that emerges the liminal problem of identity and its vicissitudes. (Bhabha 1986 117)

The ontological insecurity is present here in the need to both reinscribe and preserve the boundaries of difference towards the diseased as well as racial others. Both threaten to undermine the integrity of colonial identity. What this pattern suggests is that colonial encounters in the Pacific actualize an intensely unsettling moment of identification and repulsion. This is of course inherent in all colonial encounters that Bhabha discursively identifies as a 'place of hybridity . . . [where] the construction of a political object that is new, neither one nor the other, properly alienates our political expectations, and changes, as it must, the very forms of our recognition of the moment of politics' (Bhabha 1994 25). When Stevenson first arrived in the South Pacific in the late 1880s, European and American commerce, politics and religious interests already dominated the Islands and yet, perhaps because of this and the history of Western fantasy about the climate and peoples, Island cultures continued to both repel and attract the interlopers. This contradiction mirrors emerging uncertainties in relation to racial, class and gender difference that would gain its ultimate expression in the deliberate cultural alienation and hybridity of Modernism. The culture of fear that underlies Joseph Conrad's disturbing novella *Heart of Darkness* also lies behind the work of Stevenson and London. As Michael North observes: 'Modernism could not escape the contradictions of European colonialism; indeed it was only because it pushed these extremes that it could exist as a movement at all' (North 76). It is, therefore, in the metropolitan heartlands and the emigrant trail that we must first look for Stevenson's and London's negotiation of both class and colonial discourse.

*

The shape of this book takes the form of three interconnected sections. Chapters 2, 3 and 4 discuss examples of Stevenson's and London's travel writing in the context of contemporary discourses of national identity and attitudes towards class and racial others, particularly the way that categories of class and race can collapse into each other within a prevailing context of degeneration. Chapters 2 and 3 explore these themes through two texts that are, I would suggest, not only key to the thematic direction of Stevenson's and London's writing after their publication, but also had a significant impact on the development of their narrative technique – Stevenson's *The Amateur Emigrant* and London's *The People of the Abyss*. While both texts concentrate on largely urban environments in Britain and the United States, and the emigrant trail from Britain to and across the United States, they provide an important foundation from which to examine both authors' negotiation of the interrelated discourses of race, class and colonialism.

Chapter 4 pursues these themes as they manifest themselves in Stevenson's and London's first writings on the South Pacific, *In the South Seas* and *The Cruise of the Snark* respectively. While Chapters 2 and 3 drew out what might be called a colonial discourse in the metropolitan settings of Britain and the United States absorbed through class and national cultures, this chapter sees those ideas tested by direct encounters with Western colonialism. The focus of Chapter 4 is on the extensive attention that both authors pay to tropes and examples of illness and disease among the Polynesian Islanders of the Marquesas group who had suffered a devastating population decline following contact with Westerners. The result is a personal and discursive displacement by both authors as they negotiate their own narrative identities in an unfamiliar and disorientating cultural and colonial context. For Stevenson and London, illness in the South Pacific represented very different personal experiences, which is apparent from their narrative personas – in Stevenson's case, a return of health and relative vitality after years of invalidity; for London, progressive exposure to the tropics leads to physical and psychological collapse. By examining the development of Western images of class, disease and degeneration from the earlier travel texts examined in Chapters 2 and 3, illness and disease become part of a strategy of displacement of their own, their nations' and cultures' negative impact on the Marquesas Islands. These strategies are at one and the same time individual and markedly different in tone, and also reach comparable conclusions through the trope of and actual illness.

Chapters 5 and 6 build on the foundation of the preceding chapters to forward an extensive close reading of Stevenson's and London's major South Pacific novels – Stevenson's *The Wrecker* in Chapter 5 and London's *Adventure* in Chapter 6. Neither of these novels has benefitted from an extensive critical reading despite representing important landmarks in Stevenson's and London's Pacific writings. In Stevenson's case, this reveals a novel of not inconsiderable literary merit. While London's novel does not reach the same literary quality, it is a fascinating representation, if not a parable, of American's formal entry into the colonial South Pacific, as well as the most extensive dramatization of the South Pacific labour trade, which, from 1870 to its final cessation after the First World War, was a *cause célèbre* for missionaries and anti-slavery campaigners both in the Pacific and in Britain. Both texts explore the relationship between commercial and national interests in the South Pacific Islands and the region as a whole, taking in not only the exploitation and transportation of labourers from both the Islands and China, but also the opium trade and the development of San Francisco as an important commercial centre. Both novels trace the extent of the influence of these lines of commercial interest and this analysis interrogates the shaping and distortions of narrator, colonizer and colonized.

The relationship between a commercial exchange relation in a colonial context and the literature produced in and of that relationship is particularly revealing, as Gary Day observes: ' "literature" enacts aspects of the exchange relation and, in doing so, reveals how its logic is contradictory . . . "literature" itself becomes a means of imagining, negotiating, and even institutionalizing the mechanism of exchange' (Day 15). This idea is pursued further in Chapter 7 through examples of Stevenson's and London's shorter Pacific fiction in relation to the New Imperialism of the early twentieth century and Modernism. Neither author is generally considered in either of these contexts yet they both lived and write during key moments in the formation of both movements: Stevenson during the early emergence of a Modernist sensibility during the 1890s and London while it was at, perhaps, its greatest influence. Their relationship to both Modernism and the New Imperialism can be discerned from their anthropological interpretations of other cultures and their willingness in fiction to examine the possibilities of other ways of interpreting the world while simultaneously investigating the limits of Western subjectivity and its atavistic potential. Stevenson and London are signalling the end of one consciousness and the emergence of another, as indeed do Modernism and the New Imperialism. A consciousness whereby individual contact between colonizer and colonized is to be ultimately superseded, not by national interests, but by the influence of distant and diffuse commercial interests.

2

'Race', Class and Imperialism in Stevenson's *The Amateur Emigrant*

Introduction: Identities, Public and Private

In no sense could the events on which Stevenson's *The Amateur Emigrant* and London's *The People of the Abyss* are based be described as the result of deliberate planning. Stevenson had met his future wife, Fanny, at the French artists' colony of Brabizon near Fountainbleau in the early autumn of 1876 and a serious romance soon blossomed only to be cut short when her philandering husband, Samuel Osbourne, recalled her to Oakland, California, in June 1878 under the threat of ending his financial support. Stevenson's literary reputation was growing but was hardly profitable, which meant that he remained financially dependent on his father so Stevenson was unable to fill the breach. They parted on the understanding that Fanny would commence proceedings under the relatively liberal Californian divorce laws since Osbourne had provided more than sufficient grounds. During the interim Stevenson decamped on his tour of the Cévennes that was to provide the material for his travel memoir, *Travels with a Donkey* (1879). At the end of July 1879 he was back home in Edinburgh where he received an urgent cable from Fanny telling him that Osbourne was once more openly living with one of his mistresses in San Francisco and appealing for help. Reading this message as a call to his honour, he immediately purchased a steam ship ticket for New York and made plans for the overland journey to the West Coast. Despite having little money of his own and expecting no assistance from his parents for such a potentially scandalous object – indeed he concealed details of the trip from them – his departure struck a note of desperation and defiance to his friends as he took what seemed to be a step into an emotional and physical abyss. To his friend, Sidney Colvin, he wrote:

> No man is of any use until he has dared everything. I feel just now as if I had, and so might become a man . . . I have never been so detached from life. I feel as if I cared for nobody, and as for myself I cannot believe fully in my own existence. I seem to have died last night . . . The weather is threatening; I have a strange, rather horrible, sense of the sea before me, and can see no further into the future. I can say honestly I have at this moment neither a regret, a hope, a fear nor an inclination . . . I never was in such a state. I have only just made my will . . . God bless you and keep you, is the prayer of the husk which once contained – RLS. (Stevenson *Letters* II 72)

The emptiness and uncertainty underlying this passage – as well as the melodrama – is palpable; his will made and affairs put in order, the sea beckons like some brooding river Styx. The subject that was 'RLS' has been hollowed out by these last rites and what will come is either something new or nothingness.

The circumstances precipitating Jack London's journey across the Atlantic are scarcely so immediately traumatic. Originally commissioned by the American Press Association in mid-July 1902 to research and write a series of articles on the political and economic consequences of the Boer War, the series was unexpectedly cancelled while he was en route to New York. When he reached the city he was able instead to make tentative arrangements with Macmillan to publish a sociological study of the East End slums. Earlier that same year he and his family had made a decisive move into one of the rural areas that still at that time intermingled with the suburbs of Oakland – what he called 'the migration to the hills' (Joan London 213) – which, as his daughter and biographer Joan London notes, marked a decisive philosophical change that is significant in relation to his reaction to the East End. A few years earlier he had been strongly attracted to a city life as he observed to Cloudesley Johns towards the end of March 1899: 'I have been isolated so much, that I can no longer bear to be torn away for a long time from the city life' (London *Letters I* 259). The same letter not only refers directly to his period of wandering as a hobo, but also evokes his more recent experiences of the 'white silence' in the Yukon on which he built his early literary success. In short, we might read this as a decisive recoil from the type of freedom, isolation and human extremity that these last pockets of frontier life represented.

Ultimately his reaction to the urban was total. He wrote again to Johns in December 1901: 'I am rotting in here in town. Really, I can feel the bourgeois fear crawling up and up twining around me. If I don't get out soon I shall be emasculated. The city folk are a poor folk anyway. To hell with them' (London *Letters I* 260). A few months later this gloom had given way to joy amid the clutter of a country farmstead of chickens horses, barns and a pigeon coop expressed with unintended in the bourgeois terms of private ownership:

> Am beautifully located in new house. We have a big living room, every inch of it, floor and ceiling, finished in redwood. We could put the floor space of almost four cottages (of the size of the last one you remember) into this one living room alone. The rest of the house is finished in redwood, too, and is very, very comfortable. (London *Letters I* 260)

Thence within a year of his departure for England and the East End, London expresses both the fear that he is succumbing to an emasculated bourgeois life in the city contradicted a few months later by the evident pleasure he takes in the early material benefits his growing success was bringing him. Jonathan Auerbach has warned against overtly biographical readings of London's writings: 'Given the pull towards biography that has dominated London studies from the start, it is certainly tempting to gloss London's politics in terms of his own rise from poverty to middle-class respectability to would be gentleman' (Auerbach 120). Certainly crude biographical readings are to be avoided, but much of London's and, indeed, Stevenson's life was consciously orchestrated 'self-fashioning' creating personas that were designed to interact with their writing. This is no more so that in texts such as *The People of the Abyss* and *The Amateur Emigrant* where the author-narrators are often less concerned about poverty in the East End or on the emigrant trail to North America than the self-production of a politically aware *flâneur* or amateur ethnographer. In a commercial literary marketplace they demonstrate an awareness of their own commodification as increasingly famous authors in which a facet of their life, as much as their works, is a public narrative. As Day observes, 'the commodification of social life . . . is a class relation' (Day 173). For the moment I want to consider the implications of a realignment in Stevenson's and London's respective outlooks – for Stevenson, his journey among the steerage passengers and hoped for marriage courting both loss of caste and bourgeois moral outrage; for London, a move away from the city and his working-class origins – realignments which occurred close to the experiences that would form the material basis of their writing and in which class in general, and the working classes in particular, loom so large.

Both writers demonstrate disaffection and personal reinvention that would be explored in their subsequent textual reflections on their experience. This process in Stevenson is superficially the most dramatic provoked by the shock of the cable he received from his future wife, and still evident in the tone of his letter to Colvin. Histrionics aside – for which the younger Stevenson had a reputation – there is a clear impression of an abrupt psychological break from his earlier life. When he remarks that, 'I cannot believe in my own existence', he refers to this former conception of his life from which he has become irretrievably alienated. A similar need for reorientation can be discerned in London's new discomfiture with urban life, although the process extends more gradually over the year preceding his departure for England. Even so, disaffection with city life and yearning for rural living are accompanied by the stark contradiction between his middle-class joy in property and his earlier and apparently ongoing allegiance to socialism and the working classes that had so dominated his outlook hitherto. The physical relocation from the city coupled with this change in perspective can be seen as a means to evade the pressing contradictions that his new class/cultural position had created. Moreover, London's move into the countryside also suggests an attempt to match his newly constructed public persona as a frontiersman and chronicler of the Yukon Gold Rush and to disavow to some extent the more immediate working-class associations of his earlier life in Oakland and San Francisco which had led him to be dubbed by the local press as the 'boy socialist'. He had even stood for election as mayor of Oakland on the socialist ticket in the autumn of 1902 (receiving only 246 votes). This earlier identity as a radical socialist would be called into question by the narrative persona London constructs in *The People of the Abyss* and contained by an ascendant middle-class sensibility related to his status as a successful professional writer. 'London's identity as a socialist,' observes Auerbach, 'remains connected but subordinated to his ambitions as a fiction writer' (Auerbach 132).

Stevenson's moment of crisis also marks a changed attitude towards his writing and persona as a writer. Hitherto known more for his promise than achievement, his recent literary earnings amounted to only 'an average of nine guineas for essays, £8 for short stories, £30 for *Travels with a Donkey*, and £44.12s for the serial publications of *New Arabian Nights*' (McLynn 145). Departure for the United States and hope for marriage therefore presented him with a need to provide for himself and others rather than rely of the financial support of his father, which seemed likely to be cut off. This potentially transforms his writing from a gentleman's pastime towards professional authorship, which his father certainly feared as a loss of caste. His letter to Colvin foreshadows a new seriousness and toughness towards his writing on which he would now need to support a family. Yet the theatrical nature of his pronouncement suggests, as with London, that there are contradictions lying deeper within the abruptness of this change: there remains a sense that this is a role to be assumed rather than a life to be permanently embraced despite the all-too-real immediacy of relative poverty. For Stevenson and London their respective journeys into the world of the 'lower orders' have the rhetorical trappings of an investigation or adventure, which rather belies the personal crisis it accompanies. The ambivalence inherent in these adjustments to their public personas will bring a longer lasting awareness of distance from their subject matter – the working class and the poor – and will raise long-lasting questions about their own social identity.

In *The Amateur Emigrant* and *The People of the Abyss*, Stevenson and London are preoccupied with the material and social consequences of a dramatic alteration in their class status, which has profound implications for their conception of self. In each case their 'descent' engenders a metaphor that presents the priority and superiority of their gaze and subjective distance. This strategy is comparable to Mary Louise Pratt's analysis of colonial travel writing. The subsequent account of their journeys across class boundaries significantly shares a number of structural and ideological similarities with the travel writing she discusses, especially in the creation of a material and textual space where contact, interaction and limited understanding between the colonizer and the colonized could take place while official and more formal codes demand strict embarkation between the two. Such contact takes place against the radical imbalance of power inherent in the relationship between colonizer and colonized and this in turn establishes a subject position that enables a range of 'strategies of representation whereby the European bourgeois subjects seek to secure their innocence in the same moment as they assert European hegemony . . . he whose imperial eyes look out and posses' (Pratt 7). Pratt's use of the term 'bourgeois subjects' alerts us to the fact that this is as much a class as it is a colonial stance and practice, which underlines its relevance to Stevenson's and London's narrative strategies. As Ania Loomba, drawing on the work of R. Miles, emphasizes how such 'positional superiority' is used approaching both race and class encounters:

> The ideology of racial superiority translated easily into class terms. The superiority of the white races, one colonist argued, clearly implied that 'the black man must forever remain cheap labour and slaves'. Certain sections of people were thus racially identified as the natural working classes. The problem was now to organise the social world according to this belief, or to force the

population into its 'natural' class position: in other words, reality had to be brought into line with that representation in order to ensure the material objective of production. (Loomba 126/Miles 105)

Conversely, the indigent urban working classes could easily be forced into a naturalized racial hierarchy. This slippage between class and race is central to both Stevenson's *The Amateur Emigrant* and London's *The People of the Abyss*. The former will be the subject of the remainder of this chapter and the latter the subject of the next.

The Bourgeois Artist as Social Critic

There is no question that Stevenson's family belonged to the well-established professional middle classes. The family had produced several generations of distinguished marine engineers famous for a series of lighthouses and coastal defences around the Scottish coast and a number of technical innovations. Indeed, while London admired Stevenson's work, he did not overlook what his class background meant in material terms: 'I agree with you that R.L.S. never turned out a foot of polished trash, and that Kipling has; but – well, Stevenson never had to worry about ways or means, while Kipling, a mere journalist, hurt himself by having to seek present sales rather than posthumous fame. Stevenson received from his people 93 pounds, I believe, per year' (London *Letters* I 55). While is unclear where London came across such a strangely precise figure, it is certainly true that Stevenson was subsidized by his father for many years while he was learning his craft. His precipitate decision to set out for the United States deepened the estrangement with his parents, which had been simmering for many years, and his support was cut off entirely from August 1879 until April 1880. Having only a very small amount set aside once he had paid his fare to the steamship company, Stevenson was reduced to near pauperism. While this lasted for only a short period, for someone of Stevenson's relatively privileged background and poor health such a complete fall from financial grace represented some considerable physical and social hardship. This should not diminish the thrust of London's observation: Stevenson was very much a son of the middle classes reduced only temporarily to relative poverty, whereas London's working-class origins could only be pushed into the background once he had begun to succeed in the middle-class profession of letters. It is also worth noting that before his departure to the United States Stevenson's publications had invariably catered for the resolutely polite middle-class readership of such journals as the *Cornhill Magazine* and were subjected to the censorious eyes of his friends and parents.

Rather than respond to his enforced poverty and unavoidably propinquity with the working class by strongly reinforcing the class distinctions through his narrative, Stevenson negotiates his now rather confused status with a complexity that took him some way beyond the conventional political and social sensibilities of his established readership. Indeed, an edition of the full manuscript of his journey from Scotland to California would not find its way into print until 1966 respectable Victorian sensibilities in the form of friends and parents not being in tune with Stevenson's candid depiction of the crudities of the steerage quarters of a transatlantic steamer and still less those of an emigrant train. He recognized early that such subject matter would have a profound effect both on his outlook, but more importantly his writing style commenting that: 'M. Zola would here find an inspiration for many pages' (*Emigrant* 23), although Zola was an author whose frank subject matter and naturalist technique in novels like *L'Assommoir* he abhorred at this stage in his career. Yet it is a frankness and naturalism that informs *The Amateur Emigrant* and its truncated publication history.

The narrative persona Stevenson creates displays both sympathy and a willingness to intermingle with his new comrades while preserving a subtle class distinction through the disarming device of self-depreciating humour about his decline in social status and a refusal to romanticize his fellow passengers:

> Emigration, from a word of the most cheerful import, came to sound almost dismally in my ear. There is nothing more agreeable to picture and nothing more pathetic to behold. The abstract idea, as conceived at home, is hopeful and adventurous. A young man, you fancy, scorning restraints and helpers, issues forth into life, that great battle, to fight for his own land. The most pleasant stories of ambition, of difficulties overcome, and of ultimate success, are but as episodes to this great epic of self-help. The epic is composed of individual heroisms; it stands to them as the victorious war which subdued an empire stands to the personal act of bravery which spiked a single cannon and was adequately rewarded with a medal. For in emigration the young men enter direct and by shipload on their heritage of work; empty continents swarm, as at the Bo'sun's whistle, with industrious hands, and whole new empires are domesticated to the service of man. (*Emigrant* 10–11)

The warning that begins this passage alerts the reader that the heroic ideal of emigration does not marry with what he witnesses. Indeed, the next paragraph reveals this perspective to be an idealization largely composed of 'embellishments' since the emigrants he sees are older men with families. But note how Stevenson as the observing subject is able to oversee, reflect and interpret the situation of his fellow passengers who are silenced and serve only to point up the disappointing inversion of the heroic image they dismally fail to satisfy. They are also denied the status of imperial pioneers; not for them the epic 'civilising mission' of colonialism for they are not heading for an empty continent from which 'new empires' can be carved.

As an *amateur* emigrant Stevenson is careful not to be caught within the field of his own gaze. He re-inscribes a middle-class status by implying that it is not want that forces him to travel but his own curiosity, much like the gentleman amateur traveller/narrator of his earlier travel tales. Indeed, curiosity is one of the reasons that he advances for his presence among the steerage passengers: 'I was not in truth a steerage passenger. Although anxious to see the worst of emigrant life' (*Emigrant* 4). In doing so he creates the impression of a detached and superior ethnographic stance that systematically denies agency to his working-class fellow travellers without ostensibly claiming that role. This is striking given the romantic potential of his real reason for travelling to the United States to save the object of his affections from distress and, hopefully, to marry her. A restraint even more surprising in light of the dramatic life-or-death tone of his letter to Colvin discussed above. This role does, however, remain latent within the narrative. In fact, Stevenson's narrative strategy is considerably more complex than it might first appear, as is most clearly apparent from his depiction of the working class. Although he was keen to deny them the more romantic associations of emigration, Stevenson was willing to undermine his own resolutely middle-class perspective by considering causes for their less than heroic appearance. These were solid families forced out, not by the draw of the individualistic freedom of the frontier, but by the conditions at home: 'Labouring mankind had in the last years, and throughout Great Britain, sustained a prolonged and crushing series of defeats. I had hear vaguely of these reverses . . . But I had never taken them home to me of represented these distresses livingly to my imagination' (*Emigrant* 11). This is strikingly different to the approach taken by social imperialists like General William Booth of Salvation Army fame who would propose in his book *Darkest England and the Way out* (1890) – the title significantly echoing the explorer Henry Stanley's *In Darkest Africa* (1890) and his earlier *Through the Dark Continent* (1878) – that the poor were at risk of degenerating into a distinctly racial other. Booth's universal panacea for poverty was the dispersion through the 'empty' lands of the empire; in other words, the emigration that Stevenson tacitly questions in the passage above. Like many of his middle-class contemporaries Booth was keen to deal with consequences rather than the underlying causes of the clear distress of the working class in the second half of the nineteenth century which Stevenson at least acknowledges. Such thinking led to a presumed division of the poor into two groups, the deserving and undeserving poor, with the latter all but abandoned to their fate much like a recalcitrant, uncivilized, colonized other.

While Stevenson's equivocation towards the working classes is hardly unusual for a Victorian gentleman with liberal sympathies, his textual ambivalence directly links him to the late nineteenth-century dualistic conception of cities and their inhabitants, particularly London where the life of the well-to-do and the city's dark heart of poverty and breadline existence often existed in close proximity – as Charles Booth's poverty maps would demonstrate at the end of the century – and yet in practical terms and social terms remained worlds apart. Stevenson, like Dickens before him, had a passion for roving city streets and while the division in the Edinburgh of Stevenson's youthful wanderings had been between the Old and New Towns, the contrasting wealth and poverty would have been as evident (McLynn 258). While the question of the social stratification of cities may seem a world away from the squalor of a transatlantic crossing (and indeed the colonial South Pacific), there is a very real sense that the class sensibilities Stevenson struggles with in *The Amateur Emigrant* were both of an acute awareness of the horror that was ever only a few streets away in any British city. As Malcolm Bradbury observes:

> Beneath stability was fluidity, strangeness. If [London's] middle-class lifestyle was the object of international envy (Herbert Hoover reported it as, up to 1914, the pleasantest place in the world to live) and it was associated with the density of an achieved culture, it was also famous for its fantastic sprawl and mass. It confronted social thinkers and writers too with the problem of agglomeration and scale, the strangeness of what Gissing called its 'nether world' ... By the end of the century, as the problem of mass and the masses came to seem crucial to writers, and as the cause of social reform spread, the stark contrasts within the culture were becoming famous. (Bradbury 180)

In light of the homogenization implicit in the 'problem of the mass and the masses', the choice of the steerage passengers in Stevenson's text to take the future into their own hands confounds the stereotype of rigid class dualities. Without this ready discursive frame and the failure of his fellow passengers to live up to another stereotype, the heroic pioneer forces his narrative to focus on the conditions that pushed these people to such a desperate measure as emigration. Stevenson was certainly no political radical and intentionally removes the sting from his social commentary through a particularly scathing interpretation of the character of the steerage passengers, insisting that they were congenital failures rather than economic and class victims: 'We were a company of the rejected; the drunken, the incompetent, the weak, the prodigal, all who had been unable to prevail against circumstances in the one land, were now fleeing pitifully to another; and though one or two might still succeed, all had already failed. We were a shipful of failures, the broken men of England' (*Emigrant* 12). Stevenson will not quite allow himself to recognize without qualification that a measure like emigration for an established family is more likely to be a consequence of extreme pressure rather than fecklessness. His ambiguity towards the steerage passengers anticipates the narrative equivocation of Jacob Riis' account of the slums of New York in *How the Other Half Lives* (1890), which Jonathan Auerbach suggests influenced London's later study of the East End. Yet Auerbach's comment on Riis also reflects the dilemma of Stevenson's narrative: Riis' rhetoric gives readers a consistent feeling of sympathy precisely to the extent that the poor remain placed and categorised as others' (Auerbach 138). Choosing to take the future into their own hands by emigrating, the steerage passengers deny their 'placing' and demonstrate an agency incompatible with the idea of a passive, pitiable, other with which Stevenson can feel wholly easy.

Even more striking is Stevenson's consistent use of the pronoun 'we' that counts him among his failed, rejected and prodigal shipmates, which is rather at odds with the careful maintenance of his middle-class identity. This is, however, more in tune with the feeling of desolation in his letter to Sidney Colvin where he described himself as a 'husk', 'detached from life' and unable to 'believe fully in my own existence' (Stevenson *Letters* 72). It is this subtext of a loss of confidence and self-worth that make his observations about class distinctions so striking. What emerges is a narrative in which Stevenson makes light of his temporary fall in class status but simultaneously seeks to displace his own anxieties about personal failure onto his fellow passengers, revealing in the process rather more about himself than might initially seem to be the case. This is reflected in an acute sensitivity over class slights expressed in the form of outrage on behalf of his fellow passengers but, equally, expressive of his own anxiety. This enables him to comprehend the petty and sometimes more fundamental injustices meted out solely on the basis of class. This sensitivity is apparent from some key early episodes. First, there is the wry humour in response to the official signs of his now ambivalent class status. While he had purchased a ticket for a second-class cabin so that he had a table on which to write and perhaps to ensure he didn't become wholly of the steerage, this 'superior' accommodation consisted in little more than a sectioned-off cabin in the steerage with both first-class passengers and the crew making no distinction between the two passenger groups. Yet, as he points out:

> The last particular in which the second cabin passengers remarkably stands ahead of his brother in steerage is one altogether of sentiment. In the steerage there are males and females; in the second cabin ladies and gentlemen. For some time after I came aboard I thought I was only a male; but in the course of a voyage of discovery below decks, I came upon a brass plate, and I learned I was still a gentleman. Nobody knew it, of course. I was lost in the crowd of males and females, and rigorously confined to the same quarter of the deck . . . Still, I was like one with a patent of nobility in a drawer at home; and when I felt out of spirits I could go down and refresh myself with a look at the brass plate. (*Emigrant* 5–6)

The final sentence confirms the humorous self-depreciation Stevenson aims at his own social vanity and his class, but shares the very same perspective that would see the steerage passengers as 'a crowd of males and females'. While he is prepared to laugh at the ineffectual official recognition of status in the form of the brass plate, he and his readers *know* that he is entitled to that status as of right which is essential to the rhetorical positional superiority established within the narrative. He is more than ready to respond heatedly to what he sees as a class-based slight when a party of first-class passengers come to examine life in the steerage: 'there came three cabin passengers, a gentleman and two young ladies, picking their way with little gracious titters of indulgence, and a lady bountiful air about nothing, which galled me to the quick. I have little of the radical in social questions, and have always nourished an idea that one person was as good as another. But I was troubled by this episode. It was astonishing what insults these people managed to convey by their presence. They seemed to throw their clothes in our faces' (*Emigrant* 28). The suffix to this episode was not to appear in print until the full manuscript was published in 1966, which continues 'we had been made to feel ourselves a sort of comical lower animal' (*Emigrant* 28). Once more Stevenson's sensitivity and ire cuts both ways: he is outraged on behalf of the entire company of which he is part, and also embarrassed by the behaviour of his class.

The 'we' of this passage reflects a subtle slippage between sympathy and critique even though Stevenson most clearly associates himself with the steerage passengers. The concluding comment that under such circumstances those observed feel reduced in status to little better than animals, hints subversively at the prevailing ideology of racial regression among the working class and the poor which saw little differentiation between 'savages' and animals. Indeed, this alignment between race and class is emphasized here by the salon visitors' interest in tattered clothing as a sign of that regression, as if clothes in good repair would be in some way incongruous. While Stevenson is right to resist this stereotype, his narrative and social authority is never under threat. He is able to introduce a discourse that is progressively relative in social terms:

> Some of our finest behaviour, though it looks well enough from the boxes, may seem even brutal to the gallery. We boast too often manners that are parochial rather than universal; that, like a country wine, will not bear transportation for a hundred miles, nor from the parlour to the kitchen. To be a gentleman is to be one all the world over, and in every relation and grade of society . . . manners, like art, should be human and central. (*Emigrant* 78)

Stevenson goes to some length to emphasize that 'gentle behaviour' is a moral accomplishment rather than a class-based distinction, and then extends this to interactions between different peoples and nationalities as well. In effect he takes a pervasive discourse of otherness – in terms of both class and ethnicity – and inverts its moral polarity. Rather than assuming that the bourgeois European is inherently superior because of material and social accomplishments, he suggests that worth is gauged by the treatment of others. Inevitably, such a position is still founded on the presumed superiority of middle-class Western culture that Stevenson is certainly not going to surrender at this stage, but it is a significant check on the inherent inequality of such encounters 'usually involving conditions of coercion, radical inequality, and intractable conflict' (Pratt 6). He is also concerned here with the quantifiable difference between superficial accomplishments versus material worth expressed through deeds; the social consequences of clothing and class categorization exist on the same discursive continuum as that governing similar presumptions about the relative levels of civilization in a colonial context. A term like 'street arab' in common usage at the time in both Britain and the United States nicely encapsulates this outlook by relating the ragged appearance and itinerancy of a street child within a specific colonial framework of behavioural classification at which other extreme stands the colonized North African nomad who is assumed to be 'childlike'.

Transgression and the Threat of De/class/ification

For Stevenson, reclassification as one of the working class becomes a textual function reflecting a material condition that is involuntary, yet he introduces a note of adventure even as he comes conscious of these new social restrictions: 'Travel is of two kinds; and this voyage of mine across the ocean combined both. "Out of my country and myself I go," sings the old poet: and I was not only travelling out of my country in longitude and latitude, but out of myself in diet, associates and consideration' (*Emigrant* 72). This acknowledges that experience and adventure are gained not only by physical removal to another country, but also by migration across social barriers. Significantly, this reflection on migration approaches a position in which Raymond Williams associates with the origins of modernism albeit in an urban context:

> Thus the key cultural factor of the modernist shift is the character of the metropolis: in these general conditions, but then, even more decisively, in its general effects on form. The most important general element of the innovations in form is the fact of immigration to the metropolis, and it cannot too often be emphasised how many of the major innovators were, in this precise sense, immigrants. (Williams 45–6)

The crucial element to which Stevenson is sensitive in *The Amateur Emigrant* which Williams surprisingly does not mention is class which is at least as important as the fact of migration. Despite the evident opportunity of broadening his intellectual and experiential horizons in this encounter, in the very next sentence Stevenson immediately restricts the potential to radically alter the self by reasserting his positional superiority: 'Part of the interest and a great deal of the amusement flowed, at least to me from this novel situation in the world' (*Emigrant* 72). In essence, the experience is represented as 'fun' even if in actuality it represented some hardship and, as we shall see from London's text and later South Pacific material, access to the 'other' side of the class barrier with the attendant thrill of transgression – an adventure. However, we might also read this as a defensive strategy by which Stevenson maintains his middle-class identity. Again, humour is the chief tool he employs to defuse the very real social sensitivities that seem to be bruised while lumped together with the steerage, perhaps even concealing his shame. This is no doubt why the complete manuscript was not published in his lifetime since it both alarmed and shocked his family and friends such as his father's strongly disapproving observation that, 'I think it not only the worst thing you have done, but altogether unworthy of you' (MacKay 16). As James Hart records: 'Stevenson allowed his father to pay the publishers a hundred pounds to withdraw the work that showed the scion of a good professional Edinburgh family travelling with dirt and disease and associating with poor people' (Hart xlii).

The introduction of an adventure theme into the narrative register raises an expectation of cliché and stereotype common to both the imperial adventure story and travel writing of the time: a series of conventions that affirm the superiority of the protagonist as middle class, male and white. 'Adventure', writes Richard Phillips, 'was generally – but not universally – motivated by a clear political agenda: broadly speaking, imperialism' (R. Phillips 12). Phillips' qualification here is important when considering *The Amateur Emigrant*. Stevenson's reflections on his Atlantic crossing are structured as a considered social critique that is all the more powerful because it emerges from within the very middle-class discourse that it questions. In doing so, the narrative strives not to alienate its ideal reader to the extent that s/he would cease reading on the grounds of obvious ideological provocation. Through a careful shift in perspective he achieves a real sense of defamiliarization for readers from his own class. By contrast, while Stevenson certainly takes as much care to retain his positional superiority *vis-à-vis* his working-class objects, he never seeks to conceal his class status from his fellow passengers which gains him some acceptance. Indeed, Jones, a steerage passenger with whom Stevenson struck up a friendship, complimented him on how he 'managed to behave pleasantly' to the working-class passengers. Though Stevenson noted this was also an acknowledgement of his essential difference: 'I could follow the thought in his mind, and knew his compliment to be such as we pay foreigners on their proficiency in English. I daresay this praise was given me immediately on the back of some unpardonable solecism which had led him to review my conduct as a whole' (*Emigrant* 77–8). It is significant that the class relationship is described in terms of 'foreignness' although the direction of this objectification is returned to Stevenson and the 'superior' classes he represents since it is they – or he as their representative – who are foreign. His situation is far more ambivalent since he is now foreign to both social groups and a strangely liminal narrator which is only partially obscured by both the self-depreciating humour and quasi-ethnographic stance. His social exclusion from the salon passengers was so total as to render him socially invisible:

> In my normal circumstances, it appeared, every young lady must have paid me
> some passing tribute of a glance; and although I had often been unconscious of
> it when given, I was well aware of its absence when it was withheld. My height

seemed to decrease with every woman who passed me, for she passed me like a dog. This is one of the reasons for supposing that what are called the upper classes may sometimes produce a disagreeable impression in what are called the lower; and I wish some one would continue my experiment and find out exactly at what stage of toilette a man becomes invisible to the well-regulated female eye. (*Emigrant* 74–5)

Despite the humour of equating his wounded vanity with a reduction in physical stature and the smirk with which his proposal for a sociological study is given, this still leaves the social criticism clear and direct in this passage. Nor is the thrust of this critique directed against women. The phrase 'well regulated' conveys some understanding of the patriarchal constraints under which Victorian women lived, suggesting that they are also victims of a broader social control played out over their bodies. Women become part of the discursive nexus Stevenson is probing here; a highly complex and diffuse range of attitudes and narrative strategies that combine/confuse attitudes towards race, nationality, class and gender brought together by replicating and shifting between the narrative perspective of an ethnographic study, an adventure yarn and light social comedy. As a matter of course, late Victorian adventure narratives vigorously reproduced contemporary doctrine on private and public spaces creating aggressively masculine textual spaces far removed from the hearth and home centred on women and children (R. Phillips 89). As Ruskin argued in 1864: 'man's power is active' and 'his energy [is] for adventure' (Ruskin 146), yet the private space of home was part of a patriarchal discourse that sought to define not only domestic relationships, but could also govern in another setting the interrelation between 'inferior' classes and subject peoples. As Ania Loomba observes: 'Initially women were described in terms taken from racial discourse, and then gender differences were used to explain racial differences' (Loomba 161). It is no accident of course that Freud adopted the same 'heart of darkness' trope in the early twentieth century to describe women's sexuality: 'We know less of the sexual life of little girls than of little boys; the sexual life of grown-up women, too, is still a "dark continent"' (Freud 34). The 'well-regulated' female gaze was, therefore, another aspect of the class discourse that serves to regulate the dangerous and potentially transgressive spaces of adventure and imperial activity. While Stevenson is able to suggest insights like this, his text reproduces much of the same restrictive social apparatus in relation to the women who are part of the adventurous realm he has created from his raw experiences. As Karen Lawrence observes: 'to varying degrees, all the studies of adventure . . . encode the traveller as a male who crosses boundaries and penetrates spaces; the female is mapped as a place on the itinerary of the male journey' (Lawrence 2). By contrast to his more open attitude towards the male passengers, the steerage women are generally notable for the extent to which they transgress patriarchal dictates of female behaviour. The cabin women are then, by implication, too superficial to identify his quality among the mass of steerage passengers and while he is willing to admit some of the steerage men into his laudably inclusive idea of gentlemanly behaviour, the steerage women do not fare so well: 'It will be understood that I speak of the best among my fellow passengers; for in the steerage, as well as in the salon, there is a mixture. The women in particular, too often displeased me by something hard and forward, by something alternately sullen and jeering both in speech and conduct' (*Emigrant* 79). The salon ladies affect not to see him and the steerage women, by their forwardness, do not afford him the 'proper' respect due to a man of the 'better classes'. There also remains the unresolved question as to whether the male steerage passengers of whom Stevenson writes so admiringly were in actuality those who deferred to his class while pretending not to do so. It is not only women of the 'upper class' whose gaze is 'well regulated', but also Stevenson's attitude towards the working class.

Imperial Critique as Class Discourse

As a prelude to the narrative of his journey across the United States, Stevenson instigates an interrogation of the assumptions behind the imperial project that is not simply filtered by the narrative persona of the social investigator/traveller, but attempts to represent the beliefs and views of the steerage passengers distinct from his own opinions and literary framing. There is, of course, a limit to how far such an attempt can actually remain uncoloured by Stevenson's own views and class position as will become evident by *how* he chooses to represent others' perspective. For this is a group who, disillusioned with Britain, are not reluctant to strike at that very source of deep nationalistic pride, the expanding empire: 'for nearly all with whom I conversed were bitterly opposed to war, and attributed their own misfortunes, and frequently their own taste for whisky, to the campaigns in Zululand and Afghanistan' (*Emigrant* 16). Having denied these 'deserters' the role of adventurous pioneers, Stevenson is reluctant to grant them the acuity to comprehend that imperial aggrandisement does not benefit the British people as a whole. Since it is the working classes who provide the majority of the troops and risk their lives for that expansion with, arguably, the least share of the resultant spoils, it is a highly rational conclusion. Stevenson suggests, however, that as a consequence of their limited comprehension and discontent, they are simply focusing on colonial expansion as a convenient issue on which to blame the consequences of their own failings. Indeed, he depicts them signing an imperialist/nationalist 'bastard doggerel of the music-hall . . . "We don't want to fight but, by Jingo, if we do"' (*Emigrant* 16) to further undermine the level of political comprehension betraying his own sensitivity to this criticism. In turn, Stevenson seeks an explanation for the allure of emigration that does not discredit the British social, national and imperial status quo. However, he is, as we have seen, willing to allow that the debilitating effect of the harsh economic conditions have fallen disproportionately heavily on the working classes (*Emigrant* 11–12). His solution to these contradictory impulses is to single out a few of his steerage companions as exemplary members of their class and to stigmatize the rest – including all the women – as inherently degenerate; not only unfit for success in Britain, but in some cases also biologically and culturally inadequate. In doing so he draws on similar class anxieties that will also be evident from Jack London's representation of the East End poor. Stevenson's use of this class-based colonial register is not yet as direct as London's, but, discursively, it provides a useful narrative device to defect the implicit criticism the emigrant poses to British society.

Drunkenness in particular is identified as the primary sign of failure and unfitness, a theme that is developed at some length with a passenger named Mackay. This man, an engineer and thence a member of the artisan class, is intelligent and well spoken, but has the fatal flaw: 'He was . . . another so-called victim of the bottle. But Mackay was miles from publishing his weakness to the work; laid the blame of his failure on corrupt masters and a corrupt State policy' (*Emigrant* 36). Note how Mackay's social criticism is represented as a displacement of his own failings reproducing the narrative strategy Stevenson made use of to undermine the steerage passengers' criticism of Britain's recent imperial conflicts. This enables Stevenson to represent Mackay, who only a few lines before was a 'pertinent debater,' as an analogue of the illogical 'savage': 'He had an appetite for disconnected facts which I can only compare to the savage taste for beads' (*Emigrant* 35). The introduction of this trope also recalls the tawdry colonial practice of trading alcohol to unsuspecting and inexperienced colonized peoples and calling the widespread drunkenness a singular mark of 'savage' degeneration ripe for saving by the moralizing white interloper.

In this instance it is just as likely that Mackay has been driven to the bottle by hardship and can be seen as a victim of the same exploitative commercial and class interests as those directly subjected to the inequities of imperial trade. There is also a latent fear of the fanatical in Stevenson's depiction of Mackay's 'pertinent debates'. This strategy of undermining the credibility of an argument by discrediting the speaker is scarcely original and of course Stevenson trained, if never practiced, as an advocate. Yet there are wider ideological issues here that can be further compared to colonial discourse. For example, in the following passage Frantz Fanon reflects upon the depiction of Africa rather than a class, but the narrative conceit he unpacks suggests much the same attitude:

> Colonialism . . . has never ceased to maintain that the Negro is a savage; and for the colonist the Negro was neither an Angolan nor a Nigerian, for he simple spoke of 'the Negro'. For colonialism, this vast continent was the haunt of savages, a country riddled with superstitions and fanaticism, destined for contempt, weighed down by the curse of God . . . (Fanon 170)

Stevenson had already characterized the political acuity of the steerage passengers as something akin to a superstition; of beliefs held but with faulty or no ability to comprehend the economic and political causes behind them. MacKay is an intelligent 'pertinent debater' whose views are dismissed from the first. Much like the construction of a colonized people, the 'savage' conveniently gives way to the morally and physically fitter white race and this is the fate figuratively assigned to Mackay: 'Although far from cherishing unfriendly thoughts towards Mackay, for the man both interested and amused me, it seems an open question whether, for the good of the race, he had not better remain poor and drink himself to death' (*Emigrant* 38). But why should this be so for the 'general interests of the race'? 'Race' here is analogous to class since it seems to be less for the good of the working classes (part of the 'race' after all) that Mackay should disappear, than for the status quo that protects middle-class interests.

Whether or not Stevenson reproduces this pattern consciously, he nevertheless manages to extricate his own class carefully from the critical frame even though this strategy acknowledges an implicit threat posed by the figure Mackay as radical artisan:

> And he plainly looked upon me as one who was insidiously seeking to reduce the peoples' annual bellyful of corn and steam-engines. I feel there is some mistake in this alarm, and that people could get through life perhaps with less of either. But when I hinted at something of this view, and that to spend less was,

after all, as good a way out of the difficulty of life as to gain more, he accused me, in almost as many words, of the sin of aristocracy and a desire to grind the masses. Perhaps there was some indelicacy on my part in presenting him with such an argument; for it is not in his class that such a movement must be inaugurated; and *we* must see the rich honest, before we need to see the poor considerate. (*Emigrant* 38; my emphasis)

The 'we' emphasized here is telling since it establishes a subject position that is neither of the poor who are 'inconsiderate' nor of the aristocratic rich who are 'dishonest'. It is the 'we' or, quite literally here, the 'middle class' who must see both reformed to achieve social harmony. This 'middle class' is further refined by a concern 'about the continued property and power of many unworthy capitalists' (*Emigrant* 38) who are excluded from Stevenson's own class identification. So, who belongs to this 'middle class'? Certainly Stevenson is careful to maintain his positional superiority aboard the ship as the commentator who can dissect it as a microcosm of class ills; an identity critical of the haughty cabin passengers who pick their way among the steerage passengers and, yet, from whom he craves recognition reinforcing the need to distinguish himself from the same steerage passengers who suffered the class insult.

Stevenson's narrative persona is politically conservative, sensitive to slights and quietly supportive of empire, and also incorporates a liberal social conscience that supports a critical stance that is quite pointed on occasion with a reformist thrust. Yet he is chilled when a working man for whom he evidences some respect insists that 'capital, by some happy direction must change hands from worse to better . . . to rend the old country from end to end, and from top to bottom, and in clamour and civil discord remodel it with the hand of violence' (*Emigrant* 55). Despite his alarm at this prospect, Stevenson does allow the inevitability of reform and is willing to accept what he views as an extremist course from a man of this calibre, who 'was calm; he had attained prosperity and ease; he was a gentleman' (*Emigrant* 55). Indeed, these credentials would almost seem to co-opt this prosperous, level-headed radical to Stevenson's 'middle class', an appropriation that provides some clue to the discursive coordinates of Stevenson's position. His emphasis on culture and manners recalls Matthew Arnold's social commentary in *Culture and Anarchy* (1869), where he castigates the ruling classes for both their materialism and selfish indifference for the sufferings of the poor. This, he argues, had led to the disaffection of the poor and working classes from the nation and cultural degeneration as a fearsome mob, alien in culture and interests. Arnold's argument was to reclaim the working classes to the national project by a diffusion of English (middle-class) culture through State-sponsored mass education that would encourage national cohesiveness and thereby hold off revolution born of resentment and exclusion. This approach is not, however, unique, having been tried and tested as an aspect of imperial governance long before Arnold adapted it for the poor and working classes of the motherland. For example, Macaulay puts forward much the same strategy in his famous 'Minute on Indian Education' of 1835. The only difference is that Macaulay calls for the education of an intermediary class to mediate British culture and power to a foreign population, whereas Arnold calls for middle-class culture to be taken directly to the no less foreign working-class masses of Britain:

> We must at present do our best to form a class who may be interpreters between us and the millions we govern; a class of persons, Indian in blood a colour, but English in taste, in opinions, in morals, and in intellect. To that class we may leave it to refine the vernacular dialects of the country, to enrich those dialects in terms of science borrowed from the Western nomenclature, and to render them by degrees fit vehicles for conveying knowledge to the great mass of the population. (Macaulay 61)

Stevenson adds a more Social Darwinist edge to this Arnoldian discourse by contrasting Scottish labourers who enjoyed a more liberal education system to the equivalent English farm worker:

> I was already a young man when I was fort brought into contact with some of the heavy labours of Suffolk; and only those who have some acquaintance with the same class in Scotland, can conceive the astonishment and disgust with which I viewed the difference. To me, they seemed scarce human, but a very gross and melancholy sort of ape. (*Emigrant* 85)

Stevenson's point here is less to emphasize Britain's internal rivalries (although the standard of education in Scotland as a whole was superior and far more egalitarian than that available in England throughout most of the nineteenth century), than to underline his Arnoldian theme of the benefits of education and cultivation. As a contrast to his Suffolk labourer, he introduces an anecdote recounting an encounter with a Scottish labourer and the ensuing discussion that exemplifies the possibility of communication over a mutually shared cultural vocabulary, while maintaining an absolute material and class inequality. Here a colonizing positional superiority is unnecessary since both parties know their place in the social scale and share allegiance to a common cultural ground.

If nothing else, the vision is curiously feudal in terms of its fixed social roles, and no doubt owes something to Victorian Britain's fascination with all things medieval – not least in literature from Walter Scott's *Ivanhoe* (1820) to Stevenson's own *The Black Arrow* (1888). It does, nonetheless, betray a comprehension of the dehumanizing effects of what amounts to colonial as well as class relationships that he uses to interpret contemporary class antagonisms. The apelike quality of the Suffolk labourer emphasizes this discursive connection in terms of their potential 'racial' otherness by hinting at a colonial register that echoes the very worst type of racial slur.

It is at this point that republican America, the great melting pot of peoples and cultures, begins to represent an external threat by holding out an alternative social structure as well as a safety valve for the social pressures of Britain. Stevenson does not allow that America in fact offers anything better to the working man; quite the contrary, it is merely the allure of a place where success might be had in the face of failure at home: 'the true reasoning of their [the steerage passengers] souls ran thus – I have not got on; I ought to have got on; if there were a revolution I should get on. How? They had no idea. Why? Because – well, look at America' (*Emigrant* 80). Stevenson's response to the fact and cultural signification of the United States is as equivocal as his attitude towards the steerage passengers and broader interclass relationships. As discussed earlier, he locates a common 'racial' destiny predicated on a shared culture for Britons and Americans founded on westward expansion, but much of the ambivalence he reveals towards the motivations for emigration are, by extension, displaced onto the United States. Stevenson even though he is only an 'amateur' emigrant, becomes entangled by his own ambivalence towards the United States when he counts himself among this collection of 'failures and misfits' seeking a new beginning. Just as his narrative carefully differentiates between himself and the social misdemeanours of all classes represented aboard the ship, so he extricates himself at the last from the company of Britain's rejected: 'emigration has to be done before we climb the vessel; an aim in life is the only fortune worth the finding; and it is not to be found in foreign lands but in the heart itself' (*Emigrant* 34). So this 'emigrant' has a purpose and a life-defining one, that of marriage. His emigration is of the heart, of his emotional centre and, most importantly, a quest to define his social identity as a family patriarch in contrast to the mere physical relocation of the feckless emigrant searching for more material improvement. For Stevenson, this is a journey towards adulthood. On one level he implies that it is the inability of these 'broken men' to change themselves which will make their failure a certainty in the New World as in the Old, leaving them perpetually childlike in the eyes of a commentator like Stevenson. Such an attitude echoes contemporary assumptions about the lower classes, women and the colonized and is, indeed, the very attitude he later adopts towards the Polynesians in the South Pacific. This journey towards maturity and power is somewhat at odds with the positional superiority of the authoritative traveller/ethnographer/social commentator/colonist that Stevenson's narrative variously establishes as his persona. Moreover, the contradictory dialogue he maintains over the virtues and failings of the steerage passengers that follow this observation suggest an internalized debate concerning both his own worthiness – is he to be counted among the 'broken men'? – and whether he can make the emotional and social transformation that is required of him. This is discursively reinforced by the latent adventure theme of the text that casts Stevenson as the questing knight errant racing to succour a damsel in distress, with maturity and marriage as his ultimate goal. Yet there is an undertow of resentment in this image, one that suggests Stevenson has lost control over his own destiny if a mere word from Fanny can draw him involuntarily half way around the world perhaps explaining why this role remains largely latent in the narrative. Yet it is this personal subtext which conditions the ambivalent response to the steerage passengers. Is Stevenson simply drawn to a change of scene and life as a new beginning, or as the consequence of an illusionary idealization of the Promised Land held out by America/marriage? The risk is confirmation of his own status as a broken man or perpetual adolescent. If so, does his own self-esteem require that he find at least some of the steerage passengers admirable should he be counted among them in more than a physical sense, while also maintaining his distance from both them and the haughty cabin passengers. There is no possible reconciliation between these positions within the text since this lies beyond the narrative – what happens once he is reunited with Fanny? As a consequence, the text combines public discourses of colonialism and class with an intensely personal dialogue in which America is figured as both as a potentially redeeming space and a perversely seductive image. The resentment and unease at the heart of these idealizations reflect real personal anxieties as well as a negative reaction to the operation of class boundaries and colonialism which become more overt within the narrative as Stevenson advances further both physically and culturally into America. Not for the first time Stevenson anticipates Joseph Conrad, particularly in his ability to 'employ some of the most commonplace conventions of the adventure yarn – the journey or quest – to suggest moral and psychological conflicts with power, subtlety, and variety' (Kiely vii). Stevenson had written in 1883 of two great rival traditions in fictional narrative – realism and romance:

> The idealist, his eye fixed upon the greater outlines, loves . . . to fill up the interval with detail of the conventional order, briefly touched, soberly suppressed in tone, courting neglect. But the realist, with fine intemperance, will not suffer the presence of anything so dead as convention; he shall have all fiery, all hot-pressed from nature, all charactered and notable, seizing the eye . . . the immediate danger of the realist is to sacrifice the beauty and significance of the whole to local dexterity, or . . . to immolate his readers under facts . . . The danger of the idealist is, of course, to become merely null and lose all grip of fact, particularity, or passion . . . But though on neither side is dogmatism fitting . . . yet one thing may be generally said, that we of the last quarter of the nineteenth century, breathing as we do the intellectual atmosphere of our age, are most apt to err upon the side of realism than to sin in quest of the ideal. ('A Note on Realism' 239–40)

While often associated with the romance side of the equation with novels like *Treasure Island* and *Kidnapped*, Stevenson was crafting a narrative style that maintained an uneasy balance between realism and romance – 'on neither side is dogmatism fitting' – that is particularly evident in *The Amateur Emigrant*. While the structure – a journey quest – is a popular adventure form, the topic and eye for detail reflects the influence of realism. The result is a narrative that is able to carry and interrogate complex discourses as well as a strong emotive force. Ultimately the critical voice of the text is not, at root, directed at America but the wider Anglo-American 'race'. The 'ideal' that is flawed is not simply the idea of America but the myth of the Anglo-Saxon race. Threatened and uncertain himself in the text, his sympathies shift more decisively towards the victims of the conqueror despite his ambivalent attitude towards the emblematic class 'victims' he identified among the steerage passengers.

Stevenson asserts that as much as economic and social conditions are flawed on both sides of the Atlantic – there is no promised land here – Britons and Americans are determined by what is, despite superficial differences, effectively the same culture and demonstrate the same failings as a consequence. And yet the draw of the West, of that Promised Land – a way of life 'still conducted in the open air, and on free barbaric terms' (*Emigrant* 90) – remains. The residual image retained from the steamer is of a motley collection of very unheroic colonial pioneers attracted to migration because of an inability to succeed, and the careful reflection on conditions in Britain that produces this restless migration suggests a conception of colonialism as an inherent cultural/racial discontent:

> The talk in the train, like the talk I heard on the steamer, ran upon hard times, short commons, and the hope that moves ever westward. I thought of my shipful from Great Britain with a feeling of despair. They had come 3,000 miles, and yet it was not enough. Hard times bowed them out of the Clyde, and stood welcome then at Sandy Hook. Where were they to go? Pennsylvania, Maine, Iowa, Kansas? These were not places for immigration but for emigration, it appeared; not one of them, but I knew a man who had lifted up his heel and left it for an ungrateful country. And still westward they ran. (*Emigrant* 136–7)

And yet as with his depiction of the steerage passengers, Stevenson is unwilling, or unable, to recognize that it is the economic structure that creates both class antagonism and the prevailing conditions that leaves so many people without the means to prosper. The relentless spur to occupy more land in search of that prosperity provides grist to the mill that fuels the same process of economic and thence social inequality. Where the people spread, capital followed. As J. A. Hobson argued in his 1902 study *Imperialism*, capitalists unable to find sufficiently profitable outlets for investment at home needed a constant supply of new lands and peoples ripe for colonization and new opportunities to place funds in railways, factories and the like, and the entry of 'big business' in turn creates a new working class from the original settlers and then a further emigration to escape the exploitation and inevitable failures this entails. Indeed, the completion in 1871 of the very transcontinental railway to San Francisco on which Stevenson travelled in 1879, far from bringing the anticipated new age of economic expansion to the West Coast, brought a flood of the unemployed and low-cost commodities from the East precipitating economic collapse and a fierce competition for jobs. As Robert Schwendinger observes: 'The ranks of the unemployed swelled with men fleeing the East for the empty promises of the West: Civil War veterans seeking new lives in a marketplace that had no room for them; displaced workers whose skills were rendered useless by labour-saving technology; immigrants who had first sailed to New York and found disappointment; and the chronically unemployed' (Schwendinger 95).

While this is of itself scarcely a full-fledged explanation of the relationship between class and colonialism, it does seem to be the issue that provides *The Amateur Emigrant* with its narrative energy. Even though Stevenson acknowledges this migration, he locates its impetus in the congenital laziness of the

'Anglo-Saxon race': 'It is not sufficiently recognized that our race detests to work. If I thought that I should have to work every day of my life as hard as I am working now, I should be tempted to give up the struggle' (*Emigrant* 83). This observation is prefaced by two anecdotes: the first relating the complaint of an old American frontiersman, now an established farmer, who claims that he has had no time for improving his education due to pressure of work and whom Stevenson then observes working only 'at the extreme outside, for five hours out of every twenty-four' (*Emigrant* 82); the second the tale of a party of Aberdeen slaters who employ a man in the curious operation of 'tapping' to simulate their work while they had adjourned to the public house. Again, Stevenson ostensibly includes himself in the 'we' of 'our race' and it is significant that his two examples draw together members of the British working class with the American frontiersman turned farmer. This raises again his categorization of the 'broken men' and would be colonists of the steerage in a way that implies that Britain has exported this laziness to the New World via its surplus population of 'failures'.

Once again though, regardless of the 'we' of his characterization, Stevenson's own narrative subject position is preserved from such a simple categorization. He is neither worker nor settler, but to what purpose? It is certain that by developing a narrative strategy based on the adventure genre, Stevenson – much as Conrad was able to do later – managed to advance an interrogation of colonialism and racism which he witnessed in the raw on America's West Coast, while evading the implications of that criticism on his own identity as a member of the middle class of the most powerful imperial nation of his day – an imperialism of which he was broadly proud and supportive for most of his life. From this discursive position he was able to deliver an, at times, scathing criticism while continuing to extricate himself from the rhetorical 'we' of the narrative as is illustrated by the following encounter with a Native American family:

> ... the noble red man of old story – he over whose hereditary continent we had been streaming all these days. I saw no wild or independent Indian; indeed, I hear such avoid the neighbourhood of the train; but now and again at way stations, a husband and wife and a few children, disgracefully dressed out with the sweepings of civilisation, come forth and stared upon the immigrants. The silent stoicism of their conduct, and the pathetic degradation of their appearance, would have touched any thinking creature, but my fellow-passengers danced and jested around them with truly Cockney baseness. I was ashamed for the thing we call civilisation. We should carry on our consciences so much at least, of our forefathers' misconduct as we continue to profit by ourselves. (*Emigrant* 141)

Significantly, the key characteristics of Stevenson's earlier class-based observations resurface here as a direct attack on the behaviour of the white passengers: firstly, colonization has clothed the Native Americans in material signs of their 'degradation', which echoes the gaze of the cabin passengers who visit the steerage for signs of bedraggled clothing as a mark of their condition; second, Stevenson introduces his own class-informed criticism of the steerage passengers by depicting the white settlers' behaviour as 'truly Cockney baseness'.

The shame he feels at this scene once more ensures that he is carefully situated outside the taunting crowd, and yet he participates fully in the recognizing and categorizing the 'degradation' of their appearance, which in turn leads to a class-based slur. 'Cockney baseness' reflects a level on Stevenson's scale far below that of the stoic Native American. At the risk of belabouring the point, this passage further reinforces the association of Americans and would-be Americans with the lowest point of Anglo-Saxon culture as he views it. Moreover, in a by-now familiar twist of discursive extrapolation, these characteristics are generalized across the 'race', its conscience and its civilization. Indeed, his final sentence is highly suggestive and approaches recognition of the contradictions of the stance he maintains in the text. While not a direct participant in either class or colonial objectifications, and still less in any way materially active in colonial activities, he recognizes that he is the beneficiary of both: 'We should carry on our consciousnesses so much at least, of our forefathers' misconduct as we continue to profit by ourselves' (*Emigrant* 141). At this late stage of the text, Stevenson brings himself and his class decisively into the frame. He and they do not prosecute the dirty work of colonialism, but remain at home and reap the glory of imperial aggrandisement and share in the enormous profits of empire. Nor do they directly possess the rack-rented slum dwellings for the poor cordoned off into working-class ghettos like the East End. A position that is materially present but never directly responsible is ultimately an untenable position as Stevenson's text reveals.

3

Jack London's *The People of the Abyss*: Socialism, Imperialism and the Bourgeois Ethnographer

In the introductory chapter to *The People of the Abyss* titled 'The Descent' Jack London reinforces the 'abyss' metaphor of the text's title. Like Stevenson some 20 years earlier, both titles communicate the sinking down from European civilization suggested by Stevenson's phrase 'Cockney Baseness'. Such is the interrelation between class and racial discourse that this descent is even more directly reminiscent of a colonial perspective as the author/protagonist meets with astonishment and ignorance when he seeks directions to the East End from his middle-class friends as if this part of the city is some vague, even far off, land of depravity and savagery into which only a madman would venture. Indeed, this is just how London describes his English friends' reaction, 'painfully endeavouring to adjust themselves to the psychological processes of a madman who had come to them with better credentials than brains' (*Abyss* 11). The colonial analogy is made explicit when he seeks direction and assurance of future identification from Thomas Cook & Son, a sarcastic vignette deliberately designed to expose the absurdity of the situation:

> But Cook, O Thomas Cook and Son, pathfinders and trailclearers, living sign-posts to all the world, and bestowers of first aid to bewildered travellers – unhesitatingly and instantly, with ease and celerity, could send me to Darkest Africa or Innermost Thibet, but to the East of London, barely a stone's throw away from Ludgate Circus, you know not the way. (*Abyss* 11)

This introduces and satirizes a well-established literary and sociological trope, which equated the East End slums with the dangers and potential degeneration of the 'savage' imperial frontier – 'Darkest Africa' – and also another frontier marked by an insurmountable exotic difference, 'Innermost Thibet'. The 'darkest Africa' trope was well established by the time London was writing. It actualizes images of racial differences and a way of life once concealed but now brought to light, visible to and possessed by the imperial gaze of the intrepid bourgeois explorer from the comfort of his own armchair. By the end of the 1890s, Joseph Conrad had established a narrative connection between the mystery, savagery and racial difference of the imperial frontier and the East End of London as a direct measure of relative cultural advancement in his novella *Heart of Darkness* (1899). In the framing narrative, the central character, Marlow, looks across to the Thames riverbank to the crowded heart of the imperial trade network and famously reflects: 'And this also has been one of the dark places of the earth' (Conrad 18). The temporal distance established by the past tense has, by the conclusion of the story, been whittled away until 'The offing was barred by a black bank of clouds and the tranquil waterway leading to the uttermost ends of the earth flowed sombre under an overcast sky – seemed to lead to an immense darkness' (Conrad 123–4).

Unlike Conrad's text, London is overtly satirical; it is the ignorance of his English friends and the Dickensian spluttering of the Thomas Cook clerk – 'the human emporium of routes and fares' (*Abyss* 11) – that are risible in a way which directly imputes their competence implying its they, and not London as social investigator, who manifest some form of psychological aberration through their pointed ignorance of the East End of their own city. Moreover, it is their competence as men of affairs that is also under scrutiny. Failing to find the help he requires from Thomas Cook's chief office, he applies to the American consul-general and immediately finds a man prepared to provide the necessary official contact should anything go wrong: 'at last I found a man with whom I could do business' (*Abyss* 12). Even before describing any direct experiences of the condition of the poor in the East End, London has established a powerful discursive position which defines the British ruling classes and the great commercial institutions like Thomas Cook & Sons as representatives of an imperialism which displays an astonishing ignorance, ineptitude and ridiculousness. Imperial Power seems to rest on rather shaky foundations. Robert Peluso argues that this is part of a broader strategy to discount British imperial success in favour of an emerging American colonialism:

> Effectively marginalising Great Britain via an epistemological-ideological colonisation, which uses narratives of America as a land of opportunity and abundance to understand the extreme poverty existing, by all accounts, in the very centre of empire, Jack London's *The People of the Abyss* replaces narratives of empire dominated by British agency with a version grounded in American agency. (Peluso 59)

Yet London's narrative strategy is indicative of a considerable discursive struggle. While American imperialism seems to be promoted over the British variety, this promotion is carried on alongside criticism of the ignorance and ineptitude of the (English) middle classes. Since American imperialism might also be characterized as a bourgeois project, this appears to contrast strangely with the overall tenor and subject of this text that would suggest more socialist or at least liberal-inspired concerns inimical to the interests of this class, but not to London's own history. As a consequence the reader is left questioning the class and political alignment of London's narrative persona. Nor is it possible to resolve this contradiction by assuming that a straightforward nationalist point is being made at Britain's expense, since as a member of the middle class of another imperialist nation he would be subject to his own criticism. This contradiction is not restricted to the text. On 31 July 1902 during his Atlantic crossing, he wrote to Anna Strunsky that 'I Meet the men of the world, in the Pullman Coaches, New York clubs, and Atlantic-liner smoking rooms, and truth to say I am made more hopeful for the [Socialist] cause by their total ignorance and non-understanding of the forces at work. They are blissfully ignorant of the coming upheaval, while they have grown bitterer and bitterer towards the workers' (London *Letters I* 304). Here it is not the British middle classes under scrutiny and charged with ignorance and ineptitude but Americans. There is no mention of imperialism in the body of the letter, but it is suggestively signed 'The Sahib'. While this might simply reflect the unusual relationship he had with Anna Strunsky at this time – he seems to have been wildly, and publicly, in love with her much to the anguish of his first wife – it also implies a positional superiority towards his subjects expressed in a recognizably colonial form. Yet, he is also one of the 'men of the world' enjoying the privileges of the smoking rooms afforded by first-class travel, just as in the British capital his class status gains him letters of introduction and easy access to Thomas Cook's higher management and the American consul.

Whatever the contradictions lying behind London's narrative and personal identity, the rhetoric needed to establish this position demonstrates marked similarities to Stevenson's narrative drawing on two distinct genres that are signalled within the first few pages of the text – adventure and ethnography. The latter was widely practiced by social investigators of urban poverty as well as colonial explorers, administrators and travellers. Significantly, London had read a number of quasi-scientific sociological works on the poor in the East End and Britain in preparation for his own study, a fact not disclosed in the text itself but clear from its structure. As Auerbach observes: 'Throughout *The People of the Abyss* such authority draws on London's role as a naturalist reporting from the field – a close, sensitive, yet objective observer committed to documentary (human) nature acting out its biological imperatives in a fatal (social) environment' (Auerbach 14). The result, as we saw with Stevenson, is simultaneous practices of 'racializing' the working classes and the identification of the non-European peoples of the Western empires as a kind of colonial working class. As Helen Carr argues: 'The West has regularly expressed its relation to the rest of the world in class terms, a metaphor which has been a powerful element in colonialist discourse' (Carr 15). To anticipate the direction of the argument somewhat, London effectively employs two discursive modes to hold at bay the central contradictions of his own narrative. He creates a position whereby he can register a class-based outrage while drawing on a discourse of ethnicity that relies on contemporary notions of a racially othered working class. The first working-class people he observes on the way to Stepney are 'a new and different race of people, short of stature, and of wretched beer-sodden appearance' (*Abyss* 13). He extends that analogy, by association, to the British ruling classes whom he can then ridicule by constructing their role as a despotic local elite. In narrative terms, he creates a rhetorical stance that maintains both superiority and, as Pratt suggests, innocence enabling him to impute guilt solely to the British ruling classes despite the contradiction of his own recently attained middle-class status and the imperial ambitions of his own nation.

This is supported by and complimentarily to the other genre on which he draws to create his narrative persona – adventure fiction. This is not to perpetuate the idea that London's oeuvre should be defined by the immense success of his adventure fiction; like Stevenson, his work is considerably more diverse than this. It is, however, important to recognize that the name he had made for himself before turning his attention to the East End derived from his Yukon stories, which are dependent on the narrative devices of adventure fiction. Indeed, immediately after returning to California and while completing *The People of the Abyss*, he penned perhaps his greatest work in this genre, *The Call of the Wild*, both texts appearing in the same year, 1903. While the novel does not have a colonial setting – although even here, displaced and bitterly resentful Native Americans haunt the novel – the late Victorian adventure genre was overwhelming influenced by imperialism and the colonial frontier. Moreover, London served his apprenticeship as a short story writer devouring the works of Stevenson, Kipling and Conrad. Some popular writers like H. Rider Haggard drew directly from contemporary anthropological studies, and as Richard Phillips observes, 'popular literature was directly connected to colonialism, not just representing or legitimizing colonization. And adventure stories were often explicit and specific in their promotion of colonialism' (R. Phillips 69). Indeed, the connection was acknowledged even then. In 1891 Stevenson's friend and leading British anthropologist of the period, Andrew Lang, observed that 'men of imagination and literary skill have been the new conquerors, the Cortés and Balboas of India, Africa, Australia, Japan and the isles of the southern seas' (Lang 198). This is not to suggest that *The People of the Abyss* reads like a popular adventure narrative, but London was a master of the adventure form and thence part of his narrative repertoire. Like the rhetorical stance of the objective and all-seeing ethnographic narrator, the adventure hero relied strongly on his/her positional superiority in relation to the colonized, or potentially colonizable, others. Yet unlike the ethnographic subject, the subject of imperialist adventure narratives overtly promotes not only cultural superiority, but also physical and technical strength, qualities of personal bravery, a sense of justice and fair play even though such texts could represent its heroes as purveyors of the most extreme violence. Thence when London identifies the reaction of his British acquaintances to his intention to see first hand the conditions in the East End as an 'insane American who *would* see the East End' (*Abyss* 12), he actualizes a quasi-scientific empirical stance which contrasts on the one hand the effete reliance on irrational hearsay about the East End among the British middle classes, and on the other emphasizes his personal bravery and adventurousness, which is, moreover, specifically American. This also provides another perspective on the prominence London gives to his experience with Thomas Cook & Sons. This firm was relied upon by the British as a matter of course to arrange convenient transport to the far-flung corners of the empire and the world beyond, whereas he carries the flame of exploration of the true adventurer, daring to enter the place which the British ruling classes fear most and of which they are apparently most complacently ignorant. This stance not only promotes the vitality of American colonialism, but also allows London to combine the rhetoric of the imperialist 'civilizing mission' to the 'dark places of the earth' with that of the enlightenment of the East End poor thence preserving something of his socialist credentials while creating what is effectively an imperialist subject.

Clothing, Status and Deception

Like any good explorer or ethnographer embarking on field work, London dwells at length on the necessity of equipping himself for his descent into the East End 'abyss'. Yet the theatricality of the situation has the opposite effect, accentuating the implication that London is in fact donning a costume for some elaborate game. The process of haggling with the proprietor of a Whitechapel second-hand clothes shop is mildly comic:

> But I disputed with him over the outrageous difference between prices and values . . . and he settled down to drive a hard bargain with a hard customer. In the end I selected a pair of stout though well-worn trousers, a frayed jacket with one remaining button, a thin leather belt, and a very dirty cloth cap. My underclothing and socks, however, were new and warm, but of the sort that any American waif, down on his luck, could acquire in the ordinary course of events. (*Abyss* 14)

Just as the American consul was a man with whom London could 'do business', here we find his own business acumen altogether too much for the English shop man. Further, he considers the ill assorted garments outrageously overpriced at the ten shillings he finally agrees to pay, falling far short of the standard that even an 'American waif' would be able to acquire. It is worth pausing here to consider exactly what purpose this scene serves in the narrative at this point. The shopkeeper would, no doubt, try to get as high a price as possible from his working-class customers, but probably only tries to get an inflated value here because London appearing in middle-class, well-to-do guise is obviously more than able to afford what is being asked. Thence the dispute over the 'outrageous difference between prices and values', as he describes it, misses the point. The dispute is over prices and the ability to pay; value is relative in this type of negotiation. What London demands here is that prices should be forced as low as possible and be measured only on the basis of absolute value. Yet his basis for comparison is resolutely middle class. Being well clothed and fed the items he purchases seem to be of little value. As a consequence his commentary derives more from the attitude of a tourist than a politically committed investigator. This in turn offers an opportunity for interclass comparison but instead he only manages to make a nationalist point by asserting that the poor of the United States could acquire what he is being charged ten shillings for as a matter of course. In doing so he makes no connection between his middle-class insistence on the right to the lowest prices and the consequences of this for the working class he is supposedly here to investigate in terms of low wages. After all, he singularly fails to ask why a second-hand clothes shop is necessary in Whitechapel. The mention of a generic 'American waif' seems far more ideologically revealing than the simple tone of comparison might at first suggest.

Clothed in his new costume he is, like Stevenson, immediately struck by his change of identity and social status evident from the attitude of passers-by:

> No sooner was I out on the streets than I was impressed by the difference in statue effected by my clothes. All servility vanished from the demeanour of the common people with whom I came in contact. Presto! In the twinkling of an eye, so to say, I had become one of them. My frayed and out-at-elbows jacket was the badge and advertisement of my class, which was their class. It made me of like kind, and in place of the fawning and too respectful attention I had hitherto received, I now shared with them a comradeship. The man in corduroy and dirty neckerchief no longer addressed me as 'sir or 'governor'. It was mate now – and a fine and hearty word, with a tingle to it, and a warmth and a gladness, which the other term does not possess. Governor! It smacks of mastery, and power, and high authority – the tribute of the man who is under the man on top, delivered in the hope that he will let up a bit and ease his weight, which is another way of saying that it is an appeal for alms. (*Abyss* 15)

As a criticism of British interclass relationships and the signification of clothing in the representation of class status, this passage appears at first glance to be transparent reportage more or less coloured by a laudable social critique. What is also present, however, is a celebration of London's ability to convincingly pass as a 'native' fooling the 'common people' and the 'man on top' with equal measure. This skill is almost magical, 'Presto' and he is one of *them*, and in a similar 'twinkling of an eye' he can transform himself back into his true class which, like Stevenson's narrative persona, is an/other neither implicated in nor responsible for the class system he reviles. More troubling he revels in the double life this gives him the opportunity to lead which, as Jonathan Auerbach suggests, hints at the central conflict of Stevenson's *The Strange Case of Dr Jekyll and Mr Hyde* (1886) in his ability to transform into one of the 'beasts'. The inherent superiority of his position is maintained by his presumption of comradeship contrasted with the emasculating servility of the British working class towards the 'man on top' compounded by the impulse to beg for a little alleviation of that oppression. This also suggests that it is the inability of the British working classes to assert their individualism or to initiate collective action; they continue to defer in a way 'that it is an appeal for alms' and this continues to keep them in a miserable condition. This blame displacement is similar to Stevenson's dismissal of the steerage passengers' political comprehension and Mackay's arguments – they are to blame for their own faults. In London's text this strengthens the sense of his individualism, strength and superiority founded not on a criticism of the ruling classes, but on the weakness of the poor. His feeling of comradeship and solidarity with the East End poor therefore strikes a false note by suggesting their oppression is partly of their own making.

London's claim to counterfeit convincingly the appearance and manners of the working class parallels the exploits of colonial figures such as the explorer and Orientalist, Richard Burton, whose most celebrated exploit was to disguise himself as an Indian Muslim doctor and undertake a pilgrimage to Mecca at a time when discovery would have meant his death. Edward Said's commentary on Burton's account of his exploits captures the contradictory impulses that are also a factor in London's own 'native' masquerade: 'Burton thought of himself both as a rebel against authority (hence his identification with the East as a place of freedom from Victorian moral authority) and as a potential agent of authority in the East. It is in the *manner* of that coexistence, between two antagonistic roles for himself that is of interest' (Said 195). London is certainly not representing the East End as a place of freedom from an oppressive moral code, unless it is to free himself from the clamour for alms as an American tourist. Yet by emphasizing his American origins he certainly claims a moral authority that both rails against the ruthless exploitation by the ruling classes and also points to what he interprets as a lack of moral strength among the poor by introducing a compromised socialist framework to imply the need for a social revolution, which the oppressed, too demoralized and degenerate, are unable – or unwilling – to initiate. The way the register of the text slides between that of a detached social investigator, engaged political radical and self-made man never quite coalesces and resembles another contemporary social investigation, W. E. B Du Bois *The Souls of Black Folk* (1899). Here the intellectual, resolutely middle-class, African-American college professor constantly switches between racial solidarity, outrage, detached commentary and class-based criticism of Southern blacks. While London and Du Bois have quite different aims – there is nothing like the investment Du Bois places in the talented ten per cent to resolve social inequalities for example – there is a similarity in their narrative strategies. Both writers empathize with the objects of their texts, but are acutely conscious of what separates them and that sense of separation expresses itself though a consistent and sometime overt criticism in contradiction to their sympathy.

London's credibility as a political radical is further compromised by the evident pleasure he takes in the practical liberation that his masquerade allows him: 'This brings me to a delight I experienced in my rags and tatters which is denied the average American abroad. The European traveller from the States who is not a Croesus, speedily finds himself reduced to a chronic state of self-conscious sordidness by the hordes of cringing robbers who clutter his steps from dawn to dark, and deplete his pocket book in a way that puts compound interest to the blush' (*Abyss* 15). These 'cringing robbers' can only be poor street tradesmen – costermongers – or beggars, a phrase which sits uncomfortably with his professed solidarity and outrage on behalf of the poor once they have made this middle-class traveller feel 'sordid'. Further, the 'average American' while not a Croesus is wealthy enough in comparison with the East End poor to feel uncomfortably guilty: 'In my rags and tatters I escaped the pestilence of tipping, and encountered men on the basis of equality' (*Abyss* 15). This of course merely reinscribes the true inequality that exists in such encounters. Like a colonial adventurer, he finds a way to cast off – or fool – the crowding, grasping natives. Indeed, it is no coincidence that physical disguise is a staple of imperial adventure fiction where the European temporarily 'goes native' to further the colonial project. A contemporary fictional example of this type of colonial deception can be found among the many masters of disguise in Kipling's *Kim* (1901). The disguise trope is a device that allows the observing subject's power while enjoying a pleasurable sense of temporary – but of course reversible – rebellion; materially for individuals like Burton and as a popular thrill for the stay-at-home reader of adventure fiction.

Robert Peluso suggests that London's narrative is a production of 'knowledge of East End poverty through metaphorical relations that confirm the correctness of . . . fundamental American values, meanings, and ideals – indeed, the rightness of America itself' (Peluso 67). Yet as Said observed of Burton's masquerades, the multiple identifications London shapes for himself are mutually antagonistic and resist the reduction of this text to a nationalist-inspired tract. This is true of his narrative persona too since when in Britain, free from the material and social restrictions of middle-class American life, he is able to criticize a comparable social structure closely related to his own and yet, like Burton's ultimate belief in the superiority of European culture, his rebellion takes the form of a reassertion of middle-class American values. Given the contradictions of London's narrative identity in *The People of the Abyss* and the radical change in his opinion on the enervating effect of city life in his letters to Cloudesley Johns, his narrative dilemma becomes all the more intriguing. His revulsion could be seen to stem from his unwillingness to confront the consequences of not just an increasingly bourgeois lifestyle, but also a strong reaction to the inhabitants of the city which includes both rich and poor. Indeed, the unavoidable inequalities of cities suggest that this is the cause of his reaction: he desires the middle-class lifestyle but is unable to reconcile the social and economic inequality on which it is based. The result is an antagonism directed towards both the ruling and working classes in Britain. Moreover, the invisibility and acceptance that his disguise seems to give him with the poor is a means of leaving these immediate contradictions behind, at least within the narrative. No longer challenged by the material reproach of the importune solicitations of the poor he is able to deflect the implication of class culpability in the neglect he witnesses. His true identity and class status are a knowledge generally only known to himself and the reader, and through this textual relationship the narrative persona 'Jack London' attempts to maintain a sense of class superiority without complicity in the appalling scenes of poverty in which he, and of course the reader, participate.

Yet concealment always courts the risk of exposure. The wrench back to oneself demands an extreme reorientation of narrative focus which is carefully managed in *The People of the Abyss*. When London emerges in his disguise as a member of the working classes the adventure narrative is replaced by first person sociological reportage, and the excitement and sensation of infiltration give way to a presentation of cold facts of 'scientific' observation. An example of this stylistic shift occurs in an episode when London is in the company of an elderly carpenter and a carter while frantically searching for admittance into a workhouse for the night in character as a penniless sailor. Considerable pace and suspense are created by pressing need and a swift tramp through the dark, cold, threatening streets, the haunt of Jack the Ripper in recent memory, only to be rejected by a surly workhouse porter creating a tense expectation of some tragically dramatic resolution. Instead, London recalls he has a gold sovereign sown into his jacket for emergencies and working it loose he metamorphoses from putative hero of the tale into a middle-class ethnographer: 'Of course I had to explain to them that I was merely an investigator, a social student, seeking to find out how the other half lived. And at once they shut up like clams. I was not of their kind; my speech had changed, the tones of my voice were different, in short, I was a superior, and they were superbly class conscious' (*Abyss* 40). Note how blame for the sudden awkwardness is pressed onto the two workingmen whose silence and unease is due to their unhelpful class consciousness according to the narrator. One can only wonder if this episode is based on an actual incident how far the sudden silence concealed anger over the deceit that had been practised on them and whether London would have retained their company if it had not been for the promise of a good meal and a bed for the night.

Class Discourse as Imperial Critique

London attended the coronation procession of Edward VII in character as one of the unemployed poor. His analysis is significantly located at the narrative and physical centre of the text strategically exercising considerable thematic authority. Indeed, the positioning of this chapter mirrors the physical location of his experience, Trafalgar Square ' "the most splendid site in Europe", and the very innermost heart of empire' (*Abyss* 60). Both the textual and material spaces re-enact the 'abyss' trope of London's opening chapter. What he reports is, from his perspective, essentially irrational. While he detects an inversion of established hierarchies, this is not the disempowered poor temporarily throwing off the temporal authority of the dominant classes and their institutions, but that very ruling caste's celebration of an inversion of moral structures that leaves so many destitute in the midst of such wealth and power. He is 'perplexed and saddened. I never saw anything to compare with the pageant, except Yankee circuses and Alhambra ballets; nor ever did I see anything so hopeless and tragic' (*Abyss* 60). It is striking that he uses a comparison with American mass entertainment to trivialize and undermine the import of British State ceremony, which is as much about the expression of imperial might than it is about celebrating the ascension of a new King. While his disgust at the oppression and misery the ceremony masks is certainly not misplaced, he ultimately makes a rather more self-serving point. He proceeds to construct a complex metaphor in which the military might of empire which kills and conquers in the name of imperial aggrandisement is also an agent for the impoverishment and parasitic extraction of life from the East End poor and, by implication, Britain as a whole:

> And it was thus at Trafalgar Square, so it was along the whole of the march –
> force, overpowering force; myriads of men, splendid men, the pick of the people,
> whose sole function in life is blindly to obey, and blindly kill and destroy and
> stamp out life. And that they should be well fed, well clothed, and well armed,
> and have ships to hurl them to the ends of the earth, the East End of London,
> and the 'East End' of all England toils and rots and dies. (*Abyss* 61)

London's repulsion is powerfully expressed hinting at an older image of imperial despotism of Nero fiddling while Rome burns or, in this case, 'toils and rots and dies'. This is further enhanced by recounting in parable form the Old Testament story of the Israelites' desire for a king 'like all the nations' who, granted their wish, find they have simply created a parasitic despot who taxes them. A direct link is then made to the 'five hundred hereditary peers [who] own one-fifth of England;

and they, and the officers and servants under the King, and those who are to compose the powers that be, yearly spend in wasteful luxury $1,850,000,000 or £370,000,000, which is thirty-two per cent of the total wealth produced by all the toilers of the country' (*Abyss* 62). Interestingly, London has an entirely different perspective on British history than another popular American writer, Mark Twain, who witnessed the Jubilee procession for Queen Victoria barely five years earlier in 1897 and was deeply impressed by its ability to convey a narrative of progress and success: 'Many things about it will set one to reflecting upon what a large feature of the world England is to-day, and this in turn will move one, even the least imaginative, to cast a glance down her long perspective and note the steps of her progress and the insignificance of her first estate' (Twain 193). At the risk of generalization, the very different positions here demonstrate the contradictory significance the British Empire had for these two Americans. For London it is violent, despotic and expansive, the very anathema of American freedom; for Twain an admirable, apparently benevolent, progressive success in which Americans can share – it is not insignificant to observe that Twain would become one of the most outspoken critics of America's own imperial expansion after 1898. From this perspective London's reaction to the coronation procession seems to bear out Peluso's argument that for London, Britain represented the negation of fundamental American values against which he 'legitimizes a rapidly developing American imperialism' (Peluso 55). It is significant that Twain's view of the British Empire reflects the more positive view once expressed by London in letters to his friend Cloudesley Johns (see introduction).

The real significance of the gulf between Twain's and London's responses reflect different attitudes towards historical progression and regression. For London, the system of government that simultaneously creates such imperial might, aristocratic privilege and abject poverty is almost feudal, harking back to an earlier stage in Western social and economic development. It is, therefore, a regressive system of governance; an historical anachronism even. While this might seem to reflect the ascendency of London's more socialistic views, it is nothing of the sort. What is missing is a reference to the very class who have perhaps gained most from the empire and, indeed, considerable influence on the national and imperial government – the commercial entrepreneurs of middle-class origin. It is this class that is largely invisible in State ceremonials as Twain noted in 1897:

> As far as mere glory goes, the foreign trade of Great Britain has grown in a wonderful way since the Queen ascended the throne . . . but the capitalist, the

manufacture and the working man were not officially in the procession . . . Cecil Rhodes was not in the procession; the Chartered Company absent from it. Nobody was there to collect his share of the glory due for the formidable contributions to the imperial estate. Even Doctor Jameson was out, and yet he had tried hard to accumulate territory. (Twain 400)

From London's debatably socialist-informed perspective, he could have been expected to believe that the real power behind the throne was the bourgeoisie and had been so since the English Civil War, not the largely honorific residuum of an ancient aristocracy regardless of their inherited landholdings. Indeed, the agricultural estates of the aristocracy at the turn of the nineteenth century comprised only a relatively minor part of Britain's economy despite the capital value the land represented. Between 1811 and 1851 the contribution of agriculture to the gross national product had fallen from one-third to one-fifth, and by 1891 it had fallen to only one-thirteenth, a decline that was to continue into the twentieth century (Hobsbawm 195). It was in industry and the vast export market of the empire where the real wealth lay, and this was most visibly in the hands of the wealthiest of the bourgeoisie who had become indistinguishable from an aristocracy that had internalized their values as John Galsworthy was to reflect in the third of his Forsyte novels *To Let* (1921):

> The time had come when the Forsytes might resign their natural resentment against a 'flummery' not their by both, and accept it as the still more natural due of their possessive instincts. Besides, they had to mount and make room for all those so much more newly rich . . . They had become 'upper class' and now their name would be formally entered in the Stud Book, their money joined to land. (Galsworthy 887–8)

London's omission or lack of perception therefore has some significance. One might argue that it is the lack of depth of a younger man but this does a disservice to his usual intelligence. But it remains as Galsworthy suggests that the aristocracy had been colonized by the most successful commercial families in a process also noted by Hobsbawm: 'The wealthiest capitalist could certainly, upon shedding his more provincial crudities – and from Edwardian times even without shedding so much as his accent – win his knighthood or peerage; and his children slid into the leisure class without any difficulty whatever' (Hobsbawm 183). Certainly the contradictions of London's narrative reflect the difficulty he experienced directly attacking a class of which he was now a member. In 1905 in an interview with a reporter from the left-wing newspaper, *Common Sense*, he described his own achievement as a successful author and adoption of an affluent middle-class professional lifestyle using the very parasitic image he displaces onto the titular aristocracy of the coronation procession: 'I have become a parasite. But I have not always been one' (Kershaw 161). Indeed, one might observe that he spent many years accumulating a large estate in California completing the cycle noted by Galsworthy and Hobsbawm.

The Coronation chapter also revisits the transformation motif from his earlier encounter with the carpenter and the carter. This time he befriends a man and a woman attempting to sleep along the Thames embankment and to whom, as before, he offers to provide a meal while he questions them. The juxtaposition between the bacchanalian excesses of the coronation celebrations and the desperate situation of the man and woman could not be starker. London makes a clear differentiation between the destitute and the working classes. This man and woman are not representatives of the working classes whom he sees along the procession route 'about me, tear sin their eyes . . . tossing up their hats and crying ecstatically, "Bless 'em! Bless 'em!"' and in 'the public houses . . . a-roar with drunkenness, men, women, and children mixed together in colossal debauch' (*Abyss* 63). He is unable to comprehend the working class response to this national symbolism; being at one and the same time alienated by cultural difference and class displacement, leaving him with only the utterly dispossessed as a non-disruptive recipient of his self-affirming charity and outlet for his antagonism. It is this sense of alienating difference that forms the keynote of this chapter and resonates far beyond London's local disjunction from a foreign national symbolism leading him to reformulate a pervasive colonial image even as he is asserting his horror of the imperial and social despotism of those he perceives to be the rulers of Britain and the empire. This discourse draws on a lexicon of racial difference to externalize his confusion textually. Ironically juxtaposed with the colonial contingents of the procession who are ethnically different in a more material sense, and the working classes who rush from the public houses to cheer 'the swarthy allegiance' and then to return to the carouse' (*Abyss* 63), London focuses on the 'imperial oligarchy' around the 'King-Emperor':

> But hark! There is cheering down Whitehall; the crowd sways, the double walls of soldiers come to attention, and into view swing the King's watermen, in fantastic medieval garbs of red, for all the world like the van of a circus parade. Then a royal carriage, filled with ladies and gentlemen of the household with powdered footmen and coachmen most generously arrayed. More carriages, lords and chamberlains, viscounts, mistresses of the robes – lackeys all. Then

the warriors, a kingly escort, generals, bronzed and worn, from the ends of the earth come up to London town, volunteer officers, officers of the militia and regular forces; spans and Plumer, Broadwood and Cooper who relieved Ookiep, Mathias of Dargai, Dixon of Vlakfontain; General Gasalee and Admiral Seymour of China; Kitchener of Khartoum; Lord Roberts of India and all the world – the fighting men of England, masters of destruction, engineers of death! Another race of men from those of the shops and slums, a totally different race of men. (*Abyss* 62–3)

London is both repelled by the working men and women and the support they give to this alien ruling class – 'a totally different race of men' – which, in turn, leaves them 'racially' different again 'from those of the shops and slums'. It therefore becomes increasingly difficult to identify London's attitude towards the working class at this key juncture in the text. There is a decided alienation from this class towards the destitute and long-suffering poor represented by the couple on the Thames Embankment; and yet London uses a similar register of racial difference to characterize these very same people a few chapters later: 'A new race has sprung up, a street people. They pass their lives at work and in the streets. They have dens and lairs into which to crawl for sleeping purposes, and that is all' (*Abyss* 94). As Jeanne Reesman observes 'What often emerges as 'race' in London frequently pertains, of course, also to class' (Ressman 11). Moreover, just as the coronation procession suggests an aristocratic, violent decadence supported by foreign conquest and enslavement, so the 'ghetto folk' are becoming, quite literally, biologically as well as culturally different and an indicator of both racial and national decline: 'Brutalised, degraded, and dull, the ghetto folk will be unable to render efficient service to England in the coming struggle for industrial supremacy which economists declare has already begun' (*Abyss* 94). Despite expressions of sympathy and outrage throughout the text, London as a narrator is clearly alienated from every level of British society. His use of racial categories brings to mind the evolutionary bifurcation between the Eloi and the Morlocks of H. G. Wells' *The Time Machine* (1895). Yet rather than draw on a discourse that privileges the great surge of American imperialism to undermine the foundations of British imperial claims, London is in fact no more than echoing what British commentators had been arguing for the preceding two decades. One can see a certain conceptual and rhetorical debt to publications like James Cantile's *Degeneration Amongst Londoners* (1885) and J. Millar Fothergill's *The Town Dweller* (1889) and others.

If, therefore, London is, at least in part, repeating British anxieties to embellish his narrative, how does this affect a reading of his narrative experiences and opinions – indeed, the text itself? A few years later in 1906 London was to describe the research methodology for *The People of the Abyss* to Bailey Millard, editor of *Cosmopolitan Magazine*, thus: 'Between ourselves, and not to be passed on, I gathered every bit of the material, read hundreds of books and thousands of pamphlets, newspapers and Parliamentary Reports, composed *The People of the Abyss*, and typed it all out, took two thirds with my own camera, took a vacation of one week in the country – and did it all in two months' (*Letters II* 548–9). This is a crucial revelation concerning the composition and sources for *The People of the Abyss*. To begin with, it is strikingly at odds with his description of the work to his publisher, George Brett, following his return to the United States in 1902, it 'is simply the book of a correspondent writing from the field of industrial war . . . while it is often unsparingly critical of existing things, that it has proposed no remedies and devoted no space to theorizing – It is merely a narrative of things as they are' (*Letters II* 549). 'Things as they are' we learn from the later letter to Millard is in fact a synthesis of a large volume of other textual material and far from any theorizing, the uneasiness evident between apparently first-hand experiences in the East End and his narrative persona have been shaped from the numerous theories that he *has* absorbed as part of his research. Indeed, some British reviewers of the book were quick to detect the gap between his claims of reportage and the information needed to establish authority, such as C. F. G Masterman in the *London Daily News* of 28 November 1903: '[Jack London] has written of the East End of London as he wrote of the Klondike, with the same tortured phrase, vehemence of denunciation, splashes of colour, and ferocity of epithet. He has studies it "earnestly and dispassionately" – in two months! It is all very pleasant, very American, and very young'. What the reviewers did not know of course is the amount of research London had done for his study. Masterman notes the upper hand given to the register of adventure fiction to dismiss London's claims about conditions in the East End. In effect, by suppressing the fact of his research and by incorporating structural elements from a genre not much respected for its ability to pose serious questions, London has curiously forfeited discursive authority.

The numerous contradictions that result arise as much from a lack of discursive reconciliation of the material as ideological inconsistencies. As Reesman notes: 'Scholars who have tackled London's contradictory ideas on individualism and socialism note that London was a socialist nearly all his life, despite the inconsistency it posed to his racial theories' (Reesman 7). Ostensibly, London's critique of the British as a 'race' in physical and moral decline is founded on their neglect of the working classes. That there were signs of imperial decline and very real neglect of both the working classes and especially the poor are matters of contemporary and historical note, but London's reading of what he witnessed is a highly individualized collage of various discourses, experiences and personal associations wed together in a way unique to him. Indeed, as unique as his narrative style. What results is a text that at one and the same time presents a widespread view of poverty in Britain and a picture of the decline in the racial stock that is specific to London self-conception or, perhaps more accurately, public self-fashioning, rather than an accurate representation of the East End slums. As the *Daily News* reviewer observed, that identity is readily associated with the public identity of the Klondike adventure writer. When Jonathan Auerbach suggests that *The People of the Abyss* is a 'hybrid text' he certainly draws attention to one of its most important characteristics. Yet his suggestion that this hybridity arises as a consequence of 'the strange mixture of commentary and improvization' fails to adequately respond to the intertextual nature of London's narrative identity (Auerbach 117). Robert Peluso argues that London 'invented a new subjectivity for himself and a new "structure of discourse" that would win consent for a new set of actualities (namely American imperialism)' (Peluso 60). This position becomes problematic in light of the intertextuality of the work as a whole. Rather than an external – specifically American – analysis of British imperial decline, London adapts a series of themes from his research that reflect concerns very much from within the British imperial 'structure of discourse' which Peluso suggests he attempts to supersede. These contribute to creating a specific narrative identity that is unique and specifically American while generating considerable narrative tension as a position formed from British sources. The decline of the 'physical stock' of the common people had long been a concern of the British social imperialist, but it was the Boer War, on which London had originally been commissioned to report, that had placed this question very much on the national and imperial agenda while London was actually resident in the East End. As Gareth Stedman Jones writes:

> While Britain continued to enjoy imperial triumph abroad, interest in social questions remained small and the wave of imperialist sentiment that swept over the country on the outbreak of the Boer War appeared to set back all hopes for social reform for a decade. But when the war continued to drag on after 1900, assurance gave way to panic and doubt. After a series of defeats and frustrating campaigns, General Maurice's revelations about the low standards of recruits for the war raised once more the spectre of physical deterioration and racial degeneration. (Stedman Jones 330)

Reflecting on the repulsion London expresses while viewing the coronation celebrations and the slum conditions to be found in the East End raises the question whether this is a broader reaction to the nationalist-fuelled imperial enthusiasm that only a few years earlier had swept his own country in the period leading up to and following the Spanish–American War of 1898. Indeed, practically conterminous with the Boer War, the United States had been involved in a bitter colonial war against the Filipinos who were striving to gain independence following the defeat of the Spanish and which, like the Boer War, dragged on for years only ending in 1901 but not before the Americans had committed upwards of 60,000 troops to the field. By 1899 alone casualties had reached four thousand, which was more than that suffered in the war with Spain (Kiernan 117). The course of what was for the first time for the Americans a colonial conflict, like the British conflict in South Africa, saw a dramatic change in public opinion and invites direct comparison between British and American imperial methodologies. As May points out: 'as reports filtered back that captives had been tortured for information, potential rebels had been herded into concentration camps and troops had been sent to pro-rebel with orders to make it a "howling wilderness," some of same papers criticized the administration for tolerating such inhumanity' (May 217–18). *The People of the Abyss* is influenced by several aspects of the imperialism debate that had been taking place in the United States since 1898. While the anti-imperialist lobby never enjoyed the broad popular support, many prominent politicians, writers and intellectuals did protest. These included W. J. Bryan, a presidential candidate in 1896 (defeated by McKinley), Mark Twain and William James. Like London's study, the debate itself was both progressive and retrograde as Kiernan argues:

> . . . the practical effect of all racial speculation was likely to be retrograde. Bryan was putting the idealist case against imperialism when he said in 1899 that 'This nation cannot endure half republic and half colony – half free and half vassal.' In other words, there should be no first- and second-class citizens under the American flag. In fact there were already, inside the U.S. many millions of third-class citizens. It was unfortunate that anti-imperialists found it easiest to get a hearing by harping on the danger of American life becoming adulterated by alien stocks. (Kiernan 122)

Rather than encouraging Americans to take up the imperial baton now loosely held by Britain in moral and racial decline as Peluso proposes, London's reading of the coronation procession and the conditions he finds in the East End related to the enervating results of imperialism is just as applicable to his own country.

Indeed, London's representation of the British upper class as alien and as exotic as their imperial subjects suggests that they have become foreign to the social fabric of Britain resembling their erstwhile subjects by assuming the trappings of what Marx – betraying a decidedly Eurocentric outlook – designated 'oriental despotism' (Marx 306). Moreover, the drunken working-class customers of the public houses are transmogrified into 'cruel fanatics' incapable of rational thought common to many colonial readings of non-Christian peoples, particularly the Muslims of North Africa and the revolutionaries of the Indian Mutiny. The entire imperial social structure is, from top to bottom, subsumed into its other.

Yet comparisons between the good conditions in the United States and the horror that is Britain are constantly reiterated throughout the text. Beginning with the poor quality of the clothes that he purchases as part of his disguise (*Abyss* 14), he continues with the cramped conditions of his lodgings (*Abyss* 18); the small stature of British working class (*Abyss* 29); the plentiful, well-paid work available in the United States (*Abyss* 44); the better conditions in the American merchant marine (*Abyss* 55); even how life as a tramp is better (*Abyss* 56) and this selection is far from exhaustive. While this is certainly a variety of nationalist rhetoric as Peluso argues, none of these comparisons are made with the massed poor and working classes of the East Coast and mid-West industrial cities that were the engines of America's economic growth and the source of the nation's growing international status. The thrust of London's comparisons are ever westwards in metaphorical and actual retreat before the advance of industrialization from the east; a metaphorical journey he exemplifies by introducing the 'experience' of the 'English workman' in America: 'The proof of it is when the English workman comes to America. He will lay more bricks in New York than he will in London, still more bricks in St Louis, and still more bricks when he gets to San Francisco. His standard of living has been rising all the time' (*Abyss* 96). Note how Britain is the epicentre of this degeneration and oppression only partly alleviated in New York, a little more by St Louis until ideal conditions are met in San Francisco. London's comparative frame is not 'America', but the West and specifically a certain version of California; a land of not only economic prosperity, but of racial strength and virility as well: 'And I, walking head and shoulders above my two [British] companions, remembered *my own* husky West, and the stalwart men it had been my custom, in turn, to envy there' (*Abyss* 29; emphasis added).

Indeed, one might observe that this is less a nationalist-inspired assertion of a young, vital America over a tired, degenerate Britain, than a recession from the metropolitan centres of both 'empires' echoing London's own withdrawal from metropolitan life in California. It is, moreover, an idealized withdrawal or evasion of class conflict since the source of racial vitality on this frontier is the apparent absence of class divisions that scar the metropolitan/imperial centres. As Gregory Nobles writes in paraphrase of F. J. Turner: 'On the frontier, common people were free to fashion new social and political relationships that reflected their desires for personal independence and local self-government' (Nobles 7). The future of the Anglo-Saxon 'race' is among those settler colonies which follow this pattern: 'Blood empire is greater than political empire, and the English of the New World and the Antipodes are as strong and vigorous as ever' (*Abyss* 127). This is just the discursive locale London inscribes for himself. In effect, he manages to carve out a middle-class identity that evades responsibility for both the urban poor and industrial conflict of the metropolitan centres, as well as the despotism of imperial conquest. Indeed, the metropolitan centres are refigured as a colonial hinterland inhabited by strange and savage peoples differentiated by class and neglect in Britain, and class and immigration in the United States. By 1900 over one-third of New York's population was registered as foreign-born, almost all of whom were concentrated in the industrial working classes (Weisberger 174). With London's recorded aversion to the eastern industrial cities, it is easy to see how quickly he assumes a narrative stance towards the poor of the East End that constructs them as an alien people. The immigrant who is to be found in large numbers in the great cities is a threat to 'American' jobs making it possible to comprehend how London's socialism can sustain the contradiction of racial rather than class antagonism. He was not alone in this, and such feelings can be related directed to U.S. imperial expansion. Samuel Gompers, leader of the American Federation of Labor, spoke of the Filipinos as savages, but the most salient example is the anti-Chinese prejudice of long-standing in the West and witnessed by Stevenson in the 1880s (Kiernan 122). Indeed it is no casual rhetoric that sees London locate the vigour of the 'Anglo-Saxon race' in the newly settled lands beyond the cities, nor that he expresses his allegiance to this idea of racial elite in class terms. In short, the complexity and flexibility of this identification simultaneously combines class, economic, moral and, above all, racial superiority that enables London to criticize both Britain and, by implication, the metropolitan areas of the United States, in equal measure.

Missing, of course, from this frame are the indigenous peoples who have been variously massacred, decimated by disease, or simply displaced to make way for the white settler. While London's yeoman idyll itself is founded on a history of violence that also conveniently elides the history of African-American slavery, which originally cleared the East Coast for settlement. In essence, one must pass through much of what London attacks in *The People of the Abyss* to arrive this class and racial purity. Subsequent chapters will tackle these themes of sympathy and superiority, projected anxieties and narrative tension, in Stevenson's and London's South Pacific writing. These two texts – *The Amateur Emigrant* and *The People of the Abyss* – are key to understanding their responses to later encounters with the Other and the renegotiation of class and racial identities that will come under even greater pressures in a colonial environment. The elisions evident in London's and Stevenson's texts in this chapter by which they maintain the unity of their narrative identifications even when attacking the institutions upon which that 'positional superiority' relies and will become increasingly untenable.

4

Death, Disease and Paradise: A Parable of Imperial Expansion

'Out of My Country and Myself I Go'

This chapter will explore Stevenson's and London's first narrative encounters with the South Pacific in their travel books *In the South Seas* (1896) and *The Cruise of the Snark* (1911) respectively. Both texts feature a pronounced motif of disease and illness throughout, but particularly in relation to their land-falls on the Marquesan Islands in the actual and literary footsteps of Herman Melville's novel *Typee* (1846). Rod Edmond's pioneering work on this motif in Stevenson's and London's South Pacific writing is invaluable to this dis-cussion. As he observes: 'At the heart of the European paradise of the South Pacific, a counter-discourse of the diseased Pacific began almost simultane-ously' (Edmond 194). While the region had unique diseases – like the dis-figuring elephantitis – of particular actual and symbolic significance is the communication of European diseases that was a feature of Western contact with the Pacific from the very earliest days such as Cook's vain efforts to prevent the spread of syphilis to the Islanders from his sailors. As this suggests, the opposing tropes of the paradisal versus diseased Pacific are not just the stuff of European cultural imagination, but rather more prosaically the dissemination of disease with the growth of commerce, proselytization and colonization was a very material fact. The effect of continental diseases in the Pacific was the direct result of the technological advances that made the colonization, settle-ment and exploitation of the South Pacific possible, commercially viable and strategically important.

As well as being a significant motif of modernity, colonization and migration, exposure to disease is a profoundly disturbing personal experience that goes to the heart of the two texts under consideration in this chapter. Illness is a state which, literally and figuratively, cannot be detached from physical being, social meaning or symbolic circulation. As well as being materially devastating, it is also discursive or, perhaps more properly, metaphorical. As a liminal experience Sander Gilman observes that: 'The construction of the image of the patient is . . . always the playing out [the] desire for a demarcation between ourselves and the chaos represented in culture by disease' (Gilman 4). In a colonial context, the possible combinations of encounter of this ground are: (a) the healthy white man and healthy 'native'; (b) the diseased white man and the healthy 'native'; (c) the healthy white man and diseased 'native'; and (d) the diseased white man and diseased 'native'. The volatile element added to Gilman's proposition is ethnicity. While in (c) the relationship can preserve both racial and disease demarcation, the situation is markedly confusing and threatening in situations (b) and (d). Situation (a) is also not entirely free of a possible threat to disease/ racial demarcation although in this case the language of degeneration may be used to preserve the integrity of presumed white superiority over the 'native'. This formulation is also suggestive in relation to class boundaries and is a long proven literary technique to break down class barriers using disease tropes to produce pointed social commentary, for example the uses of illness in Dickens' *Bleak House*. However, in a Pacific context given the equal vulnerability of the colonizer to tropical diseases and the indigenous peoples' vulnerability to Eurasian diseases, one can begin to understand the potential for discursive disruption. Taking Gilman's idea one step further, the discourse that surrounds the idea of the 'patient' or 'Other' in a colonial context not only carries with it the usual stigma of illness, but also the idea of a colour line artificially preserving difference based on skin pigmentation when there is little actual biological distinction at issue. Gilman also identifies the origins of eugenics in these categorizations that have a specific 'good of race' motivation that we saw emerge in a different form in the last chapter in both Stevenson's and London's writing. Such thinking contrives to conflate discourses of race, degeneration and illness. As Gilman argues:

> These 'illnesses' are not only deviations from an absolute aesthetic norm, they 'disfigure' the body politic through the 'infection' of the individual. By the end of the nineteenth century individual beauty comes to have significance as a sign of the healthiness of the race. Here, to no-one's surprise, the notion of healthy and beautiful race has evolved into the discourse of eugenics, that can restore the beauty of the body politic. 'Race', however, is only a placeholder for the idea of the 'healthy' and 'beautiful' collective that must be preserved. (Gilman 54)

Nietzsche directly links the opposition between good/beautiful and bad/unhealthy in a racial/class-based discourse in *The Genealogy of Morals* (1887): '[it is] the Jew who, with frightening consistency, [has] dared to invert the aristocratic value equations good/noble/powerful/happy/favoured-of-the-god and maintain that only the poor, the powerless are good; only the suffering, sick, and ugly, truly blessed' (Nietzsche 167–8).

Illness then can also be a metaphor for racial difference in a colonial context and much more as material evidence and as a trope that exposes the ideological underpinnings of claims to Western superiority. Northrop Frye's description of the function of metaphor in society is useful in modifying Gilman's proposition in this respect: 'Metaphor . . . arises in a state of society in which a split between a perceived object is not yet habitual, and what does in that context is open up a channel or current of energy between human and natural worlds' (Frye 111). Illness then is a natural fact that has social meaning emblematic of an underlying and unresolved sense of difference that both distances (the patient is an object of fear and quarantine) and conveys an essential identification (the 'Other' – 'it could be me'); a split that is always threatening resolution, connection, but never does. Given the similarities with discourses of racial segregation as well as the implicit fear of the observing subject (the colonizer), images of disease are relatively common in colonial writing of this period (see, for example, Kipling's *Kim*; Rider Haggard's *King Solomon's Mines* and, of course, Conrad's *Heart of Darkness*). Thence the counter-discourse of the 'diseased Pacific' that Edmond identifies conveys a series of contradictory anxieties reflecting a real fear of disease, of maintaining racial and cultural distinctiveness, justification of the exploitation of the Islanders and the passing of new diseases to them. Foucault's extension of the notion of 'Otherness' to cover criminality, madness, disease, foreigners, homosexuals, strangers, women etc. (Derrida's suggestive name for these excluded is the 'remainder') is significant in a colonial context. The violence inherent in this process of marginalization is a key aspect of colonial discourse. As Foucault argues: 'Humanity does not gradually proceed from combat to combat until it arrives at universal reciprocity, where the rule of law finally replaces warfare; humanity installs each of its violences in a system of rules and thus proceeds from domination to domination' (Foucault 85). So, one might look upon the regulatory regimes of both disease and colonization, and race and class, along the same continuum. Yet the manifestation of illness is always uniquely devastating and personal; it can never become wholly abstract and habitualized. Disease not only calls for the regulation of the body, it also emanates from within and challenges that regulation much as the trivial bio-logical variations of ethnicity provide an outward physical marker for a colonial regime on which to focus and yet challenges that regime of othering by the essential similarity of subject and object.

Both Stevenson's *In the South Seas* and London's *The Cruise of the Snark* began life as letters; letters written with intent to fulfil publishing obligations certainly, but letters nonetheless that have a particular immediacy with the subject engaged. The editor Samuel McClure, a pioneer of press syndication, was one of the first to hear of Stevenson's proposed voyage in the South Pacific and recorded in his biography, '[I] thought at once of a "An Inland Voyage" and "Travels with a Donkey" and told him that if he would write a series of articles describing his travels, I would syndicate them for enough money to pay the expenses of the trip' (McClure 191). Yet *In the South Seas*, the rather uneven compendium of the letters produced for McClure, bears a greater resemblance to *The Amateur Emigrant* than these two earlier and lighter travel narratives. Indeed, as discussed above, it would have been impossible for Stevenson to have written in the same vein after the hard knocks that his conception of self and his art had taken during his 1879 transatlantic crossing. McClure recorded the dismay of the editors of American journals to which they had been syndicated – the South Sea letters were 'a disappointment to newspaper editors [for] it was the moralist [in Stevenson] and not the romancer which his observations in the South Seas awoke in him, and the public found the moralist less interesting than the romancer' (McClure 192). Even Fanny, Stevenson's wife, was scornful of his attempt to represent the colonial South Pacific with some objectivity and sympathy, an anthropological approach even:

> Louis has the most enchanting material that anyone ever had in the whole world for his book, and I'm afraid he is going to spoil it all. He has taken it into his Scotch Stevenson head, that a stern duty lies before him, and that this book must be a sort of scientific and historical impersonal thing, comparing the different languages (of which he knows nothing at all really) and the different peoples . . . the whole thing to be impersonal, leaving out all he knows of the people themselves. And I believe there is no one living who has got so near to them, or who understands them as he does. Think of a small treatise of the Polynesian race being offered to people who are dying to hear about Ori a Ori, the making of brothers with cannibals, the strange stories they told and the extraordinary adventures that befell us: – suppose Herman Melville had given us his theories as to the Polynesian language and the probably good or evil results of the missionary influences instead of Omoo and Typee . . . (*Letters VI* 312)

As Neil Rennie observes, Fanny seems to forget that Melville's *Typee* and *Omoo* do in fact contain discussions of Polynesian language and the missionary influence (Rennie xiii). Of interest in this passage, however, is the conflict between the commercially viable travel writing and Stevenson's insistence on an early example of anthropological method. Of the possible modes of representation available to him there is romance, scientific (anthropological) and confessional (private letters). These generic boundaries, if we consider them all as forms of representational writing, can of course collapse into the other being effectively maintained only by the exclusion of the others but even so, all three draw upon the same experiences. A dramatic example of how such exclusions maintain a boundary between the perception of objective (scientific) discourse and the more subjective memoir format in a Pacific context is the striking contrast between Bronislaw Malinowski's landmark anthropological study, *Argonauts of the Western Pacific* (1922), and the personal torment evident from his field diaries published in 1967 to some notoriety as *A Diary in the Strict Sense of the Term*.

What ultimately made *In the South Seas* such a difficult text for Stevenson's friends, family and readers is that these generic boundaries are not in practice strictly maintained. While the material that was eventually published in book form as *In the South Seas* is incomplete and is generally considered to reflect severe problems of coherence as a text, this lack of respect for generic boundaries was part of Stevenson's original conception:

> My book is now practically modelled: if I can execute what is designed, there are few better books now extant on the globe; bar the epics, and the big tragedies, and histories, and the choice lyric poetics, and a novel or so – none. But it is not executed yet; and let not him that putteth on his armour, vaunt himself. At least nobody has had such stuff; such wild stories, such beautiful scenes, such singular intimacies, such manners and traditions, so incredible a mixture of the beautiful and horrible, the savage and civilised. I will give you here some idea of the table of contents, which ought to make your mouth water. I propose to call the book – *The South Seas*; it is rather a large title, but not that many people have seen more of them than I; perhaps no one: certainly no one capable of using the material. (*Letters VI* 334–5)

It is tantalizing to imagine what *The South Seas* would have become from the fragment that made it into print as *In the South Seas*. In the face of various objections, Stevenson abandoned the original project and even refused to revise what he had written: 'I am now so sick that I intend, when the letters are done and some more written that will be wanted, simply to make a book out of it by the pruning knife' (*Letters VII* 101–2). In a striking analogue to the fate of *The Amateur Emigrant*, the pressure of commercial viability, the disapproval of family and friends and personal illness all shaped *In the South Seas*.

The genesis of Jack London's *The Cruise of the Snark* was written with few of the generic considerations or ambition that beset Stevenson. London was never shy of writing for no motive other than money and accordingly he was quick to arrange sale of his correspondence in advance with Bailey Millard the editor of *Cosmopolitan Magazine*. Indeed, the very grounds that he puts forward to vouch for his ability to produce quality reportage is his method of synthesizing secondary material for *The People of the Abyss* discussed in the preceding chapter. The full pitch is worth quoting at length:

> Now to business. I shall be gone a long time of this trip. No magazine can print all I have to write about it. On the other hand, it cannot be imagined that I shall write 50,000 words on the whole seven years [the cruise was originally planned as a circumnavigation], and then quit. As it is, the subject-matter of the trip divides itself up so there will be no clash whatever between any several different publications that may be handling my stuff. For instance, there are three big natural, unconflicting divisions: News, industrial, and political articles on the various countries for newspapers; fiction; and, finally, the trip itself.
>
> No the question arises, if you take the trip itself (which will be the cream), how much space will *The Cosmopolitan* be able to give me? In this connection I may state that *McClure's* and *Outing* are after me; and as I am throwing my life, seven years of my time, my earning-power as a writer of fiction, and a lot of money, into the enterprise, it behoves me to keep a sharp lookout how expenses, etc., are to be met. And one important factor in this connection that I must consider is that of space.
>
> And while I am on this matter of space, I may as well say that it is granted, always, that I deliver the goods. Of course, if my articles turn out to be mushy and inane, why I should not expect any magazine to continue to publish them. I believe too much in fair play to be a good businessman, and if my work be rotten, I'd be the last fellow in the world to bind any editor to publish it. On the other hand, I have a tremendous confidence based on all kinds of work I have already done, that I can deliver the goods. Anybody doubting this has but to read *The People of the Abyss* to find the graphic, reportorial way I have of handling things . . . (*Letters II* 548–9)

While believing 'too much in fair play to be a good businessman' this letter shows London commercially astute enough to hint at other publishers' interest in the letters and to betray a preoccupation with covering his expenses and expected loss of income from writing fiction. But like Stevenson, the projected range of his material is just as ambitious and the volume just as capacious although in London's case more material equalled more space in magazine columns then paid at a word rate. The project is also an avowed repetition of his method in *The People of the Abyss* in contrast to his other writing in the intervening period. The commercial consequences of London's connection with *The Cosmopolitan* profoundly shaped the resulting collection of essays. Close on the heels of concluding his agreement with the magazine (3 April 1906) came the great San Francisco earthquake (18 April) and the cost of constructing a yacht for the cruise skyrocketed. As his wife, Charmian, writes in her two-volume tribute to her husband *Jack London* (1921) this plunged him into substantial debt: 'The Great Earthquake proved very expensive to Jack London. Primarily because of it, the yacht-building, which he had calculated would cost seven thousand dollars, or at most ten, incredibly squandered some thirty thousand' (C. London 156). The circumstances surrounding the building of the *Snark* so influenced London that it is the subject of the second chapter of the book, 'The Inconceivable and the Monstrous'. Another consequence of the connection with the magazine is recorded in the 'Backword' that London wrote after his return to California and convalescence which again dwelt on costs: 'I built the *Snark* and paid for it, and for all expenses. I contracted to write thirty-five thousand words descriptive of the trip for a magazine [*The Cosmopolitan*] which was to pay me the same rate received for stories written at home. Promptly the magazine advertized that it was sending me around the world for itself. It was a wealthy magazine. And every man who had business dealings with the *Snark* charged three prices because forsooth the magazine could afford it' (*Snark* 337–8).

Despite these difficulties, London had no trouble comparable to Stevenson's from friends and family with getting the letters and subsequent book into print, but what of the text that resulted. Charmian refers to it as relating 'in more or less disconnected fashion, some of the main happenings and observations incident to the cruise' preferring instead her own journal of the cruise published by Macmillan as the more coherent guide to the journey (C. London 156). Reviewing the contexts of the book, one is struck by its range – from inconsequential first experiences of surf boarding and other tourist activities; reflections on racial characteristics and Social Darwinism; thinly veiled aspirations of American colonialism in the South Pacific; a description of near-slaving activities of labour recruiters among the Solomon Islands; and of course observations and commentary on 'native' life, local languages and pidgin. Above all the text is punctuated by London's preoccupation with his own health and the ravages he sees among the Pacific Islanders. The narrative register throughout the text is more reportorial rather than literary but when compared to Stevenson's *In the South Seas* a strikingly similar range of issues are covered, although by contrast the textual identity that emerges is quite ugly and with some justification. London's most recent biographer has called this period in his life his 'heart of darkness' (Kershaw 190–209).

Pacific Travellers and Travel Writing

Before advancing a more detailed analysis of the contents it is useful to consider the status of the texts as travel narratives. The generic variety of both texts and the very strong sense of self-fashioning is a particularly modern attribute that signals these texts as the successors to *The Amateur Emigrant* and *The People of the Abyss*. As Nicholas Thomas writes: 'modernity itself can be understood as a colonialist project in the special sense that both the societies internal to the Western nations, and those they possessed, administered and reformed elsewhere, were understood as objects to be surveyed, regulated and sanitized' (Thomas 4). Moreover, travel writing in a colonial setting has in recent years come to be recognized as a particularly complex genre as Steve Clark argues:

> The genre [travel writing] obviously overlaps with numerous other discourses of colonialism – bureaucratic instruction, demographic report, geographic mapping, military order, journalistic propaganda . . . and the journey itself obviously encodes inevitable ideological aspects: spiritual pilgrimage (Mandeville), mercantile prospectus (Hakluyt), mercenary campaign (Steadman), colonial expedition (Doughty). These do not however exhaust the potentialities of travel writing as a form: the self-reflexivity of the journey/quest motif; its intricate layering of temporalities; and its allegorical resonances with regard to the travellers own culture. (Clark 3)

Clark's observations are a useful summary of the characteristics evident from *In the South Seas* and *The Cruise of the Snark*, but what is unusual is the internal disjointedness of both texts. Certainly, the episodic nature of the original travel letters upon which they are based gives some explanation for this, but it is striking that Charmian London should refer the reader of her husband's book to her own account of the cruise if she or he seeks chronological order, an implicit criticism also evident from the following letter from Fanny Stevenson to her husband: 'Parts of it are very fine, but it loses immensely in not being a personal consecutive narrative. It gives too much the feeling of that you had got your information second hand, and it is only convincing in parts' (*Letters VII* 85). So, is the impersonality and episodic nature of the texts a consequence of the commercial constraints of the need to write and submit letters in the first instance in conflict with personal expression, or is it a personal expression that breaks down the conventions of colonial travel writing as the personal. The latter seems most likely for another possible cause for the disjointedness of the travel narrative of these texts is that the writing itself was punctuated by periods of serious illness and disorientation. These texts are very unconventional travel narratives in that though they inevitably give expression to a particular colonial identification, they provide a remarkably candid representation of acute stress which emerges both structurally and through the content.

Tim Youngs has usefully defines travel writing in a colonial context thus: 'Travel writing, especially in an imperial or colonial context, is an expression of identity based on sameness to and yet remoteness from the members of the home society'. Like Youngs this analysis will 'investigate the use of textual, physical, and cultural space for an exploration and affirmation or reconstitution of identity' (Youngs 3). However, while Stevenson's and London's travel narratives strive towards this affirmation and reconstitution on one level, they singularly fail to achieve this level of consistency. The example of Conrad's Kurtz as an alternative model of the progressive traveller and Westerner gone bad and mad looms behind both these narratives for the modern reader – London was a keen student of both Stevenson's and Conrad's writing and, while Stevenson's text predates Conrad's career, the latter was a firm admirer of Stevenson's South Pacific writing and particularly acknowledged his debt to Stevenson's *The Beach of Falesá* and *The Ebb Tide* for his own Western Pacific novel and *Lord Jim* (1899–1900) and of course *Heart of Darkness*. Indeed, in his edition of Stevenson's letters, Sidney Colvin recorded that 'I may perhaps mention here that there is a certain many-voyaged master-mariner as well as master-writer – no less a person than Mr Joseph Conrad – who . . . prefers *In the South Seas* to *Treasure Island*' (Colvin 262). What *In the South Seas* and *The Cruise of the Snark* point to is a deeper psychological malaise in the colonial subject at the turn of the nineteenth century that is also revealed in their related South Pacific fiction and Conrad's most famous stories.

Textual Encounters, Real Lives – The Marquesas Islands

The discursive formulation of the colonial South Pacific, while reflecting the uniqueness of the region, also relates to and challenges broader formulations that bring together the representation of illness and disease with various metropolitan and personal anxieties specific to the two authors and more widely to colonial writing in general. Of particular interest in how Melville's earlier fictional travel novels *Typee* and *Omoo* – widely believed to be factual when published – influence the autobiographical travel narratives of Stevenson and London. All of the texts use literary devices for Melville, Stevenson and London are all masters of their craft, but the fine line between narrative fiction and narrative fact is an intriguing question in relation to the South Pacific, which even today is heavily fictionalized as a terrestrial paradise in popular perception. Julia Swindells in her study of nineteenth-century literature and autobiography suggests that the literary, which encompasses the genres fiction, melodrama and romance, was used as a means to structure life histories 'as if "the literary" itself is the key (possibly the only) means of construction of self . . . The heroine, the victim, the martyr are the only means of representing an experience unprecedented in discourse (the working man by the working woman) but they are also signifiers of lack, of what is missing' (Swindells 140). Of course, Stevenson and London as writers would be expected to produce very different work if they had been consciously writing an autobiography; rather a travel narrative is a text that has autobiographic elements. For this reason Swindell's point is useful in that the narrative personas of *In the South Seas* and *The Cruise of the Snark* can be characterized as a fictional realization of self within a factual genre. This is a crucial distinction from Melville's fictional realization of self within a fictional genre. The difference is neatly underlined by Stevenson's view of the relationship between a work of art and life: 'Life is monstrous, infinite, illogical, abrupt, and poignant and a work of art, in comparison, is neat, finite, self-contained, rational, flowing and emasculate' (McLynn 243). What becomes evident from both *In the South Seas* and *The Cruise of the Snark* is the ability of 'life' to disrupt the most dogged attempts at artistic order.

By the end of 1887 Stevenson was confined to Saranac Lake among the Adirondack Mountains in the hope that its climate would help with his pulmonary complaint, yet the South Pacific was on his mind. In November he suggested to Edward Burlingame of *Scribner's* 'why don't you get Charles Warren Stoddard on your magazine: has a small touch of genius; and his thing about the lepers shows he has not lost his arts' (*Letters VI* 50). The 'thing about the lepers' was Stoddard's 1885 book *The Lepers of Molokai* the famous, if not infamous, Hawaiian leper colony that Stevenson (and London after him) was to visit. Stevenson had been introduced to Stoddard by Fanny during his first visit to San Francisco in 1879/80 and had been much taken by his account of his travels among the islands of the Pacific. When he came to write of his own voyage to the Pacific it was to be associated with a motif of resurgent health:

> My dear Lady Taylor, I have to announce our great news. On June 15th we sail from San Francisco in the schooner yacht *Casco*, for a seven months cruise in the South Seas. You can conceive what a state of excitement we are in; Lloyd [Stevenson's stepson and later collaborator] perhaps first; but this is an old dream of mine which actually seems to be coming true, and I am sun-struck. It seems too good to be true; and we have not deserved such good fortune. From Skerryvore to the Galapogos is a far cry! And from poking in a sick-room all winter to the deck of one's own ship, is indeed a heavenly change. (*Letters VI* 184)

Yet by the time Stevenson wrote the opening lines of *In the South Seas*, this sense of elation and nervous energy had waned: 'For nearly ten years my health has been declining; and for some time before I set forth on my voyage, I believed I had come to the afterpiece of life; and had only the nurse and the undertaker to expect. It was suggested that I should try the South Seas; and I was not unwilling to visit like a ghost, and be carried like a bale, among scenes that had attracted me in youth and health' (*South Seas* 5). The persona Stevenson creates is at odds with his real enthusiasm for the voyage and recalls his definition of art as 'emasculate' compared to 'real life'. Thence the artistic creation, Stevenson the narrator, conjoins both the enervation and forced invalidity of poor health ('carried like a bale') with the diminishment of masculine force perhaps as a consequence of his practice within an artistic medium that he stereotypically associated with femininity.

By 1906 when London conceived the idea of sailing around the world, he planned to follow Stevenson through the South Pacific to the Marquesas, Hawaii and later Samoa. The prospect of the journey filled him with as much excitement, but rather than the diminishment of masculine force, his narrative stance anticipates a triumph of will and self-assertion as he writes in the forward of *The Cruise of the Snark*:

> Life that lives is life successful, and success is the breath of its nostrils. The achievement of a difficult feat is successful adjustment to a sternly exacting environment . . . here is the seas, the wind, and the wave. Here is a ferocious

environment. And here is difficult adjustment, the achievement of which is delight to the small quivering vanity that is I. I like. I am so made. It is my own particular form of vanity. That is all. (*Snark* 7)

A comparison between the narrative tone set by Stevenson and London in these very different opening passages encourages the belief in the common perception of these two authors: London the quintessential man of action and chronicler of humanity's battle with an unremitting natural world; while Stevenson the gentle, quaint, rather saintly, consumptive invalid, adding poignancy to his output of romantic adventure stories. Certainly, these images conform to the biographical myths that have grown around both authors, partly encouraged by popular readings of their most famous – and popular – fictions, and the careful post-mortem media manipulation by their spouses and wider family. Yet the introductory passages to *In the South Seas* and *The Cruise of the Snark* show both authors actively manipulating their narrative personas. This is not to say that they are pure artistic fabrication – these are not novels. Rather it is a deliberate strategy to provide contrast between the material that will be presented in the narratives and their actual experiences in the Pacific. The relative state of their health as it emerges in the texts themselves and the 'subtext' of their letters makes these early passages all the more intriguing. Stevenson suffered from a number of debilitating illnesses throughout his life, though the most recurrent was a lung complaint with symptoms that included haemorrhages (jocularly dubbed 'Bluidy Jack' by Stevenson) commonly presumed to have been tuberculosis although its exact nature was, and is, open to some speculation (McLynn 171–2). Residence in the South Pacific, particularly the temperate Samoa, would stabilize his condition considerably (although never fully). As he wrote to his friend Henry James in 1890: 'The Sea, the islands, the islanders, the island life and climate, make and keep me truly happier. These last two years I have been much at sea, and have never wearied; sometimes I have indeed grown impatient for some destination; more often I was sorry that the voyage drew so early to an end' (*Letters VI* 402–3).

By contrast, cruising in the South Pacific for Jack London brought progressive illness. By the time the yacht reached the Solomon Islands, it resembled a floating infirmary including numerous cases of Solomon Sores or Yaws – 'raspberry-like skin eruptions and destructive lesions' (Lunquist 60) – as well as regular bouts of fever. London was also suffering from another skin complaint that caused the skin of his hands to flake off and had the uncomfortable symptom of impaired balance which was most likely psoriasis. London had at least eight of these lesions as a time and describes with part comic, part scientific bravura in keeping with his narrative persona his attempts to doctor himself and the rest of the crew in the final chapter of *The Cruise of the Snark*, 'The Amateur M.D.'. Still, the iron constitution that had seen him through the Klondike and the horrors of the East End was now failing him: 'I was puzzled and frightened. All my life my skin had been famous for its healing powers, yet here was something that would not heal. Instead, it was daily eating up more skin, while it had eaten down clear through the skin and was eating the muscle itself' (*Snark* 315). The 'something that would not heal' recalls the plight of the narrator of Melville's *Typee*, disabled by a mysterious disease among a people renowned for cannibalism that not only 'consumes' his vitality but also skin and muscle. The inference in both cases is that being physically consumed by the people is not the only threat in this environment. There is something hidden and invidious to the white interloper that echoes the sentiment of Conrad's *Heart of Darkness* and the fever-ridden Kurtz. London's experience occurred far from the Polynesian Marquesas Islands the setting for *Typee*, but among the Melanesian Solomon Islands where the focus of Western phobia over cannibalism had shifted. Most Polynesian islands had by this time been subdued and colonized by various Western powers, but the Melanesian south-west Pacific was still the abode of a people perceived as mysterious, hostile and irredeemably savage – the inhabitants matched by a harsh climate and disease. While ritual headhunting was certainly a feature of inter-group feuds on many Melanesian islands, the acute aversion that characterized Western attitudes towards Melanesian Islanders no doubt had more to do with prevalent negative perceptions of people with black skins, while the tawny-hued Polynesians of the Marquesas – lighter skin suggesting greater levels of civilization and beauty according to contemporary racial hierarchies – were frequently admired.

London's mysterious ailment coupled with the extended metaphor of consumption focused on the skin is suggestive of a phobic sense of infection and perhaps racial denegation and class anxieties, which also echoes how the boat consumed his fortune in such a 'monstrous' fashion. Rod Edmond observes that 'His own body had become the site on which metaphors of disease and corruption that he had used to express the effects of Western settlement were literalized' (Edmond 211). It also signifies the failure of the proletarian body to inhabit the fruits of such conspicuous and wasteful spending. There is a relationship between London's own sense of physical trauma brought on by his exposure to tropical diseases and his writing – an erosion of his bodily/physical boundaries to recall Tim Dean's observation – but some caution needs to be taken over how this is seen to be mediated in the text. The physical proximity of powerfully alien cultures and London's state certainly leads to a textual unhinging of colonial tropes. The first and most obvious is that the outward sign of racial superiority and difference, white skin, has quite literally proven to be both weak and susceptible with significant metaphorical implications for the culture he represents. Edmond also observes that London in a series of leper stories written after his visit to the Hawaiian leper colony on Molokai seems to have appreciated the horror of the disease for Polynesian societies as a consequence of their belief system in which 'Skin is the boundary between self and others, between the individual and their society. It shields the self from the world and holds the contents of the body, mediating that traffic between inner and outer worlds which constitutes the individual's sense of selfhood' (Edmond 205). While this is arguably true of London's fiction, as he moves further into the alienating Melanesian Pacific it is he who is under threat. Discursively his narrated body becomes the site for a form of reverse colonization adopting a way of thinking about the body that he is exploring in his writing about the impact of colonization of the Polynesian Islanders, and draws out his response to the threat of the alien and incomprehensible Melanesian Islanders and the equally inexplicable diseases that gnaw away at his body. Despite then his hubristic celebration of the power of the will against nature in the foreword to *The Cruise of the Snark*, it is the very threat of defeat by an unanticipated natural force – illness and disease – that is transformed into the physical and cultural threat of the Melanesian Islanders. Metaphorically, the Islanders become the threat to his body. Conrad's Kurtz again springs to mind. Weakened in body and in mind, on the brink of being overwhelmed by an alien culture, he experiences a major physical and psychological collapse. Driven finally to consult doctors in Australia, London never resumed the cruise.

The trajectory of Stevenson's South Pacific voyage is towards health and vitality. When he characterizes his frame of mind at the beginning of his journey as an epilogue to his life and the prelude of another, towards death, it is also to be carried out 'among scenes that had attracted me in youth and health (*South Seas* 5). So, a journey that is in a physical sense a journey into the unknown becomes an imaginative mapping of the familiar territory of youth and restitution of health. It is the 'South Seas' rather than the South Pacific that Stevenson envisions, a literary contract that is also a colonial mapping. As Neil Rennie observes:

> Factual and fictional accounts of distant travel to different places located at
> different times on the expanding frontier of the 'known' world can be seen as

engaged in a historical process in which literary commonplaces were repeatedly displaced and relocated in geographical space, repeatedly exposed as literary fiction and discovered as geographical fact. The commonplaces of South Sea travel literature were present in accounts of real and imaginary travel long before the discovery of the South Seas. (Rennie, Preface)

Yet the idea of travel is also a long-standing autobiographical trope that reaches towards the unfamiliar through the known by adapting three genres: the spiritual journey as in Augustine's *Confessions*, Dante's *Divine Comedy* or Bunyan's *The Pilgrim's Progress* (which Stevenson mentions in *Travels with a Donkey*); the journey through life such as Wordsworth's *The Prelude* of T. S. Eliot's *Four Quartets*; as well as the travel narrative. Perhaps the closest in essence to Stevenson's narrative journey is Wordsworth's *The Prelude* – Stevenson had been an admirer of Wordsworth in his youth and early adulthood (McLynn 42). The poem recounts a number of literal journeys that become the metaphoric representation of the poet's interior quest for his earlier self and spiritual home. The conclusion of the poem brings Wordsworth to the point of a new beginning in his home in the Vale of Grasmere about to embark on his great work, *The Recluse*. Like Stevenson, this new beginning embodies and essential pessimism:

> Oh! Yet a few short years of useful life,
> And all will be complete, thy race be run,
> Thy monument of glory will be raised;
> Then, though too weak to tread the ways of truth,
> This age fall back to old idolatry,
> Though men return to servitude as fast
> As the tide ebbs, to ignominy and shame (14.432–439)

These lines strikingly encapsulate many of the themes that Stevenson introduces into his own autobiographical journey. Indeed, to look ahead for a moment, this stanza also contains the mood and a hint of the title of Stevenson's study of the dregs of Western society in the South Pacific, *The Ebb Tide* (1893). More directly, while a lament for lost youth, the poem ends with old age that Stevenson translates into the 'afterpiece of life' and a physical – even spiritual – weakness to 'tread the ways of truth'. The truth, perhaps, being the poet's attempt to recapture the essence of his own past among which Stevenson is to be 'carried like a bale' through scenes of youthful attraction. The key difference is, however, the essence of youth that Stevenson's image is intended to capture. For him it is not the passing into old age after an active life, but of nursing and immobility burdened by a serious illness that resembles the helplessness and dependency of early childhood rather than robust youth. The mingling of journey and illness tropes in Stevenson's passage creates an ambivalent preface for the work to follow, introducing the very real despair of serious illness to enable a maudlin self-dramatization as an invalid resigned to death. This is contrasted with an incessant restlessness that would take Stevenson through most of the South Pacific; a barely suppressed childlike energy that, in turn, leads to an infantilism that is both a burden and a return to youthful dreams. The subtext is Stevenson's poor health and while much improved in the South Pacific it was never that of a physically robust individual. Yet aside from the opening paragraph, Stevenson rarely refers to his state of health in *In the South Seas* despite regular bouts of sickness during his voyages. He becomes fascinated instead by the variety of illnesses that afflict the Marquesan Islanders and the population decline precipitated by Western contact and colonization. In the following passages it is possible to all these themes at work together with a backward glance towards an overpopulated Britain that incubate disease:

> When I had sat down with them on the floor, the girl began to question me about England which I tried to describe . . . explaining as best as I was able, and by word and gesture, the over-population, the hunger, the perpetual toil. '*Pas de cocotiers? Pas de popoi?*' she asked. I told her it was too cold. But she understood right well; remarked it must be very bad for the health, and sat a while gravely reflecting on that picture of unwonted sorrows . . . She began with a smiling sadness, and looking on me out of melancholy eyes, to lament the demise of her own people, '*Ici pas de kanaques,*' said she; and taking the baby from her breast, she held it out to me with both hands. '*Tenez* – a little baby like this; then dead. All *Kanaques* die. Then no more. (*South Seas* 22)

The following chapter (Chapter VI) is emphatically entitled 'Death' as if in fulfilment of this prophecy and concerns itself with a detailed inventory of imported diseases, corrupted local customs and the dramatic population decline among the Marquesans.

This passage also recapitulates the pessimistic atmosphere of Stevenson's introduction, but here the sorrow, regret and melancholy resignation to death is displaced onto the Marquesan mother, her expression variously characterized as 'gravely reflecting', 'smiling sadness' 'unwonted sorrows' and 'melancholy eyes'. This is a deft expression of the *Et in Arcadia ego* topos – I [death] an even in

Arcadia – of earlier writers on the South Pacific adapted to displace and elaborate his 'afterpiece of life'; a doomed image of an earlier, vital self destined to fade 'like a ghost' projected onto an entire people. This is another trope that has a long history in account of European exploration and colonization that is by no means restricted to the South Pacific, but had early come to have a particular resonance in representations of the region. Perhaps the most elegant example is that of Louis Antoine de Bougainville's account of his voyage to Tahiti in 1768 (see Rennie 82–108). This group had been labelled 'King George the Third Islands' by the British explorer Samuel Wallis. Bougainville promptly renamed this attractive group *La Nouvelle-Cynthére* and shaped his description of the islands by reference to a combination of classical mythology and eighteenth-century utopia literature. Yet the regret expressed on departing the islands in his published journals resembles the tone of Stevenson's introduction and his encounter with the Marqusan woman: 'Adieu peuple heureux et sage, soyez tougours ce que vous êtes, Je ne me rappellerai jamais sans délices le peu d'instans que j'ai passes au milieu de vous et, tant je vivrai, je célèbrerai l'heureuse isle de Cythére. C'est la Véritable Eutopie' (Cited by Rennie 89), he supposed discovering that the Tahitians had passed on venereal disease to his crew, an infection blamed on Wallis' British crew sparking a long controversy (Smith 38–45).

Like Bougainville, Stevenson associates regret, melancholy and imported disease with an ostensibly paradisal South Pacific locale that serves to defamilarize these otherwise out of place emotions and unpleasant realities. There are of course more subtle and telling adaptations of the trope in Stevenson's text. The melancholy of departure has been shifted to dramatize a pending departure from life, and a heightened pathos of the passing of a race and culture – the Marquesans. Moreover, there is another change of trajectory: rather than Bougainville's implication of paradise being infected by imported disease, there is in Stevenson's passage a move to regain the 'innocent' wonder of youth for the European observer by the displacement of both the debilitation of disease and the melancholy of resignation onto an entire people. Stevenson's careful arrangement of the scene with the Marquesan woman is also revealing. They all sit on the mat and, proceeding from the woman's resigned but despairing summation, he enacts a kind of mime 'piling the pan and cocoa shells one upon the other to represent houses . . . I went through an elaborate performance, shutting out draughts and crouching over an imaginary fire', while all the time 'the unconscious babe struggled to reach a pot of strawberry jam' (*South Seas* 22). In a quite literal sense they are all playing on the floor with Stevenson as the adult playing with or teaching through gesture a child. By the conclusion of the chapter a curious dissonance enters into the narrative:

> . . . and in a perspective of centuries I saw their case as ours, death coming in a tide, and the day already numbered when there should be no more Berentai [British], and no more of any race whatever, and what oddly touched me) no more literary works and no more readers. (*South Seas* 22–3)

Not only is the slow, relentless, painful decline of disease displaced onto the woman, but also Stevenson's sense of infantilism caused by his long-term ill health. The tragedy of the Marquesan woman, her child and her people is trivialized by her status as a quasi-child being instructed at the feet of the white father. Not for her the return of vitality and imagination, despite her youth. Indeed, she and her island *are* the scene of Stevenson's youthful attraction, but the 'case' and that of her people is a hopeless one. But what of Stevenson and the European interloper he signifies? He speculates that at some vague, far distant future Europeans might face a similar plight and then even usurps the infant/ child characterization to his own discursive advantage by which he, the colonizer, simultaneously claims both youthful vitality for himself and his 'race', but also the wisdom of the teacher for it is he who provides an 'elaborate performance' for the woman's edification. Conversely, the Marquesan suffers from both the ignorance of youth and the debilitation of old age facing an impending extinction supplanted by the younger, more vital European migrant.

This passage conveys a keen sense of sympathy over the common ground of illness and suffering and Stevenson does not try to deflect responsibility for the devastating diseases among the Marquesans. Significantly, the causes for him seem to originate from the poor climate of Northern Europe (specifically Britain) and the diseases it has incubated and the transplantation of those people and those diseases to the South Pacific. The discursive focus of colonialism undermines this sympathy and acknowledgement of collective responsibility since the Marquesans are a childlike colonized people – 'natives'. In narrative terms, the experience of individual and racial suffering is fractured into four autobiographical/travel metaphors. First sympathy – pain as shared experience that in some way forges a connection despite disparities of power and culture; second a recognition of the ravages brought by European contact and colonial- ism; third the reassertion of an internalized colonial ideology as the white man as symbol of paternal authority that succours the supplicant child native; and, finally, the regaining of authority that has been undermined in Stevenson's case by long-term illness and as a novelist practicing an 'emasculating' art. In many respects, illness and disease operate as a colonial 'contact zone' to adopt Pratt's phrase, that is both the assertion of colonial domination and also a social 'space' in which the negative consequences of Western contact and settlement are relatively undisguised. Stevenson's narrative is clearly sympathetic but by the same token he is complicit by deriving a personal revitalization from the very same tropes imbedded in such a staged colonial encounter.

Another factor integral to Stevenson's response to the Marquesas is that he is not, of course, the first literary visitor to this part of the island group since as already noted this is a setting for Melville's *Typee*. This novel features a Western protagonist suffering from a mysteriously debilitating ailment. Indeed, the so-called Tahitian proverb that serves as a leitmotif for the opening chapters of Stevenson's text – 'the coral waxes, the palm grows, and man departs' (*South Seas*, 8 and 27) – in fact originated with Melville and was also to be used subsequently by the French writer Pierre Loti. So when Stevenson writes of literary extinction – 'no more literary works and no more readers' – it is in the full knowledge that he is a participant in a literary history, a tradition. The implication of this comparison is that the death of the Marquesans means to death of their culture also which is transmitted by demonstration or orally from generation to generation:

> What is peculiar is the wide-spread depression and acceptance of the national end. Pleasures are neglected, the dance languishes, the songs are forgotten. It is true that some, perhaps too many, of them are proscribed by [the French colonial government]; but many remain, if there were a spirit to support of revive them. At the last feast of the Bastille, Stanisalao Moanatini shed tears when he beheld the inanimate performance of the dancers. When the people sang for us in Anaho, they must apologize for the smallness of their repertory. They were only young folk present, they said, and it was only the old that knew the songs. The whole body of Marquesan poetry and music was being suffered to dies out with a single dispirited generation. (*South Seas* 27)

Read in this context, Stevenson's imaginative sympathy which leads him to see the end of European culture is jarring since the frame of comparison is a literate Western culture in which historical and cultural records need not become extinct with the passing of the people who produced them. His play of imagination might be read as an assertion of Western cultural power which, as Stephen Greenblatt observes: 'On many occasions, this conviction [of superiority] was bound up in what Samuel Purchas in the early Seventeenth century called the Europeans' "literall advantage" – the advantage, that is, of writing' (Greenblatt 9).

This advantage enables a certain textual self-indulgence imagining personal and racial extinction with, paradoxically, no actual risk to the reflective subject, contrasted with the fate of the colonized Marquesans who face the very real prospect of disease and cultural extinction. To recall Stevenson's introductory passage, this is comparable to the intimation of his own death and debility as the 'afterpiece of life', not as a real threat of death but imaginative play; a form of ontological liberation tempered by an artful pathos that engenders literary beginnings. Both the literal and figurative occupation of the Marquesas leads to the destruction of the indigenous population and their culture onto whom, literally and figuratively, the negative tropes associated with disease and cultural atrophy has been displaced. Yet when Stevenson came to write *The Ebb Tide* (1893), the literary displacement was brought home to roost with the colonizers in a striking departure from the 'tradition' of representing the South Pacific: 'Throughout the island world of the Pacific, scattered men of many European races and from almost every grade of society carry activity and disseminate disease. Some prosper, some vegetate' (*Ebb Tide* 173).

By December 1907 when Jack London, Charmian and his crew made landfall on the Marquesas he was deliberately following in the steps of both Melville and Stevenson. Like Stevenson, he was also drawn to the implications of the Marquesans' diseased misery and depopulation that had worsened by the time of his visit, the point of departure again being Melville's *Typee*:

> Life faints and stumbles and gasps itself away. In this warm, equable clime –
> a truly terrestrial paradise – where there are never extremes of temperature
> and where the air is like a balm, kept ever pure by the ozone-laden Southeast
> trade, asthma, pthisis and tuberculosis flourish as luxuriantly as the vegetation.
> Everywhere, from the few grass huts, arises the racking cough of exhausted
> groan of wasted lungs. There is a form of consumption called 'galloping', which
> is especially dreaded. In two months time it reduces the strongest man to a
> skeleton under a grave cloth. In valley after valley the last inhabitant has passed
> and the fertile soil has relapsed to jungle. (*Snark* 163)

The individual Marquesan has disappeared from this scene leaving only the residual metonymy of coughs and cries of pain. Rather than the melancholy and creeping extinction that characterized Stevenson's representation of the islanders which conveyed a certain visible dignity despite his condescension, the Marquesans' are for all intents and purposes on the brink of extinction. Yet, probe a little deeper and the passage reveals a hesitation between implying that the Marquesans have succumbed to a congenital weakness – since the climate is so fine and all other living things flourish, it must be the people themselves like the degenerate working classes of *The People of the Abyss* – or conversely, that it is the disease itself that has flourished in this equable clime' and 'terrestrial paradise leaving a landscape inimical to human life'. This contrast between a healthy environment and parasitic vigour is repeated in London's view of the racial identity and relative virility of the contemporary Marquesan: 'A pure Marquesan is a rare thing. They seem to be all half-breeds and strange conglomerations of dozens of different races'. Initially, London ascribes what remaining vitality that the Islanders have to this hybridity, 'the one thing that retards their destruction is the infusion of fresh blood' but later switches to contempt: 'it is a wreckage of races at best' (*Snark* 163).

By looking for the causes of Marquesan depopulation among popularized ideas of racial degeneration or a hostile environment, London seems reluctant to confront the possibility that the fate of the Islanders is the direct consequence of Western contact. The blame lies with either the climate – the very thing Stevenson said of Britain – or the hybridization that he sees, contradictorily, either advancing or retarding their decline. He concludes his evaluation with the observation that, with the absence of a people to cultivate it, the landscape has reverted to jungle which no doubt leaves it empty for recovery by settlers. From the pen of an American author, this immediately brings to mind the *vacuum domicilium* justification central to the myth of the frontier. The land has defeated the indigenous people and their fall from racial purity either hastens or retards that defeat, Underlying this contradiction is London's horror of both racial impurity and the ability of nature 'red in tooth and claw' to lay humanity low, which in turn reveals both a potential ground for solidarity as part of a universal struggle with nature, or an overriding contempt for the Marquesans' weakness and racial impurity. The potential sympathy anticipates the moment when his body and will crumbles under the assault of tropical diseases. Stevenson's colonial paternalism is of course equally contradictory since sympathy is undermined by a presumption of intellectual and cultural superiority. Yet in London's narrative, paternalism has been supplanted by contempt that of course conveys none of the pastoral concern of Stevenson's text. This is explicable in the context of the differing histories of imperialism in the United States and Britain. By the early twentieth century, British imperialism was, arguably, a matter of government and administration as well as economic and strategic exploitation of peoples who were racially and culturally very different – the white settler colonies had largely gained autonomy and dominion status by this time – rather than by direct settlement, the great example being the Indian subcontinent. The history of the

United States is a history of violent displacement and concurrent bacteriological decimation of the indigenous population and then settlement. By the time the United States had itself become an overseas imperial power after the Europeans model following the Spanish American War of 1898, there was considerable uncertainty about how to govern the new possessions wrestled from Spain, especially the culturally alien Philippine Islands. Thence Kipling's call in his poem 'White Man's Burden (The United States and the Philippine Islands)' to 'Send forth the best ye breed –/Go Bind your sons to exile/To serve your captives' need' is as much a lecture in colonial technique as it is the English writer's celebration of the abandonment of the isolationist Monroe Doctrine (Kipling 323). Indeed, his lines imply very much the kind of paternalism uncovered in the passage from *In the South Seas*. Further, James Slagel suggests that the Pacific was a more immediate source of the exotic for Americans than the Orient was for Europeans, though with important differences. Drawing in the work of Edward Said, he argues that, 'where Europe sees the Orient through the nostalgic "what was" or "what was perceived to be," America has viewed the Exotic through "what could be." Both distortions show the Occident's desire to dominate; each creates a discourse based on "Western projections unto and will to govern" the culture (Said's phrase) and a virtual reality created by extrapolating from ill-formed texts' (Slagel 174).

Moreover, London is a writer from the Western United States where settlement is a matter of living memory in the early 1900s and which had a history of particularly vicious racism directed towards Chinese immigrants and earlier Mexican settlers (recorded first hand by Stevenson in latter half of *The Amateur Emigrant*). This history and other factors encouraged a highly deterministic form of naturalist writing – including, as well London, Frank Norris and John Steinbeck – that James Slagel has called 'pessimistic determinism':

> They were also informed by developments in psychology, political philosophy and science, particularly by Charles Darwin's *The Origin of Species by Means of Natural Selection* in 1859, which contributed to Naturalistic thinking not only the idea that Homo Sapiens are related to lower forms of animals but that people are capable of atavistic regression to a savage state, that behaviour can be the product of biologically determined forces, that there is nothing transcendent in human life. Life is a struggle for survival in which not the fittest but most ruthless prevail . . . Out of these ideas the dominant theme in Naturalism of pessimistic determinism, the notion that characters are the victims of promethean forces of hereditary, society and a hostile nature, powers outside the control of protagonists and for which they are not to be held responsible. (Nagel xxviii)

Certainly London's identification of Marquesan decline with racial inferiority rather than Western intervention and colonialism fits comfortably within such a discourse while also being at odds with it by the very notion of Western exceptionalism that lies behind it. The white interloper is thus absolved from any responsibility for the spread of disease and can occupy the 'empty' land unburdened by a guilty conscience, since it is simply nature weeding out the weaker race. His dismissal of the Marquesans is no more than the narrative presumption that he, the 'fitter', has prevailed in the ruthless competition. Yet the contradiction throughout this section suggests that this is a position only sustained under considerable ideological strain.

Such strain may stem from more unconscious anxieties. London's own 'race' occupies usurped land and, by the early twentieth century, the United States had become a byword as a cultural and racial melting pot. Somewhat ironically many of the people he detects in the admixture of Marquesan blood can be found intermingled in 'white' America and not least on the West Coast: 'English, American, Dane, German, French, Corsican, Spanish, Portuguese, Chinese . . . ' (*Snark* 163). Homi Bhabha's analytical reworking of 'hybridity' assists in identifying the implicit threat London's narrative attempts to subsume. Bhabha argues that the selective intermingling by the colonized 'native' of the colonizer's idioms with the indigenous culture is ontologically unsettling: 'half acquiescent, half oppositional always untrustworthy [this] produces an unresolveable problem of cultural difference for the very address of colonial authority' (Bhabha 330). This only goes so far, however, addressed as it is to the kind of imperial ideology that strove to maintain strict cultural and, thence, racial boundaries in the administration of culturally disparate colonies. What of the would-be colonist whose history is one of intensive frontier settlement, slavery and mass immigration? In that event the ambivalence is not generated by cultural hybridity – since both Stevenson's and London's Marquesans remain culturally distinct even if in terminal decline – but more directly on the grounds of miscegenation, a national neurosis for Americans of Western European descent that was the legacy of slavery. Not surprisingly, London returns later in the same chapter to this unresolved ambivalence in an attempt to reconcile his views on racial purity and hybridization. The focal trope is again illness and disease but his identification of the racial decline of the Marquesans is more direct. London proposes that Melville's Marquesans were 'physically magnificent [because racially] they were pure' (*Snark* 163). To displace the hybridity of his own nation, London conjures a broad conceptualization of a pure 'white race' but acknowledges that it was they who spread the new diseases to the Marquesas.

Yet because the 'white race' is relatively more diseased and has as a consequence developed a greater range of resistance, it must be of greater vigour; biological superiority conferred by the natural selection of disease. Disease has become a positive force:

> We of the white race are the survivors and the descendents of thousands of generations of survivors in the war with micro-organisms. Whenever one of us is born with a constitution peculiarly receptive to these minute enemies, such a one promptly died. Only those of us survived who could withstand them. We who are alive are the immune, the fit – the ones best constituted to live in a world of hostile micro-organisms. The poor Masrquesans had undergone no such selection. They were not immune. (*Snark* 170–1)

This is, of course, a flawed argument that would only pass scrutiny by the most ideologically motivated reader, although such a reader was not uncommon in the early years of the twentieth century while anticipating aspects of racial fascism. But if the 'white race' is such a paragon of evolutionary virility because of resistance to old world contagion, what of the inhabitants of Asia and Africa who enjoy a comparable resistance to many of the same diseases but were most certainly the victims of systematic Western imperialism and racial denigration since the days of the Greeks and Romans. The French historian Emmanuel Le Roy Ladurie argues that 'the relatively benign nature of contact in the Ancient World was not due to any particular kindness or treatment on the part of the conquerors but to the immunity, or at least partial immunity, enjoyed by the subject native peoples to the microbes that had been in circulation over a period of time throughout Eurasia and Eurafrica' (Le Roy 76). This ostensibly seems to bear out London's argument, but by his reasoning the racially distinct people of those continents would be every bit as refined by 'hostile micro-organisms' as the European 'we' he privileges, but his racial hierarchy would hardly accept this. So as a 'racial' distinction it does not stand up to much scrutiny.

The circle of this argument is squared so awkwardly London resorts to a cannibal joke to emphasize the distance between us (his readers) and his object: those who had such a fearsome reputation for consuming their enemies – thanks to Melville's *Typee* – were now being consumed in turn by an alien disease they had ingested. Nature's judgement on the savage Marquesan, it seems. The contradictions of his argument are not quite so easily obscured, however. Hybridity either weakens the Marquesans or confers a residual vitality; pure Marquesans were physically magnificent, but inherently weak in the face of nature in the form of disease; it is the place and climate that encourages disease, or the climate has nothing to do with it and is a balm; white people spread disease and are immune themselves thanks to natural selection, but London enjoys no such immunity. His final word on the Marquesans is also his most revealing implying an involuntary recognition of the physical and cultural consequences of Western contact and colonialism. If, London suggests, the Marquesans had been a race of several hundreds of thousands, they might have withstood the bacteriological onslaught and, indeed, prospered becoming a 'regenerated race' with strengthened immunities. Yet with no colonial expansion there would have been no contact with the Marquesans who would have continued to prosper. It is colonialism and the economic and technological determinants behind expansion which provokes an ideologically driven attempt to transfer guilt and responsibility that both absolves and privileges the carrier as a being who has advanced further along the evolutionary road mapped out, or determined, by Nature. But then, the opposite is equally true. The very discourse that rejects responsibility also creates the spectre of the white man roaming the earth disseminating disease that Stevenson identified in *The Ebb Tide*. This leaves London's own identity strikingly threatened when he almost becomes the victim of the very forces of 'natural selection' ironically and actually represented by his deteriorating white skin.

5

The Inequities of Trade: Adventure Narratives, Ethics and Imperial Commerce in Robert Louis Stevenson's *The Wrecker*

In February 1890 Stevenson wrote to his American publisher, Edward L. Burlingame of *McClure's*, with a word of explanation regarding a new project that he had outlined in a preceding letter, *The Wrecker*: 'You will already have received from me a letter about *The Wrecker*. No doubt this is a new experiment for me, being designed so much as a study of manners, and the interest turning on a mystery of the detective sort' (*Letters VI* 366). In addition to a detective plot, the novel creates a curious brew by relying heavily on imperial adventure fiction, featuring a marginal locale in the South Pacific, piracy, smuggling, murder and two eventful seas voyages. The novel is also an extended examination of class discourse and the distorted experience created by commercial ideologies. The principal character and narrator, Loudon Dodd, and the central character of the embedded mystery that he uncovers, Norris Carthew, both feel themselves to have entered into a man's estate as a consequence of their adventures. Martin Green has called the adventure genre a 'masculinist literature' in which women are absent or marginalized. That is certainly the case with this novel, which has only one significant female character and even she has limited – though crucial – narrative presence. Indeed, Rod Edmond following Elaine Showalter refers to the novel as a 'homosocial romance of adventure and quest' (Edmond 178). Yet the cathartic violence that typically accompanies such masculinist discourse is exceptionally extreme and disturbing owing to the absence of any redeeming ideal. All the principal characters of this novel are involved to varying degrees with questionable, and often criminal, activities that by no stretch of the imagination could be construed as justifiable by an appeal to the colonial 'idea' which might be expected of the adventure genre.

Moreover, despite the elements of sensationalism lent to the novel by the underlying mystery, the day-to-day description of personal relationships and colonial trading is pointedly commonplace – 'a study of manners' – in a way that presents ethical ambiguity as standard practice thence placing the whole imperial infrastructure on very tawdry foundations. Indeed, the question ultimately posed by this novel is – how can a civilizing mission proceed founded upon what is essentially petty corruption that sometimes leads to horrendous crimes? A corruption that undermines personal relationships leading to a rather more complex text than Showalter's typology of the male quest romance would suggest. The close male camaraderie of the adventure tale is transformed into a vehicle that foregrounds the reciprocal moral failings of friends and business partners – often indistinguishable in the narrative – resulting in a spiralling decline into ever more questionable activities. A pervasive atmosphere of moral ambiguity informs all of Dodd's activities and relationships, which significantly affect the overall tone of the novel since it is through his point of view that the action is recounted leading Edmond to comment on the 'thoroughly debased' adventure ethos of the novel. Conrad's Marlow would later perform a similar narrative function in *Heart of Darkness* and *Lord Jim*, but significantly with Marlow's character the ambiguity resides beyond him in the situation that he strives to comprehend. While the events that he witnesses certainly provoke confusion and ambiguity, this emphasizes both the dangers and immorality of 'mismanagement' – a faltering in the prosecution of the 'idea'. Yet in Dodd, Stevenson has created a far more disturbing narrative experience since his ethics are questionable from the beginning, although not in a manner that defines the character as bad and thence manageable on that basis, since after some pressure he can be grudgingly brought to act in an honourable way although often with inopportune timing for those who rely on him. Such an ambivalent point of view in the narrative has distinct implications for the structure and impact of the novel taking the reader into situations hardly implied by expectations of the adventure genre.

In May 1892 during serial publication of the novel, Stevenson wrote to Henry James describing the narrative as 'a machine, and a police machine; but I believe the end is one of the most genuine butcheries in literature; and we point to our machine with modest pride – as the only police machine without a villain. Our criminals are a most pleasing crew, and leave the dock with scarce a stain on their character' (*Letters VII* 292). Taking pride in retaining the remorseless pace and violence of the detective story – a characteristic significantly shared with adventure fiction – Stevenson revels in breaking the expected convention by having no explicit villain to blame despite the criminality of his protagonists' actions. While uncondemned by the 'court' of this narrative, they are still criminals; murder has, after all, been committed with extreme 'butchery'. Their acquittal relies upon a narrative perspective that provides the ideological norms of the text and which constructs a favourable view of the protagonists to the extent readers might be surprised at what they are encouraged to excuse. As Schlomith Rimmon-Kenan observes: 'the ideology of the narrator-focalizer is usually taken as authoritative, and all other ideologies in the text are evaluated from this "higher" position' (Rimmon-Kenan 81). This does not, of course, preclude questions about the reliability of the narrator, which is very much at issue in this novel. Indeed, Rimmon-Kenan is careful to place 'higher' within quotation marks indicating that a higher narrative level does not necessarily indicate factual veracity within the narrative. Alan Sandison, comparing Stevenson's *The Ebb Tide* to Conrad's *Heart of Darkness*, observes that both novellas feature an ambivalence that links both authors to early literary Modernism, but that Stevenson's text suffers because it lacks the discriminating consciousness of a Marlow. He continues: 'Their ambivalence can then become the ambivalence of novels whose subject is perception but which can then become the ambivalence of novels whose subject is perception but which can be found catalogued along with novels about moral consciousness' (Sandison 317). This is an astute observation that is particularly pertinent to *The Wrecker*, a novel much wider in scope than *The Ebb Tide* and featuring a similar mediating consciousness in Dodd. *The Wrecker* is centrally concerned with both ambivalence and moral consciousness, but also both fictional *and* factual representation.

This represents a significant development in Stevenson's art inspired by his first-hand experience of colonialism in the South Pacific. As noted above, he was a professed opponent of the naturalistic realism of writers like Emile Zola about whom he had disagreed with Henry James. While admiring the technical accomplishment he was repulsed by the subject matter. In a letter to the editor of *The Times* in early September 1886, Stevenson had made his objections public: 'M. Zola is a man of personal and forceful talent, approaching genius, but of diseased ideals; a lover of the ignoble, dwelling complacently in foulness, and to my sense touched with erotic madness' (*Letters V* 311). Yet the perspective offered by *The Wrecker* easily suits this description as criminality is represented as excusable in a colonial context. Stevenson was also conscious of the influence of this colonial milieu on his writing in a letter to Burlingame: 'I am sorry to say that Dodd, Pinkerton, Nares . . . and all the minor characters, are portraits, almost undisguised. This is not my usual method of work. I want your advice as to (a) the success and (b) the decency of this method' (*Letters VI* 376). The concern with decency here stems from the 'warts and all' realization of character portraits in the novel where character flaws dictate key directions in the plot. Yet even more shocking is how these very human flaws are magnified in a colonial context as corruption and violence materially affecting many lives. In many senses, the novel is one of character, class and cultural flaws explored in Europe and America which are reasonably harmless in those settings, but prove fatal at the colonial frontier. Structurally and discursively the connection between experience and fiction – or more properly the fictionalization of experience – reaches farther than a few character portraits as Stevenson wrote to his friend Charles Baxter: 'However, I believe the *The Wrecker* is a good yarn of its poor sort, and it is certainly well nourished with facts; no realist can touch me there; for by this time I do begin to know something of life in the nineteenth century, which no novelist in France or English seems to know much of' (*Letters VII* 192). Stevenson's claim to find both a factual veracity and an experiential authenticity that the realist writers of Europe have failed to capture is a bold one given the 'exotic' South Pacific setting that provides the destination and frame of this novel. What is the greater 'understanding' of the nineteenth century to be found so far from home? The answer is the *behaviour* of Europeans and Americans beyond their homelands: in short, the behaviour encouraged by the exploitative relationships of empire and colonial trade. In this respect the text operates less as a quest narrative than as a form of picaresque novel with Loudon Dodd and his aristocratic counterpart, Norris Carthew, realizing their manhood but at the price of learning disquieting truths about themselves and their culture. As Roslyn Jolly observes of Stevenson's South Pacific work: 'as Conrad, Kipling, Waugh, and Camus were to do after him, Stevenson . . . used the edges of empire as the setting for a modern and modernist existential drama' (Jolly xxxiii). Yet caution is necessary in gauging the level of explicit criticism. While scarcely represented favourably, there is no implicit call for the dismantling of empire and the equality of races. Rather this is, as Stevenson claimed, a study of manners among Europeans and Americans that signifies a bemusement at an imperial success founded on all-too-apparent petty frailties. No class escapes censure, and while it may be no reductive condemnation of Western colonialism, it is a rejection of the fallacies of the 'idea' that would ennoble greed and selfishness.

Indeed, a closer analysis of Stevenson's use of experience, place and character studies from among his acquaintances reveals a rather selective process. The detailed description of the Marquesas Islands in the framing narrative of prologue and epilogue is significant as it is the setting of Loudon's and Carthew's ultimate exile. The locale is Tai-o-hae French administrative capital of the Marquesas Islands of a comparable date with Stevenson's own visit recorded in *In the South Seas*, and the opening descriptive panorama is an edited version of his own entry into Tai-o-hae harbour from that text. While white traders and officials – if, indeed, they are based on actual acquaintances – are disguised, various Polynesian notables are depicted under their own names. Thence we have both Vaekehu the 'native queen' and her son, Prince Stanilas Moanatini rushing off to administrative duties. The only white personage who is depicted under his own name is the famous tattooed man who had tried, and comically failed, to win the favour of a high-ranking Marquesan woman who also finds his way into *In the South Seas*. It is significant that while Stevenson had agonized over the 'decency' of using thinly veiled portraits of his American and European friends, he clearly felt no such restraint with regard to his Polynesian friends who are reduced to little more than local colour. Similarly, the tattooed white man visibly inscribed with the cultural imprint of another culture is someone who has 'gone native' and is treated in the same way. The South Pacific episodes of the novel could, therefore, be read as little more than a setting or exotic backdrop for a tale exclusively focussed on Europeans and Americans. But why then such attention to verifiable detail or, as Stevenson put it, 'well nourished with facts'. To a lesser extent, the same process can be discerned in the other significant locales of the novel; San Francisco most readily, but also Paris and Edinburgh. Yet the narrative also features two wholly fictional – although intended to be stereotypical – places, the very English Stallbridge-le-Carthew, Norris Carthew's point of origin and ancestral home, balanced by Loudon Dodd equally fictional and very American mid-Western state capital of Muskegon. The narrative presents these stereotypical but fictional heartlands of both English and American national identity only to recede further from them by featuring locations quite marginal to secure notions of that identity. A city like San Francisco with its teeming polyglot population and Pacific-facing commercial outlook belongs to such a margin, as in a sense do Paris and Edinburgh. The Paris of the novel is not the political capital of a rival empire, but the feckless, marginal life of the Bohemian artist colony, the playground of the Anglo-Saxon aesthete; and Edinburgh, a capital without an independent nation, perpetually marginalized by the political and imperial domination of London and England.

Stevenson's claim to have created a study of manners provides the most obvious hint of an explanation, but it is a modest claim given the scope of the novel, which is no less than an interrogation of British and American national character and identity both as ideal and in practice. The American Muskegon and the English

Stallbridge-le-Carthew are fictions because we are invited to accept them as foci for abstracted 'imagined communities' to borrow Benedict Anderson's phrase. They are representative of a cultural nationalism that contains notions like the high colonial 'idea' of the civilizing mission, manifest destiny and dubious racial categories, and Anglo-Saxonism. Yet as John Hutchinson argues, alongside such idealizations lays the threat of cultural degeneration: 'The aim of cultural nationalists is . . . the moral regeneration of the historic community' (Hutchinson 124). But what to Stevenson are unquestionably scenes of moral degeneration among the British and American (collectively, Anglo-Saxon) protagonists of this tale in a manner that suggests that the 'race' was never entitled to claim the moral high ground of the redeeming 'idea' to begin with.

The Miseducation of Loudon Dodd: From New World to Old

The framing prologue of the *The Wrecker* introduces the reader to Loudon Dodd, a South Sea trader of peculiarly rarefied tastes. His cabin is fitted out with antique furniture and bookshelves adorned with Renaissance French texts while in contrast to this initial characterization by setting, he tantalizes the motley company of European traders assembled in the white-only clubhouse with hints of a career involving a number of criminal activities – 'the opium and the wreck, and the blackmailing' (*Wrecker* 14). Yet 'career' is too strong a word for the 'yarn' that follows since genuine commercial activity, licit or illicit, is clearly anathema to Dodd's sensibilities. When it is suggested that he was involved in property speculation in California, a more or less legitimate commercial venture, he reacts with the aesthete's disdain: 'Surely, I never went so far as that . . . interested? I guess not. Involved, perhaps. I was born an artist; I never took an interest in anything but art' (*Wrecker* 8). The idea of a frustrated artist turning to commerce to support himself is perhaps not unusual, but a turn to crime is an arresting idea and brings a new sense of decadence. Short as it is, this initial portrait of the mature Dodd – the narrator for the remainder of the text – is significant as it serves not only as an intriguing introduction to the story to be recounted by Dodd in retrospect, but also raises questions about the reliability of his character and how he will shape the story. Indeed, despite his strong preference for art, his personality has led him into darker pursuits that on the face of it do not seem to have been driven by financial necessity. Further, his character poses a fundamental question: is it his personality that has morally perverted the culture to which he devotes himself, or the culture that has morally corrupted him. Dodd's partner provides the capital for their business, but there seems to be less of a business the more he describes their relationship: 'I don't know that the [boat] does pay . . . I never pretended to be a business man. My partner appears happy; and the money is all his, as I told you – I only bring the want of business habits' (*Wrecker* 9). With the later talk of blackmail this relationship becomes increasingly suspect despite the assertion that he and the man whom he is blackmailing became his friend. The concluding link to the retrospective narrative that follows – 'Here follows the yarn of Loudon Dodd, not as he told it to his friend, but as he subsequently wrote it' (*Wrecker* 14) – is more than just a device to create verisimilitude, but is designed to influence the reading of the tale that follows. For in writing the tale he exposes the crime of his partner whom we learn is Norris Carthew only towards the end of the novel. The prologue/epilogue frame is, therefore, not just a convenient frame story but the logical culmination of both Carthew's crime – exposure – and confirmation of Loudon's identity as a blackmailer. The narrative is an elaborate blackmailer's confession.

The obvious flaws in Dodd's character inevitably raise questions about the nature of his devotion to art which persists as an important theme throughout the novel as a vehicle to raise much wider ethical issues. The prologue establishes an early discursive topic around the nature of work and class through a sensibility obsessed with the idea rather than the successful practice of art. As Vanessa Smith observes: '*The Wrecker*'s questions about the material base of aesthetic pursuits and the value of artistic enterprise as measured against forms of manual activity surface repeatedly in Stevenson's meditations published and private, on the art of writing' (Smith 151). Writing to Sidney Colvin as the ground was being cleared for planting on his Samoan estate, Stevenson was to make this question of relative 'value' explicit:

> To come down covered in mud and drenched with sweat and rain after some hours in the bush, change, rub down, and take a chair in the verandah, is to taste a quiet conscience. And the strange thing that I remark is this: if I go out and make sixpence, bossing my labourers and plying cutlass or the spade, idiot conscience applauds me: if I sit in the house and make twenty pounds, idiot conscience wails over my neglect and the day wasted. (*Letters VII* 20)

Smith goes on to argue that Stevenson's concern with this question stems from latent feelings of guilt over his failure to follow the family profession of marine engineering, a profession that he was both disinclined to follow and for which he lacked the necessary physical robustness. Within *The Wrecker*, however, this theme takes a rather different shape that has less to do with respect for the nobility of manual labour – although that question does arise later in the novel – but the difference between the genuine artist and the poseur, or even something worse. Dodd's fascination with art does not stem from thwarted genius but from the dilettante's fascination for the easy, decadent, life it affords the wealthy amateur. When Dodd speaks of his devotion to art – whether his insistence is to his putative reader of his confessional narrative or to acquaintances and friends within it – it is not 'art' but the life open to a particular sensibility produced by unearned income. It is an expression of class aspiration – about easy money, the means for obtaining it, and its social and personal consequences.

The embedded narrative opens with the question of his 'poor father's' character that serves as both a thematic introduction to the circumstances that have created the mature Dodd the narrator, and an insight into the cut-and-thrust world of American commerce. The description of his father reveals far more about Loudon's character than it does about his father, which creates immediate questions of his reliability as a narrator. Rimmon-Kenan observes that 'The main sources of unreliability are the narrator's limited knowledge, his personal involvement, and his problematic value-scheme' (Rimmon-Kenan 100). Dodd's limited knowledge has less to do with his status as a narrator than the necessary obscurities of the detective plot Stevenson has adapted. His personal involvement is certainly a factor because of the third item, his value scheme. This is evident from the opening description of his father. While taking satisfaction in his father's distinguished appearance, he goes to some length to diminish all that he has achieved in both the public and private realms. He is 'unhappy in his business, in his pleasures, in his place of residence, and (I am sorry to say) in his son' (*Wrecker* 15). While Dodd concedes that he is a disappointment to his father, he does so by painting a picture of a man congenitally unhappy with the entirety of life – it is not the same as saying: 'my father was a happy man disappointed in his son'. His defensive attitude seeks to deflect any blame from himself by implying that his father was fundamentally discontented and unhappy and that his disappointment in his son is inevitable – and unremarkable – as a consequence. He further questions his father's intelligence and his ethics. While the ethics of commerce is certainly not above interrogation in this text, we are presented with a picture of Dodd that reveals a wilfully narrow-minded rejection of hard work and self-sacrifice as well as an inability to recognize the possibility of constructive enjoyment in an occupation towards which he is not personally sympathetic. Yet there is an underlying resentment that goes further. His father's evident devotion to his work serves to limit the time he can devote to Loudon. In the absence of another parent – his father is a widower – Dodd seeks an outlet in an occupation and a life inimical to that source of distress, an artistic ideal that is as ephemeral as business is practical. Perhaps more discomforting is the cost to the relationship between father and son, for whom he seems to have no feeling other than a condescending pity. Another implication of this problematic relationship, which is significant because it is repeated in his friendship with another hard-working businessman, Pinkerton, is the clear displacement in illustrates. Dodd's thwarted ambition and consequent unhappiness are revealed in a series of bitter asides about himself, the first of which immediately follows his rather cruel judgement of his father:

> Unluckily, I never cared a cent for anything but art, and never shall. My idea of a man's chief end was to enrich the world with things of beauty and have a fairly good time himself while doing so. I do not think I mentioned that second, which is the only one I have managed to carry out; but my father must have suspected the suppression, for he branded the whole affair self-indulgence. (*Wrecker* 15)

The retrospective acknowledgement of his failure to achieve his primary aim – 'to enrich the world with things of beauty' – and the accuracy of his father's reading of his aims in life should not obscure the fact that Dodd persists in an attitude that has proven to be so destructive of one relationship and will endanger others. It is his father's parting remark in this section which reverberates through the text: 'But struggle as you please, a man has to work in this world. He must be an honest man or a thief, Loudon' (*Wrecker* 16). But how does the 'world' define honesty, theft and work?

When he is despatched by his father to the Muskegon Commercial Academy to learn something of 'real life,' all his prejudices against his father's value system are confirmed and become ingrained. The curriculum of the Academy is conventional instruction in the mornings and to put theory into practice in the afternoon by speculating on its mock stock and commodity market linked directly by telegraph to Wall Street and other markets using 'college paper' that has a minimal value of one cent to the dollar. As might be anticipated, Dodd's tone is sarcastic and condemnatory over the educational merits of such a system: 'It was cold-drawn gambling, without colour or disguise. Just that the impediment and destruction of all genuine commercial enterprise' (*Wrecker* 17). While by now his ability to recognize 'genuine commercial enterprise' must be open to question, he is ironically applying his father's value scheme even though it was he who sent him to the Academy. Yet the academy is also notable for its modernity; not only is there the physical link to far off New York, Chicago, St. Louis etc., but it is also held in high esteem for its innovative curriculum:

> You are a foreigner, and will have difficulty in accepting the reality of this seat of education. I assure you before I begin that I am wholly serious. The place really existed, possibly exists to-day: we were proud of it in the State, as something exceptionally nineteenth century and civilised; and my father, when he saw me to the cars, no doubt considered he was putting me straight in line for the presidency and the New Jerusalem. (*Wrecker* 16)

While such a reaction to modernity and commerce from a self-avowed aesthete is not unexpected, the clear satire on American ideas of progressive vocational education and commercial aggressiveness is especially pointed articulated by a fictional US citizen. It is tempting to suggest that Stevenson, the upper-middle class British author simply overplays his hand and clumsily reveals his own prejudices through his American narrator. Certainly it is not hard to find evidence of Stevenson's dislike for what he discerned as American commercial brashness. Indeed, he freely recorded in *The Amateur Emigrant* the 'fierce, sordid, appetite for dollars'. However, such a biographical reading does no justice to the narrative given the reservations that are early established over Dodd as reliable narrator. Moreover, he also wrote in qualification of his criticism that the 'appetite for dollars' was a component element of the fuel that feeds the 'constant kaleidoscopic change that Walt Whitman has seized and set forth in vigorous, cheerful, and loquacious verses' (*Emigrant* 90–1). Dodd's alienation from the commercial energy of his country is also an estrangement from its maturing cultural tradition represented by figures like Whitman. His outlook is an older, class-stratified rejection of both the modernity and social change represented by his own country and reflected in his yearning for a privileged lifestyle in the Old World living off his father's money where he finally succeeds in being sent after conspicuous failure at the Academy. Despite well-founded suspicion over the potential ethical compromises of commerce, he is out of step with the prevailing ethos of his country and his age. When Dodd's father is finally persuaded to send his art-loving son to Paris, it is to acquire an art education in pursuit of profit as an enrichment of both his family's fortune and the American cultural fabric: 'I took up the statuary contract on our new capitol; I took it up first as a deal; and then it occurred to me that it would be better to keep it in the family. It meets your idea; there's considerable money in the thing; and it's so patriotic.

So if you will say the word, you shall go to Paris and come back in three years to decorate the capitol of your native state' (*Wrecker* 6). As the Hugh Brogan observes: 'many of the best and brightest of their time went into business, confident that they were furthering civilization and their country's best interests by doing so. Nor were they wholly wrong. It was they who undertook the job of bringing order out of the chaos that America's exuberant industrial growth had created' (Brogan 99).

These issues are further tested through his relationship with the quintessential American entrepreneur, Pinkerton, who personifies not just speculation, optimism and energy but also, significantly, decency. It is ironic that his parents were 'from the old country' where he was also born is a reminder that America is a nation of emigrants whose pluck and determination is the offshoot of an older branch, England. Of course there have been many other nationalities and ethnicities that shaped American identity, and yet English identification is privileged and interrogated through this key relationship. The issue is a product of the popular but historically questionable notion of the shared 'racial' identity of Anglo-Saxon culture. Pinkerton's claim to fame among the British and American student population of Paris is a version of the 'thin red line' that hails back to this 'racial' solidarity:

> The second incident was that which had earned Pinkerton his reputation. In a crowded studio, while some very filthy brutalities were being practiced on a trembling debutant, a tall pale fellow sprang from his stool and (without the smallest preface or explanation) sang out, 'All English and Americans to clear the shop!' Our race is brutal, but not filthy; and the summons was nobly responded to. Every Anglo-Saxon student seized his stool; in a moment the studio was full of bloody coxcombs, the French fleeing in disorder for the door, the victim liberated and amazed. (*Wrecker* 38)

While the victim of these 'filthy brutalities' is not identified, an earlier incident involves an Armenian who defends himself with a knife. In this later episode the victim is more passive and not identified by nationality or ethnicity, but must be rescued in what is a symbolic enactment of the Anglo-Saxon 'civilising mission', protecting the weak from predatory European imperialists. The unspecified 'filthy brutalities' is an unusual expression which implies some form of sexual transgression or homoeroticism drawing on contemporary charges of effeminacy levied at those who identified themselves as aesthetes of whom Oscar Wilde would be the obvious example. While Dodd is modelled to some extent after the aesthetes, the narrative builds a distinction that the call to Anglo-Saxon students polarizes preventing their masculinity from being questioned. Clearly Stevenson's musings over the 'nobility' and sense of satisfaction brought by manual labour reflects some personal anxiety towards the perceived effeminacy of his vocation as an artist, but especially as a novelist as a medium closely associated with feminine expression in the nineteenth century. The concession that the 'Anglo-Saxon' was a brute but not a 'filthy brute' almost advances a propensity to violence as a positive virtue that will prove crucial as the plot unfolds.

This emblematic scene creates a series of complex associations, among them, class, race, masculinity and imperialism. Certainly *The Wrecker* features a series of close relationships between men that propels the adventure/detective plot. However, this is not the only determining characteristic of these genres which had, by the end of the century, begun to reflect a number of anxieties evident from this incident and throughout the novel. As Richard Phillips insists: 'Adventure stories chart masculinities contextually, in relation to particular constructions of class, race, sexuality and other forms of identity' (R. Phillips 45). While brutishness may be preferable to sexual or, worse, explicitly homosexual 'filthiness' to Dodd, the question of violence introduced here will develop into a key concern of the narrative. The English and American men violently assert themselves to establish physical domination founded on a claim to moral superiority rather than out of any compassion for the poor victim who is soon forgotten after the mêlée. The violence is an overreaction to a form of behaviour that must remain subsumed rather than public if it is to be tolerated. By comparison, the violence in the imperial adventure tale had immeasurably increased in the latter years of the nineteenth century in tandem with advances in the understanding of sexuality, particularly female sexuality. Richard Phillips observes that:

> Later nineteenth-century characters . . . were polarised along gender lines, becoming clearly masculine or feminine. The masculinization of boys was partly a response to changing ideas about what it meant to be feminine. Claudia Nelson interprets the masculinization of boyhood in light of the contemporary developments in psychology. As psychologists began to think of women as actively sexual, in the second half of the century, it became impossible to think of feminine boys as asexual, hence sexually pure, and (later on) to think of them as (in some way) homosexual . . . (R. Phillips 51)

Yet *The Wrecker* is neither juvenile literature nor simply an adventure tale. While there are two adventure plot lines intermingled with the interrogative methods of detective fiction, the narrative structure operates to actively question the central assumptions of the narrator. What unfolds is a text that probes the governing ethos of male friendship and those other nineteenth-century patriarchal constructions commerce, imperialism and racial hierarchies, as well as the fear of emasculation introduced by this episode from Pinkerton's past. Unlike juvenile adventure literature, this text not only shows the aggression and violence of these patriarchal realms, but also actively seeks an explanation – the answer that emerges is not the resolution of the mystery, but the revelation of 'brute' realities ethically circumscribed. To look ahead for the moment, Edward Said argues that '[t]he space between the bashing of other religions and cultures and deeply conservative self-praise has not been filled with edifying analysis or discussion' (Said 397), and, yet, this is the interrogatory space created between the unreliability of Loudon as a narrator, the ethical shortcomings of Euro-American commerce, and masculine violence conducted at the imperial periphery.

The broader implications of Pinkerton's character are also significant. His belief in the destiny of the 'American type' weds the American national myth to the zeal of the evangelist: 'We're all under bond to fulfil the American Type! Loudon, the hope of the world is there. If we fail, like those old feudal monarchies, what is there left?' (*Wrecker* 42). His rhetoric evokes the American belief in national 'manifest destiny' – coined by John O'Sullivan in 1845 – that had carried the United States across the North American continent. By the 1890s, the idea embodied a nascent American imperialism after the European model that led to the acquisition of Hawaii, the Philippines, Cuba and Puerto Rico by the end of the decade. The rationale behind these annexations was as much economic as political, securing important points along key trading routes. Pinkerton's dismissal of these 'old feudal monarchies' echoes both the tone and rhetorical flourish of another imperial rallying call for the revitalization of the most powerful of those old monarchies, Britain. In his inaugural address as Slade Professor of Art at Oxford in 1870, John Ruskin argued:

A destiny is now possible to us, the highest ever set before a nation to be accepted or refused. . . . Will you youths of England make your country again a royal throne of kings, a sceptered isle for all the world a source of light, a centre of peace. . . . Will you, youths of England, make your country again a royal throne of kings; a sceptred isle, for all the world a source of light, a centre for peace; mistress of Learning and of the Arts . . . There is indeed a course of beneficent glory open to us, such as never was yet offered to any poor group of mortal souls. But it must be – it is with us, now, "Reign or Die." And if it shall be said of this country, she must found colonies as fast and as far as she is able, formed of her most energetic and worthiest men; – seizing every piece of fruitful waste ground she can set her foot on, and there teaching these her colonists that their chief virtue is to be fidelity to their country, and that their first aim is to be to advance the power of England by land and sea. (Beckson 344–5)

For both Ruskin, the British art critic and academic, and Pinkerton the American businessman of 'extended interests', it is the exalted 'idea' that shapes their rhetoric and occludes the desire to protect economic and political interests. The British Empire between 1860 and 1870 had reached the zenith of its economic growth and power although anxieties of decline and eclipse in the face of the rapid industrial growth of the United States and Germany were already prophesized prompting rallying calls like Ruskin's concerned with the strategic defence of vested interests (Kennedy 172–94). By the 1890s when Stevenson was writing of Pinkerton's enthusiasm for the 'American Type' and assuming the torch of leadership from a tired Europe dominated by anachronistic monarchies, the United States was as well placed as Britain to protect her extensive economic interests. Stevenson identifies both the economic impetus of American expansion and its close link to the imperial rhetoric of an earlier generation in Britain. He also reproduces the sense that Americans had of eclipsing a nation that simultaneously held the distinction of being mother country, former oppressor and greatest commercial competitor. Stevenson had noted this sense of triumphalism during his first visit to the United States in 1879: 'they [the Americans] return full of bitterness because the English show so small an interest and so modified a pleasure in the progress of the States. Truly; but perhaps we should please them better, if they would measure the growth of America on some different standard from the decline of England' (*Scotland to Silverado* 91). He was also quick to note the sense of 'racial' and cultural identification that Americans felt for the 'Old Country', dramatized in the novel by Pinkerton's Anglo-Saxon call to arms. Again, this echoes not only historical and cultural affiliations, but also economic realities. As Hugh Brogan suggests, where their economic interests converged on the same region or industry, the United States and Britain could be fierce competitors, but each would work to exclude non-Anglo-Saxon competitors: 'There was, in fact, a partnership between England and the United States, but it was so informal, and punctuated by so many rows, that most Americans never detected it' (Brogan 449).

The 1880s and 1890s were also a period of fierce debate concerning the moral responsibility of art conducted between the extremes of high – if hypocritical – Victorian ideals of propriety and the amoral stance of aestheticism which looked to Gautier's maxim in *Mademoiselle de Maupin* (1835) of *l'art pour l'art* which is echoed in Oscar Wilde's preface to *The Picture of Dorian Gray* (1891): 'No artist has ethical sympathies. An ethical sympathy in an artist is an unpardonable mannerism of style . . . All art is quite useless' (Wilde 9). Dodd's own obsession with art shares both the aesthete's insistence on 'art for art's sake' and the bourgeois notion of a morally elevating art as the basis to criticize the apparent moral failings of materialists like his father and Pinkerton. Through this characterization Stevenson refines the focus of the debate to suggest that it is the self-serving nature of humanity that creates moral ambivalence. Thence the idea of art as an abstraction or practice is not of itself an ethical model equipped to regulate lived experience since, as discourse, it can be manipulated to create or reinforce a critical position that excuses or initiates damaging interpersonal relationships, such as Dodd's relationship with his father and later Pinkerton. Moreover, ideas like the 'civilising mission' is little more than the aestheticization of a similar self-serving motivation predicated on expansion and profit. There is both a personal and cultural selfishness that is derived from an identical moral vacuum, which produces an apparently amoral as well as a hypocritical moralizing art, a romanticized civilizing mission and a violent imperial trade. In each instance, it is the suppression of consciousness that is the source of evil, the evading of responsibility and involvement, and essential and wilful misrecognition of the consequences of personal and collective behaviour towards the Other. Dodd's artistic and Pinkerton's business myopia stem from their shared habit of self-deception rather than simply from their lack of talent, which is abundantly obvious when they each prove failures in their respective fields.

When Loudon is reduced to the real poverty of an unendowed art student in Paris following his father's death, he and Pinkerton fall to arguing over the ideals of their respective vocations, business and art, in which the key word is romance: 'To this romance of dickering [business] I would reply with the romance (which is the virtue) of art: reminding him of those examples of constancy through many tribulations, which the rule of Apollo is illustrated' (*Wrecker* 60). While Loudon mentions 'romance' to convey the mysterious, exciting quality of his endeavour – the 'idea' – the passage pivots on the ambivalence of the word to signify both a fantasy removed from the demands of real life, or a picturesque falsehood. Indeed, the older Dodd the narrator recalls his expectations of student life confronted with this reality: 'Every Man has his own romance; mine clustered exclusively about the practice of the arts, the life of the Latin Quarter students, and the world of Paris as depicted by that grimy wizard, the author of the *Comédie Humaine*. I was not disappointed – I could not have been; for

I did not see the facts, I brought them with me ready-made' (*Wrecker* 30). Note how Balzac, the grim portrayer of the day-to-day brutalities of poverty and deprivation and the hypocrisies of polite, middle-class obfuscation is a source of romantic abstraction by which reality is transposed into fantasy. It is left to Pinkerton to point to both the escapism and the immediate danger in this conception: 'But what I can't see is why you should want to do nothing else. It seems to argue a poverty of nature' (*Wrecker* 61). What Loudon views as the inherent virtue for his desire is rightly identified as a serious flaw in a character bereft of a broader ethical template other than that of his 'idea' of art; a refusal to gain a wider experience to gauge the consequences of individual actions so long as they serve the pursuit of his desires. While Pinkerton questions Dodd's obsession, his own evaluation of experience is similarly problematic, as Loudon observes, 'Reality was his romance' (*Wrecker* 92). For 'reality' read material gain. In Pinkerton's estimation, experience is only to be measured as a means of directly obtaining profit, or of supplying the necessary personal skills for doing so. He has a similarly misplaced sense of virtue: 'you can't get it out of my head that it's a man's *duty* to die rich, if he can' (*Wrecker* 60; my emphasis).

In *In the South Seas* Stevenson recorded the evaluation of *his* character by the autocratic Chief of Apemama, Tembinok – 'I look your eye. You a good man. You no lie' – which Stevenson glosses, 'a doubtful compliment to a writer of romance' (*South Seas* 218). The humour of this situation rests upon the pun on the alternative signification of the word as a picturesque falsehood. Stevenson had already conceived the idea of *The Wrecker* by the time of this encounter and suggestively, if facetiously, questions the moral ambivalence inherent in question of appearance over experience, as well as enacting the primal scene of European contact in which the Other accepts offers of friendship at face value unaware of the underlying profit motivation of the colonizer, which is, in turn, buried beneath a culturally destructive, but virtuous, ideal – the civilizing mission. Apemama might seem far removed from Paris while *The Wrecker* and *In the South Seas* are very different texts, but the comparison is indicative of Stevenson's artistic and political development towards an uncompromising realism that brings together the moral ambivalence of behaviour in the imperial metropole with the colonial periphery. Moreover, Loudon's subsequent career in Paris plays out the dynamics of the colonial encounter in which Stevenson was an uneasy participant in the South Pacific as he was writing. The episode of the café brawl that covered the Anglo-Saxon students with such honour and earned Pinkerton his fame has established a quasi-racial stance towards the French perpetrators of uncivilized 'filthy brutalities' that must be stamped out.

During Loudon's subsequent career as an impoverished art student he contracts numerous debts with French tradesmen, restaurateurs and his landlady without apparent qualm. When he turns to one of his student acquaintances for help, the questionable morality of his actions is brought into question by the wealthy Englishman Myner, who bluntly observes how Loudon has been exploiting a quirk of French custom:

> The French give a great deal of credit amongst themselves; they find it pays on the whole, or the system would hardly be continued; but I can't see where *we* come in; I can't see that it's honest of us Anglo-Saxons to profit by their easy ways, and then skip over the Channel or (as you Yankees do) across the Atlantic. (*Wrecker* 68)

Outraged by the reminder of his honour, Loudon refuses Myner's offer to pay his debts on condition he returns to the United States on the grounds that he has no 'genius' and therefore no prospects as an artist to develop by staying. To emphasize the question this raises over Loudon's character and the disadvantage the tradesmen are under, Myner reminds Loudon to make sure that whatever he does it is 'honest'. In response to Loudon's bluster, he continues: 'You seem to think honesty as easy as Blind Man's Bluff: I don't. It's some difference of definition' (*Wrecker* 69). This advice echoes that given by his father – 'a man has to work in this world. He must be an honest man or a thief, Loudon' (*Wrecker* 16) – signalling that he has in fact become a thief prepared to cheat the French tradesmen who have given him credit. His pursuit of art in virtuous poverty as an idea that mitigates this robbery is exposed for the false position that it is since he lacks the 'genius' to be a successful artist. Loudon is averse to suitable work gained through experience and honesty leading him to romance and dishonesty.

Standing on the Wall of Antoninus: Western Civilization in the Contact Zone

From the point of view of his father, Pinkerton, and finally Carthew, Loudon is something of a bad investment if his family and friends invest in him in the expectation of his loyalty to both them and their social/commercial interests. As Pinkerton enthuses when Loudon joins him in San Francisco, 'This is what I have longed for: I wanted two heads and four arms; and now I have 'em. You'll find it's just the same as art – all observation and imagination; only more movement. Just wait until you feel the charm' (*Wrecker* 96). Loudon, however, merely uses their funds to further his own devotion to art as if it is a higher calling that excuses any number of betrayals. Yet it is also clear that both sides of the relationships depicted in the novel are governed by self-interest to a degree, and that all parties are at least tacitly candid about what they desire in return, even if Loudon chooses not to honour the desires directed at him. As Michel Foucault observes: 'We never desire against our interests, because interest always follows and finds where desire has placed it' (Foucault 1977). This pattern governs interpersonal relationships throughout the novel.

San Francisco is an important location in the novel and a city with which Stevenson was personally much taken. While the spatial reach of the novel stretches back to the Old World of France and Britain and then westwards through the newly founded states of the Midwest across the Pacific to Australia and the uninhabited Micronesian island of Midway, San Francisco sits at the centre of this novel. The city had made a powerful impression on Stevenson during his short residence in 1879 which left him with the feeling that California and, indeed, the Western states in general, were not 'Anglo-Saxon' like the states in the East. A number of impressions from 1879 are repeated in the novel. Writing of his 1879 visit in his 1883 essay 'San Francisco', he had noted:

> Next, perhaps, in order of strangeness to the rapidity of its appearance, is the mingling of the races that combine to people it. The town is essentially not Anglo-Saxon; still more essentially not American. The Yankee and the Englishman find themselves alike in a strange country. There are none of those touches – not of nature, and I scarcely say of art – by which the Anglo-Saxon feels himself at home in so great a diversity of lands. ('San Francisco' 182)

This sentiment is echoed in *The Wrecker*: 'But San Francisco is not herself only. She is not only the most interesting city in the Union, [but] the hugest smelting-pot of races and the precious metals' (*Wrecker* 117). This analogy cleverly joins the 'melting pot' metaphor that was in common usage about the United States (although usually only in reference to the great entrée ports of the North), with the economic lure which created the fantastic growth of the city – the gold rush of the 1850s. In a development of his earlier theme of racial/cultural alienation, Stevenson has his narrator make an astute observation:

> I stood there on the extreme shore of the West and of today. Seventeen hundred years ago, and seven thousand miles to the east, a legionary stood, perhaps upon the wall of Antoninus, and looked northward towards the mountains of the

Picts. For all the interval of time and space, I, when I looked from the cliff-house on the broad Pacific, was that man's heir and analogue: each of us standing on the verge of the Roman Empire (or, as we call it, Western civilisation), each of us gazing into zones unromanised. (*Wrecker* 118)

Not only is the West conceived as a homogeneous imperial entity, but the specific historical reference is also significant. Antoninus was the Roman emperor who succeeded Hadrian whose more famous stone wall remains an important monument in Britain to this day. It was Antoninus who pushed the Roman border in Britain to its zenith, conquering the lowlands of Scotland and establishing a new border – and largely turf-built wall – from the Forth to the Clyde, a border that established the highland–lowland distinction of subsequent history. Following a major rebellion, this new border was eventually abandoned with the extent of Roman Britain reverting back to Hadrian's Wall a few years after Antoninus' death. The comparison invited by this image is between the old Roman Empire at the high-water mark of its military and cultural domination of Britain, and 'Western Civilisation' perhaps also at the high-water mark of its influence. Indeed, the very multicultural, non-Anglo-Saxon impression of San Francisco might suggest its permeability. Indeed, Western Civilization's border is no longer recognizable as Stevenson wrote in 1883 – it had become a 'strange country'. The comparison anticipates Conrad's *Heart of Darkness* where Marlow uses a similar metaphor to hint that Britain, too, was once uncivilized: 'imagine him here [a Roman commander on the banks of the Thames] – the very end of the world, a sea the colour of lead, a sky the colour of smoke . . . marches, forests, savages, – precious little to eat fit for a civilised man' (Conrad 19). Both authors draw upon a common rhetoric of imperial decline and social degeneration that saw analogies between the decline and fall of Rome and the periodic crises of imperial confidence throughout the second half of the nineteenth century, but more persistently towards the century's close (Morris vii). In 1891, for example, T. H. Huxley wrote of the dangers of ignoring the social misery that was the result of human failure within British society. The analogy between the British and Roman empires is clear:

It is certain that there is an immense amount of remediable misery among us; that, in addition to the poverty, disease and degeneration, which are the consequences of causes beyond human control, there is a vast, probably very much larger, quantity of misery which is the result of individual ignorance, or misconduct, and of faulty social arrangements. Further, I think it is not to be doubted that, unless this remediable misery is effectually dealt with, the

hordes of vice and pauperism will destroy modern civilisation as effectually as
uncivilised tribes of another kind destroyed the great social organisation which
preceded ours. (Huxley 53)

It is evident that Conrad's and Huxley's use of this analogy offers an
acknowledgement of the savage within while supporting the case for the benefits
of 'civilising' conquest. Stevenson's analogy by contrast suggests something
closer to Huxley's social concerns. The imperial border of both the West and
Anglo-Saxon culture has become merely a political border that no longer
reflects demographic reality, suggesting a civilization past its peak. There is little
overt *fin de siècle* anxiety over decline and degeneration in Loudon's comments;
instead he is increasingly fascinated by the polyglot San Francisco, anticipating
a fundamental change in his own outlook away from the Old World towards the
new: 'But I was dull. I looked backward, keeping an eye on Paris; and it required
a series of converging incidents to change my attitude of nonchalance for one
of interest, and even longing, which I little dreamed I should live to gratify'
(*Wrecker* 118). And yet it is possible to discern in his character and that aspect of
San Francisco that attracts him the decadence of the culture and waning power
of the Western Empire.

While San Francisco might represent the limit of Western Civilization
for Loudon, it is scarcely the archetypal colonial frontier having become a
major West Coast city. San Francisco had developed at a fantastic rate into a
commercial hub of telegraph wire, bustling port, stock exchange and densely
packed slums of numerous nationalities and ethnicities. Stevenson depicts the
city on the periphery of the Western Empire, but at the centre of a regional
economy with interests stretching across the Pacific to China and beyond.
Hugh Brogan argues that the growth of San Francisco was the culmination of
internal migration within the United States that Stevenson had experienced
during his first journey Westwards: 'immigrants were conspicuous in the great
surge of the internal American movement which was carrying the centre of
population ever Westward' (Brogan 408). *The Wrecker* not only records this
reorientation within the United States that would achieve fruition in the
twentieth century, but also the beginning of a gradual decentring of 'Anglo-
Saxon' American from their myth of the frontier. If it can be properly identified
as an ethnicity, Anglo-Saxons have become in the novel only one of many
competing elements – although without doubt the wealthiest and the most
politically entrenched – of a region united only by commerce and the lust for
wealth. Stevenson's San Francisco is a city of teeming hybridity, which again

brings to mind Mary Louise Pratt's notion of the 'contact zone' the 'space of colonial encounters, the space in which peoples geographically and historically separated come into contact with each other and establish ongoing relations, usually involving conditions of coercion, racial inequality, and intractable conflict' (Pratt 6). Conflict there certainly was as class conflict easily generated racial resentment especially against Chinese migrants in the competition for jobs and economic security. Loudon recites the greatest agitators of the day, from Kearney who called for anti-capitalist as well as anti-Chinese violence, and the vigilante leader Colman. In a characteristic moment of moral vacuity, Loudon is disappointed not to see the agitation erupt into immediate violence: 'if I was disappointed, in my character of looker on, to have the matter end ingloriously without the firing of a shot or the hanging of a single millionaire, philosophy tried to tell me this was the more picturesque' (*Wrecker* 116). The visibility of a particularly alien Chinese culture reproduces the anxieties that contributed to anti-Chinese rioting and, later, unashamedly racist immigration laws written into both state and federal statutes. While remaining aloof from what he observes with his 'artist's' perspective, Loudon is particularly sensitive to the implications of this issue in the following passage:

> Chinatown by a thousand eccentricities drew and held me; I could never have enough of its ambiguous, inter-racial atmosphere, as of a vitalized museum; never wonder enough at its outlandish necromantic-looking vegetables set forth to sell in commonplace American shop windows, its temple doors open and the scent of the joss-stick streaming forth on the American air, its kites of Oriental fashion fouled in Western telegraph-wires, its flights of paper prayers which the trade wind hunts and dissipates along Western gutters. (*Wrecker* 117)

Both the material city and the local culture it reflects are being overwritten but another cultural discourse, and the imagery suggests the strangulation of modern – American – culture by an underdeveloped people who dwell tempo-rally in an earlier epoch.

This is a common Western colonial concept that places other peoples in an/other time zone in terms of social evolutionary history charted by Johannes Fabian in his study *Time and the Other*: 'Our *temporal* dismissal of the Other is always such that he remains "integrated" in our spatial concepts of logic (such as order, difference, opposition)' (Fabian 127). Yet rather than a subordinated Other, the Chinese have gained a disruptive dominance over modern Western infrastructure and technology represented by fouled telegraph wires, a 'contaminated atmosphere' and gutters clogged with streams of paper bearing alien writing. Perhaps most disturbing to the Euro-American reader is that Loudon's description locates the alien presence not in some land over which the West is the overlord, but an alien city within the borders of not only 'Western Civilisation' but also the national boundaries of the United States. As a consequence the relationship between the imperial metropolis and the colonial periphery is discursively and materially broken down. As Fabian observes: 'While the imperial metropolis tends to understand itself as determining the periphery (in the emanating glow of the civilizing mission or the cash flow of development, for example), it habitually blinds itself to the ways in which the periphery determines the metropolis – beginning, perhaps, with the latter's obsessive need to present and re-present its peripheries and its others continually to itself' (Fabian 6). The periphery has become the metropolis in San Francisco; just as the metropolis defines the periphery so that periphery can be found on its own doorstep. Following Fabian's terminology, inside and outside have become one hybrid whole that does not establish the distancing reassurance of the 'civilizing mission' or imperial trade that takes place 'over there' rather than 'here'.

The key is trade. The threat is not the hordes of marauding Picts colourfully imagined by Loudon's Roman legionary, but traders and economic migrants seeking employment and a better life – the archetypal American Dream. The circulation of goods and capital represented by the tall ships from China, Sydney, the Indies and the Pacific Island schooners Loudon's imagination seizes upon in San Francisco Bay, necessarily leads to the circulation of peoples and cultures. Given Loudon's evident pleasure in the visible exoticism which appeals to his artistic sensibilities, his professed alienation from the world of business in such an overwhelmingly commercial city is, not unexpectedly, ambiguous since one necessarily entails the other. Loudon treats art as a privileged discourse that is not implicated in the material, but his relationship with Pinkerton focuses attention on the underlying economic imperative where the question of ethics and justification are splintered. As with his father, Loudon questions both Pinkerton's probity and his capacity, but avoids going so far in his personal criticism to threaten his own livelihood and hopes to eventually to return to Paris and the Latin Quarter where he finds it easier to maintain his fantasy life as an artist:

> But the trouble was that such differences continued to recur, until we began to
> regard each other with alarm. If there was one thing Pinkerton valued himself

upon, it was his honesty; if there were one thing he clung to, it was my good opinion; and when both were involved, as was the case with these commercial cruces, the man was on the rack. My own position, if you consider how much I owed him, how hateful is the trade of the fault-finder, and yet I lived and fattened on these questionable operations, was perhaps equally distressing. If I had been more sterling or more combative things might have gone extremely far. But, in truth, I was just base enough to profit by what was not forced to my attention, rather than seek scenes: Pinkerton was quite cunning enough to avail himself of my weakness: and it was a relief to both when he began to involve his proceeding in a decent secrecy. (*Wrecker* 99)

The phrase 'decent secrecy' neatly encapsulates the hypocrisy required to maintain a semblance of peace between the two friends and, from a broader perspective, peace in a society founded on exploitation secure in its moral and racial superiority. This broader perspective is brought into clearer view when Pinkerton questions one of the great commercial institutions of imperial Britain duly stripping it of its aura of probity using a similar narrative strategy to Jack London representation of Thomas Cook & Co in *The People of the Abyss*: 'I tell you Lloyd's is a ring like everything else; only it's an English ring and that's what deceives you. If it were American, you would be crying it down all day' (*Wrecker* 100). Why, Pinkerton asks, should he be held to greater business standards than the pinnacle of Western, if not Anglo-Saxon, civilization? The difference is, of course, the cultural mythology which cloaks the operations of Lloyd's – the romance of empire and the civilizing mission. There are both social and personal costs to be weighed against the maintenance of such a deception since it defects attention away from other ills as Patrick Brantlinger argues: 'imperialism functioned as an ideological safety valve, deflecting both working-class radicalism and middle-class reformism into non-critical paths while preserving fantasies of aristocratic authority at home and abroad' (Brantlinger 35). On a personal level, Loudon's and Pinkerton's friendship incorporates an element of deceit and half-truth that persists in varying forms for the remainder of the novel. Indeed, it becomes a defining characteristic of their relationship. Moreover, in as much as the 'idea' or 'romance' of empire deflects attention away from social pressures at home, so the romance of adventure found in a colonial business venture comes a short-term safety valve for the strain in their relationship. But in doing so, personal deceit is translated into an involvement in perhaps the most ethically insupportable imperial trade institutions of all – the opium trade.

Opium: The 'Reality of Romance' and the Wreck of the *Flying Scud*

Early during his residence in San Francisco and partnership with Pinkerton, Loudon calls his friend's frenetic energy 'the reality of romance' which, like the romance of the adventure story, conjures visions of epic struggles against long odds in far-flung lands: 'as he thrust his bold hand into the plexus of the money market, he was delightedly aware of how he shook the pillars of existence, turned out men (as at battle-cry) to labour in far countries, and set gold twitching in the drawers of millionaires' (*Wrecker* 93). This series of images not only evokes the excitement of imperial trade, but also its innate violence as Pinkerton rummages in the entrails of the money market, or issues calls to arms. There is also an element of bathos in this passage – 'he shook the pillars of existence' – consistent with Loudon's amused condescension. But dangerously for someone whose livelihood is invested in a firm grasp of material conditions, the 'romance of reality' all too easily becomes a romance of the imagination: 'In the early days . . . he consulted me without reserve, [pacing the room, projecting, ciphering, extending hypothetical interests, trebling imaginary capital, his "engine" (to renew an excellent old word) labouring full steam ahead' (*Wrecker* 98). It is fitting, therefore, that the story of the *Flying Scud* should begin with the auction of its wreck among a shady cartel. The purpose of the ring is to fix the price of wrecked ships that are sold off for salvage by the insurers who are significantly in light of Pinkerton's earlier comment, Lloyd's of London. The opportunity to purchase the ships is shared out among the members of the ring in turn, while the others ensure that the auction price is set at a minimum by freezing-out any other potential bidders. Pinkerton, of course, is a member of the ring and has profited from the arrangement once before in a deal that drew criticism from Loudon. With his name at the top of the list again, he expects to obtain the wreck of the *Flying Scud* and her valuable Chinese cargo at the usual knock-down price. This time, however, there is a surprise bidder who cannot be intimidated by the ring; a down at heal lawyer named Harry Bellairs representing an absent principal. Excited by the sense of romance surrounding a wreck – 'reflecting to myself that of all forms of the dollar-hunt, this wrecking had by far the most address to my imagination' (*Wrecker* 131) – Loudon throws his fortune behind Pinkerton only for them both to become perplexed as the price runs up into the thousands. Since the visible cargo has limited value, the answer must be smuggling; and with a

China-bound ship this can only mean one thing – opium: 'this must be the secret. I knew scarce a ship came in from any Chinese port, but she carried somewhere, behind a bulkhead, or in some cunning hollow of the beams, and nest of the valuable poison' (*Wrecker* 137).

The description of opium as the 'valuable poison' is no casual rhetorical flourish; it was the slang term for the opium business in the Pacific region (the 'trade' in Chinese coolies was known as the 'pig trade') (Booth 176). The phrase records the negative perception of the 'trade' as a whole which was a legitimate business in both American and Britain during the nineteenth century if not a reputable one. The only official illegality represented by the smuggled narcotic on the *Flying Scud* is an attempt to evade import duty. While the trade in opium during the nineteenth century by no means attracted the general opprobrium that affixes to the production, distribution and use of narcotics today – botanical and medical prizes were awarded for successful attempts to cultivate the opium poppy in Britain – the trade did attract considerable resistance from the 1870s. The objection was not on the grounds of its abuse as a narcotic in Britain since it was the staple pain killer and soporific of its day. It was entirely unregulated and as a consequence freely prescribed and even sold over the counter in grocery shops until late in the century. Resistance was instead focused over a particular point of the morality of the imperial trade. The worldwide cultivation and production of opium was dominated by British India whose export duties made a substantial contribution to the expenses of not only that colony, but also the empire at large. It was the Chinese who paid the humanitarian and social cost. As Eric Hobsbawm observes: 'India controlled the trade of the Far East through its export of surplus within that area; the exports consisting largely of opium, a staple monopoly that the British fostered systematically (mainly for revenue purposes) almost from the start. As late as 1870, almost half of China's total imports consisted of these narcotics, kindly supplied by the liberal economy of the West' (Hobsbawm 148–9). More recently, Carl A Trocki has gone further by arguing that 'opium was crucial to the expansion of the British Empire during the late eighteenth and early nineteenth century, without it there may have been no empire at all' and 'the opium trade laid the foundation for the global capitalist structure, both in its nurturing of European imperial capital and its international merchant class' (Trocki 10).

Stevenson had written of the evils of the drug in a colonial context in *In the South Seas*, duly noting the acute moral difficulty that he finds in criticizing the

French government of the Marquesas for their lax control of the substance as a subject of an empire which virtually monopolized production:

> French officials shake their heads when opium is mentioned; and the agents of the opium monopoly farmer blush for their employment. Those that live in glass houses should not throw stones; as a subject of the British crown, I am the unwilling shareholder in the largest opium business under heaven. But the British case is highly complicated; it implies the livelihood of millions; and must be reformed, when it can be reformed at all, with prudence. This French business, on the other hand, is a nostrum and mere excrescence. No native industry was to be encouraged: the poison is solemnly imported. No native habit was to be considered: the vice has been gratuitously introduced. (*South Seas* 54–5)

Stevenson's choice of words is revealing: 'nostrum' suggests that there is no legitimate medical demand for the narcotic in the Marquesas and implies that the drug is imported solely for the use as a narcotic. 'Excrescence' suggests that its introduction into French Polynesia is an unnatural development, while British maintenance of the trade because of the traditional cultivation and production in pre-British India and Chinese knowledge of the narcotic effect of opium was an evolutionary development. What this ignores, however, is that pre-British production of the drug in India and narcotic abuse in China was relatively limited in comparison with the highly organized and recognizably industrial production and distribution by the British during the nineteenth century. In essence, Stevenson has shifted the moral responsibility for the existence of the trade onto the Indians and Chinese with whom the British cannot tamper without bringing ruin to their traditional economies; their societies are, it seems, inherently decadent and ripe for eventual 'civilization' once the economic issues have been resolved. While Stevenson registers abhorrence for the trade and acknowledges a certain degree of shame for his country's role in it, he resorts to a recognizably imperialist argument to distinguish British colonialism from the French variety in a manner that resembles the deflection away from Britain of the anti-imperial message of Conrad's *Heart of Darkness* by focusing on poor management by the Belgium crown rather than the 'idea' of colonialism. Yet the sense of unease is not entirely subsumed by this evasion, which is notably defensive. As Trocki asks: 'How could a system based on the trade in this product, acknowledged even then as an evil, be morally squared with the ideas of the "best" of the empire builders?' (Trocki 5).

The introduction of opium at this juncture in the novel echoes the growing moral objections to the opium trade in China, but it can also be read as enacting the evasion and displacement Stevenson presents in *In the South Seas*. Since Pinkerton and Loudon are Americans who intend to deal in smuggled opium, British readers might easily believe that their involvement 'is a nostrum and mere excrescence' dealing *only* for profit rather than a belief that it is an imperial necessity. While Americans were not directly involved in the production of opium, they were among its most enthusiastic shippers and became the principal importers of Turkish opium in an attempt to circumvent the British monopoly, an action which had the knock-on effect of encouraging an increase in British Indian production in an attempt to lower prices and freeze the American merchants out of the market. As Robert Schwendinger observes: 'Americans developed a monopoly of Turkish opium, bootlegging into China as much as twenty per cent of the total import, challenging and spurring the British on to higher cultivation and sales' (Schweninger 8). The significance of opium smuggling in the novel might provoke unease by raising this spectre of an aspect of colonialism and economic imperialism that both Britons and American would prefer not to contemplate – much like the silence that grows between Pinkerton and Loudon over morally ambivalent business ventures from which they both profit – and instead focusing on national aggrandisement and economic growth that a belief in an ostensibly 'civilizing' trade brings to the world. This returns the narrative to the significance of the Chinese community of San Francisco, which tracks the end point of the international trade in opium. With the great migration of Chinese workers throughout the Pacific region in response to the labour demands of Western colonialism (including the settlement and development of the Western United States), they carried with them the habit of opium abuse instilled in them at home thoughtfully supplied by Western commerce. Thence opium abuse spread throughout the Pacific colonies and, in the case of America, directly into the national hinterland. The hand of both Britain and American in this spread was mostly lost on the average American providing ammunition for the racialist case against further Chinese immigration as ostensibly demonstrating their low morality. While not directly approached in the narrative, there is a further history of exploitation buried beneath this apparent cause and effect. For many migrant Chinese workers the recourse to opium was a reaction to the harsh, near slave, conditions of the work they were asked to do under their indenture. Trocki, while he writes specifically of the Malay Peninsula, succinctly outlines conditions that would have been familiar to many of the Chinese workers dispersed throughout the Pacific region during the course of the nineteenth century: 'Swallowing a bit of opium in the middle of the day eased the pain in his muscles and made it possible to go on working through the heat. It also dulled the pain of standing for hours at a time knee-deep in bone-chilling jungle streams and mining sluices shovelling mud to separate out the ore' (Trocki 144). While addressing the plight of the Pacific Islander rather Chinese indentured workers, Jack London explores the morally debilitating effects of such labour contracts on both employer and employee in the Pacific in *Adventure*.

The migration of labourers and the spread of opium abuse went hand in hand with Western commerce and development. Rather than an exceptional circumstance of the maintenance of a traditional, indigenous industry and pre-existing trade, in reality, it was the engine that drove colonization across the Pacific and South East Asia, an agent of social degradation cloaked in the calculated ignorance of the 'civilizing mission'. Thus when Loudon reflects upon his new role as an opium smuggler, it is not to undergo the tortures of conscience he is earlier fastidiousness over Pinkerton's enterprises might have led the reader to expect, but to register surprise at how little he is bothered by his conscience: 'It shows how much I had suffered morally during my sojourn in San Francisco, that even now, when our fortunes trembled in the balance, I should have consented to become a smuggler and (of all things) a smuggler of opium. Yet I did, and that in silence; without protest, not without a twinge' (*Wrecker* 147). As if to underline the fundamental dangers of an America – perhaps even Western civilization – underwritten by a colonial vice, he imagines a Chinatown riddled with opium dens dangerously undermining the foundations of the city: 'China Town . . . was doubtless undermined with opium cellars, and its blocks pierced, after the similitude of rabbit-warrens, with a hundred doors and passages' (*Wrecker* 150). A cursory reading of this passage simply suggests a repetition of the contemporary Californian paranoia of an unclean, swarming 'yellow peril' that occasionally appears in Jack London's work. Yet it is, at further remove, Western colonialism and commerce that is supplying both the opium and the demand for cheap, readily exploitable labour. The disintegration of the city imagined by Loudon is the logical development of the activities of its 'Anglo-Saxon' elite, and charts a comparable anxiety centred on late nineteenth-century Aestheticism's adoption of Oriental imagery as a sign of decay and alien exoticism. Here too the danger is not the imagined devolutionary dangers of a Far Eastern culture that has 'infected' the cultural consciousness of the West, but a subconscious displacement of degeneration that looks to the consequences of the opium trade that has established an association between repressed guilt, languorous narcotic dissolution and Chinese culture.

From Midway Island to Middle England:
The Mystery of the *Flying Scud*

The departure of Loudon to recover the wreck of the *Flying Scud* from Midway Island marks an intensification of the adventure/detective fiction structure of the narrative. Within this action-oriented framework the figurative interrogation of a number of critical questions is sustained. Uppermost is the image of the ship itself. While Pinkerton attempts to keep their business afloat by relying on tenuous lines of credit, their salvation rests on the suspected illegitimate cargo of the grounded ship, which in turn representative of the global reach of Western imperial commerce, good and bad. Loudon is entirely uninterested in the legitimate trade goods carried by the ship, which, when the time comes, will simply be cast into the sea in the frantic search for opium. The correlation between a business adrift on a highly speculative, if not strictly illegal, certainly morally bankrupt, venture and an imperial trade system, which sustains activities like the opium trade, emphasizes the perversity of the value system of not only the two partners but also Western commerce as a whole. The narrative points towards contemporary debates over imperialism that argue that there was a tacit agreement between the unscrupulous businessman intent on profit with the minimum of government restriction and ethical pressure, and the vested interests charged with that very same government (of which the ostensibly upstanding businessman of the insurance ring provide an interesting example). More often than not, these were identified as the same people or concerns. As the economist J. A. Hobson wrote in 1902, 'the vested interests at the same time protect their economic and political supremacy' (Hobson 142). The secrecy surrounding the true nature of imperial trade is an amplification of the 'decent secrecy' that developed between the partners in the wake of Loudon's fastidiousness over some of Pinkerton's activities. To underscore the duality of a legitimate and morally edifying trading empire that brings economic prosperity and 'civilization' while engaging in practices of a reprehensible and self-serving nature, when Loudon becomes frustrated by his inability to uncover the opium, it is the Chinese cook who comes forward to relate back to the colonizers their own smuggling tricks: '"Captain," he began, "I serv-um two year Melican navy; serv-um six year mail-boat steward. Savvy plenty." "Oho" cried Nares, "you savvy plenty do you? (Beggar's seen this trick in the mail-boats, I guess)"' (*Wrecker* 224). Significantly it is the official lines of colonial communications that have been used to smuggle opium with apparent impunity. This episode is also highly ironic when juxtaposed with the images of Sino-phobic San Francisco – it is the Chinese cook who is aware of the smuggling activities of the white crew of the official mail boat but is not complicit; much as the association of the Chinese with opium is the consequence of Western trade not Chinese moral torpidity.

When after following the suggestion of the cook the opium is recovered, it proves something of an El Dorado and does not amount to enough to save the partners from bankruptcy, but Loudon proceeds with Pinkerton's instruction to peddle the drug to contacts among the white planter community of the Hawaiian Islands. The recent history of these islands embodies the ethical duplicity of both colonialism and imperial trade. In 1890 they were still eight years away from annexation by the United States and nominally ruled by an indigenous monarchy. The importation of opium to the group was expressly illegal according to local statute, but it had been subject to licensed importation for the use of Chinese labourers in the past. In 1886 the Hawaiian King sought to reintroduce the licence to buttress the monarchy's finances. This would lead to scandal when the scheme came to light and provide the justification for a coup led by white planters and the establishment of a planter-dominated republic in 1893. A request for formal annexation when submitted to the United States Government was rejected and the action repudiated because of the acknowledged illegality of the coup. Yet while the white plantation owners on Hawaii had vested interest in ensuring a supply of opium to the kingdom for the use of their Chinese labourers, the legislation allowing its importation for this use was used as evidence for the unfitness of the indigenous government. When Stevenson first visited the islands in the 1880s their independence was already compromised by white settlement and economic and political domination. Moreover, the towns and villages were recognizably American in appearance from the 'humming city' streets of Honolulu to the smaller villages, 'the States would be the closest parallel; and it is a moderate prophecy to call it so already' (*South Seas* 187). Loudon calls attention to this feature of the islands when he pointedly refers to 'the metropolitan island of Hawaii' (*Wrecker* 235). So the peddling of the opium from the *Flying Scud* is illegal but who are Loudon's Hawaiian conspirators?

> The two (I learned afterward) were frequent partners; Sharpe supplied the capital, and fowler, who was quite a character in the islands and occupied a considerable station, brought activity, daring, and a private influence, highly necessary in the case. Both seemed to approach the business with a keen sense of romance; and I believe this was the chief attraction, at least with fowler – for whom I easily conceived a sentiment of liking. (*Wrecker* 236)

The notion of drug smuggling as a game is profoundly troubling but Loudon's identification with both the 'romance' of crime and his identification with one of his co-conspirators is not. The situation anticipates Hannah Arendt's summation of colonial identity: 'Outside all social restraint and hypocrisy, against the backdrop of native life, the gentleman and the criminal felt not only the closeness of men who share the same colour of skin, but the impact of a world of infinite possibilities for crimes committed in the spirit of play, for the combination of horror and laughter, that is the full realisation of their own phantom-like existence' (Arendt 190).

The motivation of 'play' rather than profit absolves the 'gentleman' of responsibility for his actions: if the motivation is correct, one is not a criminal but a romantic adventurer within an imperial adventure story. Likewise the criminal can become tied to the morally 'justifiable' work of empire. It is intriguingly as if the genre is being used by characters to create a false consciousness to convince them that their venality is permissible. The rather aptly named Sharpe and Fowler with their political and financial prominence and respectability suggest that this is an attempt to make a strong political observation rather than hide behind the exaggerated fantasy of adventure fiction. This has been a feature of the novel's debate of 'romance' throughout, but in the latter stages of the narrative it is clear that it is at the character level that the fantasy at the heart of the genre (and of empire) operates, not at the level of the text which emerges as a grimly unflinching examination of how individuals can commit the worst of crimes, but remain at ease with their consciences and maintain their position in society. Loudon does not see two criminals but gentlemen enamoured of 'romance' even when it is clear that Sharpe is a thoroughgoing hypocrite when it is revealed that he 'lunched . . . in a private apartment of the Hawaiian Hotel – for Sharpe was a teetotaller in public' (*Wrecker* 247). It is also the sort of class recognition for which Loudon yearns. Even the Pacific Islands for so long the repository of Western fantasies of paradise offer only the bleakness of Midway Island and the hypocrisies of urban Hawaii – *The Wrecker* increasingly becomes a troubled and troubling text. Perhaps most disconcerting is that having crossed the boundary into unequivocal criminality, Loudon enthusiastically buys into the myth, the romance, of this work including the discovery within him of a willingness to resort to violence which he problematically associates with claiming his mature masculinity: 'And from that moment, I date myself a man of rounded experience: nothing had lacked but this, that I should entertain and welcome the grim thought of bloodshed' (*Wrecker* 177). This is, of course, another aspect of Loudon's personal self-deception that has made him such a problematic narrator from the beginning. The quality of the personal relationships he has been able to form have certainly been lacking as is his questionable obsession with art and integrity. It is worthwhile to contrast Loudon's new-found aggression with Pinkerton's violent moral outrage at the student hazing over which they first met. This earlier episode at least upheld some sort of moral principle even if violently resolved, whereas Loudon's resolve centres purely on a matter of illicit profit, commercial survival and amoral entertainment. However, Loudon's experiences during the voyage do build on Pinkerton's outlook:

> I believe, if things had gone smooth with me, I should now be swollen like a prize-ox in body, and fallen in mind to a thing perhaps as low as many types of *bourgeois* – the implicit or exclusive artist. That was a home word of Pinkerton's, deserving to be writ in letters of gold on the portico of every school of art: 'What I can't see is why you should want to do nothing else.' The dull man is made, not by nature, but by the degree of his immersion in a single business. And all the more if that be sedentary, uneventful, and ingloriously safe. More than one half of him will then remain unexercised and undeveloped; the rest will be distended and deformed by over-nutrition, over-cerebration, and the heat of rooms. And I have often marvelled at the impudence of gentlemen, who describe and pass judgements on the life of man, in almost perfect ignorance of all its necessary elements and natural careers. Those who dwell in clubs and studios may paint excellent picture or write enchanting novels. There is one thing that they should not do: they should pass no judgement on man's destiny, for it is a thing with which they are unacquainted. There own life is an excrescence of the moment, doomed in the vicissitude of history, to pass and disappear: the eternal life of man, spent under sun and rain and in rude physical effort, lies upon one side, scarce changed since the beginning. (*Wrecker* 220–1)

The high rhetoric of Loudon's claims for the ennobling nature of the world of action and physical labour are disingenuous at best. The frame story which introduces the contemporary Loudon shows that rather than the man of action he would be, he has in fact grown rather corpulent, sedentary and ingloriously safe. While a traveller and nominal South Pacific trader, a wealthy patron meets his needs and the main cabin of their trading vessel is furnished in the manner of the comfortable, pretentious, drawing room of the very bourgeois he scorns. The use of the word excrescence is intriguing in this context suggesting that those who lead a sedentary, secure life are an unnatural outgrowth of civilization. In the process, Loudon's unethical activities as a smuggler are neutralized and given purpose as well as historical significance.

These tawdry and criminal activities are a source of masculine virtue beyond the judgement of the sedentary reader secure within the imperial homeland. The passage contrives to evoke discourses of evolutionary theory, degeneration and colonial migration. The stay-at-home adventurer leads an unnatural life that must fall foul of Spencer's 'survival of the fittest' doctrine to give way to the men of action and destiny battling at the fringes of civilization. Loudon's bourgeois is thus then also a figure of cultural degeneration, the 'implicit or exclusive artist' wedded to a notion of art for art's sake whose torpidity signifies both cultural decline and a waning evolutionary energy demonstrating the extent to which his previous views have changed, echoing the views of such contemporary commentators as the English psychologist Henry Maudsley: 'What an awful contemplation, that of the human race bereft of its evolutionary energy, disillusioned without enthusiasm, without hope, without aspiration, without an ideal' (Maudsley 64). In short, Loudon reconstructs the 'idea' that obscures the motivations and justifies the consequences of his descent into criminality. Yet, when Loudon despairs, Stevenson returns the reader to the duality of his earlier reverie as the representative of an empire that stands at its high water mark on the cusp of imminent decline. This is a carefully calculated irony aimed at the historical significance of the myth of manifest destiny in contemplation of the ruins of another culture to whose decline he has contributed by the supply of opium:

> . . . it was revealed to me suddenly, how the bungalows [on Hawaii], and the Fowlers, and the bright, busy town and the crowding ships were all children of yesterday; and for centuries before, the obscure life of the natives, with its glories and ambitions, its joys and crimes and agonies, had rolled unseen, like the mountain river, in that sea-girt place. Not Chaldea appeared more ancient, nor the Pyramids of Egypt more abstruse; and I heard many times measured by the 'drums and trampling' of immemorial conquests, and saw myself the creature of an hour. (*Wrecker* 249)

The quoted phrase is from the fifth chapter of Sir Thomas Browne's *Hydriotaphia, Urn Burial, or a Discourse of the Sepulchral Urns lately found in Norfolk* (1658) which develops an extended funerary meditation on man's mortality. The sentiment and purpose of the passage are of course similar to Stevenson's reflections of the fate of the Marquesans in *In the South Seas* and here, as there, the rhetoric insulates the Western observer.

This brief but pivotal episode on Hawaii marks the beginning of the unravelling of the mystery of the *Flying Scud* and the final demystification of

Western expansion and cultural and economic domination by leading to the very individual who has brought about his and Pinkerton's financial ruin. This surprising turn of events has a great deal to do with Loudon's desire to make good his loss of moral and class standing or, rather, since his ethical compass has been circumscribed throughout the novel, the reconstruction of his own self-image in a manner that satisfies his own expectations and the social/cultural group with whom he indentifies. Ironically, that social group is that of a second-generation commercial bourgeois that he scorned during the voyage to Midway Island. The process begins when he learns by chance that the Scandinavian first mate of the *Flying Scud* was in fact an Englishman, Norris Carthew, who has recently entered into a considerable estate. The centre of this new mystery lies with the doctor of a British warship who rescued the crew of the wrecked trading ship. Learning that Loudon is asking questions, the doctor contrives to have him invited aboard his ship. The subsequent encounter opens the door of what Loudon will become in the framing story, at one and the same time marking his fall into blackmail accompanied by a need for class recognition: 'I am not at all the person to forgo an advantage; I have much curiosity. But on the other hand, I have no taste for persecution; and I ask you to believe that I am not a man to make bad worse, or heap trouble on the unfortunate' (*Wrecker* 258). The vagueness of the entreaty offers an excuse for almost anything, indicating that Loudon is grasping for some financial advantage and also anxious to regain the form of class and caste rather than expose the truth that has led to his and Pinkerton's financial ruin. The doctor naturally responds to this tacit offer enigmatically offering 'great excuses' while maintaining the secret to which he is pledged as a gentleman. What Loudon has learnt is that it is possible to have an identification as a criminal and a gentleman, and despite his intimations of 'unmistakably evidences of foul play' he is willing and eager to accept the doctor's offer to enter into this class-levelling pact of silence: 'I cannot convey a sense of the rugged conviction and judicial emphasis of Dr Urquart's speech; to those who did not hear him, it may appear as if he fed me on enigmas; to myself who heard, I seemed to have received a lesson and a compliment' (*Wrecker* 258–9). Given Loudon's demonstrable capacity for self-deception and the limitations of his point of view as a narrator, it is not difficult to discern that he hears what he wishes. Certainly, when he extends his hand to Urquart, the mark of gentlemanly agreement between equals, the doctor refuses to take it laying his hand familiarly on his shoulder instead. This is enough for Loudon, but it is mark of patronage rather than the class validation he believes it to be. Later when he presents himself at the Carthew family seat in English, the servants express a comparable class-based caution to his presumption of status: 'He [Carthew] had no pride about him, I was told; he would sit down with any man; and it was somewhat woundingly implied that I was indebted to this peculiarity for my own acquaintance with the hero' (*Wrecker* 305).

This situation mirrors and reverses Loudon's attitude towards Pinkerton, who, despite clearly having capabilities that he lacks – such as action, energy and fidelity – is more than often the source of condescending amusement. As Pinkerton's wife observes when it is apparent that he is keeping Cathew's secret from his now-broken former partner 'you were always sneering at my James; you always looked down upon him in your heart, you know it!' (*Wrecker* 268). Brought up in privilege, the son of a wealthy businessman, Loudon's tastes and sympathies aspire to his interpretation of aristocratic tastes. Measured against Carthew, a real aristocrat, or the imposing Dr Urquart, he is found wanting but not in his desire to belong. His behaviour mimics rather than genuinely obtains the characteristics of an aristocracy that affected to look down upon a commercial class even as they benefitted from the wealth and power of empire. Yet his desire also represents the process by which that aristocracy had always been able to replenish its ranks with the wealthy and powerful:

> One important effect of this continuity – part reflection of the established power of the old upper class, part deliberate unwillingness to exacerbate political tensions among the men of money and influence – was that the rising new business classes found a firm pattern of life waiting for them. Success brought no uncertainty, so long as it was great enough to lift a man into the ranks of the upper class. He would become a 'gentleman' doubtless with a country house, perhaps eventually a knighthood or peerage, a seat in parliament for himself or his Oxbridge educated son, and a clear prescribed social role. His wife would become a 'lady', instructed in her duties by a multitude of handbooks of etiquette which slid off the presses from the 1840s. (Hobsbawm 82)

Yet Loudon is (however reluctantly) the offspring of American commerce and lacks the 'clear social role' that British society provided for better or ill, giving his perspective a penetrating critical edge when he does come into contact with the real thing. While the United States had spawned its own prominent revolutionary war elite and its own fantastically wealthy 'robber baron' class able to buy the material signifiers of the Old World aristocracy (there was even a lively marriage market between the old and new world elites), Stevenson anticipates some of the characteristics of a Jay Gatsby in Loudon interested more in the outward display of wealth and position as a marker of stature than in birthright and tradition.

The multiple contradictions of Loudon's outlook – a desire for the culture of the Old World offset by a New World respect for naked achievement but not for the physical toil that comes with it – is all the more exposed when he resorts to an Old World signifier of self-worth that is less immediately tied to personal success and wealth – class. This governs his relationship with his father and Pinkerton who both enjoy, at least for a time, success in the more meritocratic American social system, while being congenitally unable to follow them as he regards himself as a gentleman with aristocratic taste and sentiment rather than a mere businessman. However, this heritage emerges to considerable narrative effect when confronted with the inherited wealth and position of the Carthews in England as he contemplates the family portraits:

> To an American, the sense of domination of this family over so considerable a tract of earth was even more oppressive; and as I considered their simple annals, gathered from the legends of engravings, surprise was mingled with disgust. 'Mr. Recorder' doubtless occupies an honourable post; but I thought that, in the course of so many generations, one Cathew might have clambered higher. The soldier struck at Major-General; the Churchman bloomed unremarked in an archdeaconate: and though the Right Honourable Bailly seems to have sneaked into the Privy Council, I have still to learn what he did when he had got there. Such vast means, so long a start, and such a modest standard of achievement, struck me a strong sense of the dullness of that race. (*Wrecker* 300)

Despite the clear critical edge of this passage, which relies for its effect on Loudon's American background, and putting aside for the moment the matter of 'so long a start', the rather modest achievement of this family shine a light on Loudon's personal aspirations and achievements in contrast to the energy of his own nation. Thence the impression of the undeserved wealth and power of the Carthews is also true in microcosm in the way that Loudon's modest talents have been funded in turn by his father, Pinkerton and as we learn from the Frame story, a blackmailed Carthew. While the Carthews' status has been dignified by time and tradition, this in itself does not confer moral legitimacy. And yet nor does Loudon's more immediate backers all of whom come by their wealth in less than ethical circumstances as Loudon has consistently reported: his grandfather, father and Pinkerton are sharp businessmen whose activities do not bear any sustained ethical examination. If we take Loudon with his aristocratic cultural aspirations and reliance on inherited and gifted wealth, he is emblematic of a metropolitan bourgeois content to benefit from ethically questionable profits at several removes from their generation on the fringes of empire. This is true of the Old and New Worlds and reproduces the outward trappings, manners, education and privileges of minor aristocracy like the Carthews that the bourgeoisie aspire to that is even further sanitized by time and tradition; as Pinkerton observes of the insurance market Lloyd's of London, 'it's an English ring, and that's what deceives you' (*Wrecker* 100). The Carthew house sits at the centre of a web of empire-spanning interests subtly suggested by the family's global correspondence to be found in the butler's stamp collection: 'the obsolete triangular Cape of Good Hopes, Swan Rivers with the Swan [Australia], and Guianas with the sailing ship' (*Wrecker* 307). The wealth of the Carthews is drawn from dividends derived from their demesne in England and investment in the activities of the British Empire. How far the one relies upon the other is a historical issue that Hobsbawm touches on above.

In the final act of a narrative that persistently peels away the ideological obscuration of empire, the mystery of the *Flying Scud* is the story of the youngest son of the Carthew house removed from the imperial centre to the colonial frontier to re-encounter first hand the violence and ethical vacuity of the West's commercial dominance. Carthew, like Loudon, asserts a desire to follow the arts not, as his position demands, as a patron but as a practitioner. This draws the ire of his father since this is contrary to the dignity of his position; the Carthews collect works of art, not manufacture them. Unlike the well-meaning concern of Loudon's father that he be equipped to earn a livelihood, it is the weight of family tradition that bears down on Carthew and, in contrast to the brash modernity represented by the Muskegon Commercial Academy, he is dispatched to Oxford. Compared with Loudon's modest failure at college, Cathew's 'lack of zeal and fear' deliberately antagonizes his tutors while his debts infuriate his father before he is eventually sent down (*Wrecker* 319). Failing in the diplomatic service and contracting a huge gambling debt, he is sent into family exile in Sydney, Australia, on an annual pension of £300 on the understanding that he never return home in ironic echo of the conditions under which convicts were sent to the colony. Unlike Loudon's dislike of actual work, Carthew discovers that he has a genuine capacity for honest physical labour when he becomes a railway navvy. Carthew's experience recapitulates the social engineering behind the convict foundations of the colony, and also the ground on which the colony would eventually reject the inequalities of the mother country in its own national consciousness in succession to the class politics of the Old World. A potentially dangerous underclass is removed from the body politic and planted in new ground to gain redemption through hard work and opportunity, the colonizers' ideal of nobility and independence. Yet the suggestion that a similar process can lead to redemption of an unremarkable and stale aristocracy is radical: 'Plenty of open air, plenty of bodily exertion, and continual instancy of toil, here was what had been hitherto lacking in his [Carthew's] misdirected life, and the true cure of vital scepticism' (*Wrecker* 326). There is, of course, an important difference. Stevenson clearly intends the pioneering colonization of Australia to be an ennobling ideal, close to the 'idea' of the civilizing mission taming a wilderness and spreading the benefits of productivity and modernity (Carthew is laying railway track after all). The Australian Aborigines, the chief losers in this process, do not feature in the narrative and are thus not allowed to cloud this rosy picture. Loudon, however, is involved directly in one of the great scandals of imperial trade, the distribution of opium, and becomes a torpid blackmailer as the reader knows from the Marquesan-set frame narrative. While distinctions are constantly muddled in the patterning of the text, this seems to be an attempt to create a contrast between a good colonialism involving the 'honest' cultivation of 'empty' land like Stevenson's plantation on Samoa, and a bad colonialism based on the second-hand dealings of shady commerce.

Yet the narrative does not rest there. Enticed into entering in a partnership with a foppish friend Tommy Hadden, Carthew enters into a new career as a Pacific Island trader. Hadden could be read as an exaggerated form of Pinkerton and this is how Loudon reads him: 'He was a kind of Pinkerton in Play. I have called Jim's the romance of business; this was the Arabian tale' (*Wrecker* 331). However, this description better suits Loudon's enthusiasm for his South Pacific venture in quest for smuggled opium and later career as the simulacrum of a trader. The partnership is involved in a single fantastically exploitative – and fantastically profitable – transaction with Islanders but they are wrecked on Midway Island only to be picked up by the ill-founded *Flying Scud*. Encountering a captain as rapacious as they are, he tries to extract a passage fee as exorbitant as their trade with the Islanders, one of their crew stabs the captain and a massacre of the rest follows. In a powerful ironic twist, the crew member who initiates the violence is an Irishman who has no financial interest in the venture whatsoever beyond his seaman's pay. His characterization as a man prone to sudden outbursts of violence is tied to that Irish identity and his hybridity as a colonized subject: 'the stormy inconstancy of Mac's behaviour had connection with a gill or two of wine; his passions, angry and otherwise, were on a different sail-plan from his neighbours; and there were possibilities of good and evil in that hybrid Celt beyond their prophecy (*Wrecker* 360). This massacre is the mystery; a tawdry act of violence over an already tainted profit extracted from those who are unable to assess the value of either the goods or the honesty of the purveyors. Yet it is not only the colonial subject who is subject to the violence and moral aporia of imperial trade. Carthew brings the moral vacuum home to where it originates – the celebrated shires of England. As Amié Césaire observes: 'colonisation works to *decivilize* the colonizer, to awaken him to buried instincts, to covetousness, violence, race hatred, and moral relativism' (Césaire 13). This novel is not only about the rapacity and violence of the colonized zone and its local victims, but the deep corruption of personal relationships obscured by blurring the lines of profit and responsibility. The manner in which this narrative cleverly replicates and tests its reader's presumptions by scrutinizing to the same ethical consequences from subtly different perspectives is a discursive and aesthetic triumph belying the relative critical obscurity of this text. It deserves a place alongside Conrad's *Heart of Darkness* as one of the most significant analyses of class and empire of its epoch.

6

The Indignity of Labour: Jack London's *Adventure* and Plantation Labour in the Solomon Islands

Jack London's novel *Adventure* has scarcely found favour with his modern critics. Indeed, Clarice Stasz who has provided the only extended attempt to read the novel to date is at pains to excuse a work that 'competes for the nadir of London's longer tales', on the grounds of the stressful conditions under which London was writing. A similar sense of unease is reflected in her reference to the 'most disagreeable part of the plot, its unadulterated racism' that stands in strong contrast to London's other South Sea tales in this regard' (Stasz 178). Much the same position is taken by Jeanne Campbell Reesman although she specifically links the quality of the plot to the aborted voyage of *The Snark*: 'It is as though *Adventure*, with its weak romantic plot and its rampant racialism was London's revenge on the Solomon Islands for his defeat there' (Reesman 162). Stasz is also disappointed with the portrayal of the central female character, Joan Lackland, whom she reads both in relation to London's wife, Charmian, and the turn of the century New Woman. Certainly, the novel represents what is unquestionably a racist perspective from a twenty-first-century viewpoint and is an inferior literary effort compared with Stevenson's *The Wrecker* and even in comparison of with much of London's other South Pacific writing. Despite questionable literary merit and a lack of social progressivism, the novel is significant in relation to early twentieth-century questions of identity, racial difference, class and imperialism. Stasz's essay deserves praise for pioneering a serious examination of a discomforting novel, and her reading of the biographical antecedents of the text is valuable and informative, but it is necessary to explore the historical and cultural contexts of the novel without relying too much on a biographical frame as the primary organizing principle and source of critical judgement, convenient as this may be to excuse the offensiveness of some of the content and the dent this puts in London's literary reputation.

That is not to say that London's experiences of colonialism in the Solomon Islands and the physical distress that brought his cruise to an end are not significant to a reading of the novel. They are important in much the same way that Conrad's experiences in the Belgium Congo were important to *Heart of Darkness*. Indeed, as the title to this chapter suggests, the plantation labour system that London encountered in the Solomons and represented in both *Adventure* and the posthumous *Jerry of the Islands* (1917) will be significant in understanding the context of the crude racism of the narrative. However, both London and Conrad express far more than their individual prejudices and beliefs in their respective novels, even if a clear idea of their opinions could in some way be objectively resurrected. In this respect, the implied author of *Adventure* is not the Jack London of biographical fact and speculation. As Rimmon-Kenan argues 'An author may embody in a work ideas, beliefs, emotions other than or quite opposed to those he has in real life; he may also employ different ideas, beliefs and emotions in different works' (Rimmon-Kenan 86). It is only the reader and potentially the critic who looks for consistency and a questionable causality between individual works and what is known of the author. As is evident in the preceding chapters, such contradictions can reveal the conflict embedded in colonial, racial and class identities. Despite the relative simplicity of the plot – and I certainly agree with Stasz that this aspect of the novel is no aesthetic triumph – London nonetheless engages with a remarkable range of highly contentious issues, including: the nature and justifications of colonialism; racial and class hierarchies; the emergence of the United States as a colonial power and rapprochement with, and also implicit critique, of Great Britain; the changing role of women; and, above all, the definition of slavery at the beginning of the twentieth century.

These are themes that Stasz also identifies but seeks to relate them to London's life and beliefs as isolated individual issues rather than broader cultural constructions with which the novel engages. It is important to consider not only the material conditions of London's experiences in the Solomon Islands but also the way the material is organized and encoded within the novel. In this respect, London deploys two highly popular genres, the colonial adventure story (once again) and the romance. In doing so the novel manages to unsettle the cultural and ideological foundations of both. 'Genres,' writes Claire Colbrook, 'could be understood as regular ways of proceeding; authors write in certain forms in order to gain cultural recognition. Each act of literary production, while taking part in that regularity, also uses and reconfigures that genre' (Colbrook 99). Further, such reconfiguration opens up new ways of understanding the underlying cultural and ideological constructions with which it is associated, as Richard Phillips argues in relation to adventure fiction: 'Adventure's realistic images are capable of articulating critical ideas that cannot be expressed in more abstract terms, whether because they are not precisely formulated, because they might be censored, or because they would be less readable, therefore less effective in that form' (R. Phillips 113). London's depiction of colonialism in the Solomons and the racial attitudes held by the white planters both valorize their practices and views, and also brings them into question through a conscious confrontation with the more sordid and violent aspects of colonial practice generally obscured by representations of 'moral fortitude and personal valour' typical of the colonial adventure story of the time, just as his introduction of the New Woman exposes some of the less palatable realities of marriage even when women demand and gain greater agency within a culture of violence and repression.

The Pacific labour trade has scarcely attracted much attention since its discontinuation in the early 1900s and might be said to be all but forgotten beyond the Pacific Islands themselves but for the notable exception of a few obscure academic histories published in the late 1960s and early 1970s of which Edward Docker's *The Blackbirders: The Recruitment of South Seas Labour for Queensland, 1863–1907* of 1970 is by far the most distinguished. Overshadowed today by contemporary interest in the history and legacy of transatlantic slavery, in its time the Pacific labour trade generated considerable controversy at the highest levels of the British imperial government both at home and their Pacific colonies, even provoking debates on the floor of the House of Commons and generating a considerable body of legislation from its inception in the 1860s through to the time of London's visit to the region in the 1900s. Moreover, the trade provoked outrage among the various missionary societies active in the Pacific, as well as the British and Foreign Antislavery Society and the Aboriginal Protection Society that could both trace their origins back to the original British anti-slavery movement. Yet other than the minor popular Australian novelist Louis Becke whose work occasionally refers to the labour trade (and who had been a recruiting agent), Jack London is the only novelist of note to leave us a literary examination of the trade and its consequences. Even though the British claimed to regulate the trade that principally existed to serve their colonies in the region, all of the major colonial powers in the Southwest Pacific were involved to a greater or lesser extent. French and German nationals were active as recruiters to supply their own nations' plantations as well as those of the British. U.S. citizens were also active recruiters, but only to supply the demands of other nations. Despite the regulation of the 'trade' – known as 'blackbirding' locally – it was characterized by a history of appalling abuse, violence and inhumanity. The practice had begun in 1863 to supply the plantations of Queensland and later Fiji with an inexpensive source of labour from the Melanesian Islands of the Southwest Pacific, particularly from the New Hebrides (now Vanuatu) and the Solomon Islands, but later also British New Guinea. From the outset charges of slavery and slave trading were made, which despite increasing legislation – notably British imperial legislation in the form of the Pacific Islanders Protection Act of 1872 – continued until the trade to Queensland ended in 1908 and to Fiji in 1911 (Docker 180).

The resemblance of the trade to slavery was indeed striking with respect to the dubious methods of recruitment and the term of the so-called contract with which the Islanders were bound. The abuses perpetuated by recruiters including trickery, kidnapping and violence to induce Islanders to embark of the plantations. One highly questionable practice involved the giving of 'gifts' to compensate chiefs and families for the loss of their young people, an arrangement that easily degenerated into an unabashed slave trade when an enemy captured in war was sold into bondage, or an autocratic and greedy chief would connive with the recruiter to force some of his subjects to sign up to provide the means to acquire Western goods, particularly firearms. Recruiters were also known to auction Islanders to the highest bidder and were not above murder as several well-documented massacres of unwilling 'recruits' demonstrate. The resemblance of these practices to the old African slave trade scarcely needs emphasizing, or the stark contradiction between high-minded British claims to have outlawed the African trade while regulating another practice that closely resembled it, as Edward Docker observes: 'to the average merchant trading in the South Seas a speculation in Kanakas was no different from a speculation in pork, or shrunken heads' (Docker 53). Imperial and colonial regulation was concerned with minimizing abuses that occurred during the recruiting process itself although tellingly there was never legislation to extend the Slave Acts which outlawed the African slave trade to the Pacific and abolish the practice altogether. There were later regulations to govern the treatment of Islanders on the plantations themselves, such as the provision of very basic medical facilities, although mortality rates among the Islanders was always higher than that among the local white population. Yet such regulations did little to alter the essential relationship: a contract was typically for three years with an annual wage of £3 for Fiji and £6 for Queensland (usually paid in kind via overpriced trade goods purchased from the employer), including a very basic diet and 'free' repatriation to their home island at the end of the contract. Superficially, these terms resemble conditions under which Indian-indentured labourers were shipped throughout the British Empire, including Fiji, although by modern standards even this arrangement was a system of outrageous exploitation. In contrast to the plight of the Pacific Islanders, the Indian-indentured labourers' conditions of work were negotiated and overseen by the British Indian Government and, even though this was itself a colonial institution, it could and on occasion did bring its influence to bear if abuses occurred. By contrast, once 'recruited', Islanders were very much at the mercy of the planter and local laws; escapees were as likely to be shot as recaptured and subjected to arbitrary punishment.

The social ramifications of the trade were often disastrous for the home islands and contributed to the depopulation of many smaller islands while cultural patterns were disrupted and sometimes irreparably destroyed by subsequent upheaval. One by-product of the trade that contributed to both population and cultural degradation was the practice of supplying returning labourers with firearms thereby adding a deadly edge to the almost constant ritualized feuds characteristic of many Pacific island cultures that had, until then, been relatively bloodless affairs. The trade in people and arms had spread to the New Hebrides (Vanuatu) and the Solomon Islands in the early 1880s, an area that, by the time of London's visit, had had twenty years' experience of dubious recruiting practices and the consequent supply of arms. This build-up of weapons and resentment returned to haunt both traders and recruiters alike, since the 'Solomon Islands had an unenviable notoriety for murderous attacks on ships' (Morrell 331), signalling an increasing ability by the Islanders to defend themselves and their way of life from encroaching colonizers. As O. W. Parnaby observes:

> From the beginning the relations of black and white in the Pacific had been marred by crimes of violence, but these had become more frequent since Europeans began recruiting labour. Many natives were murdered by recruiters and others were recruited by force, and for this the natives took indiscriminate revenge. Ironically, the Europeans, by selling firearms to natives, provided them with the more effective instruments of revenge. (Parnaby 166)

It is into this world that *Adventure* plunges the reader from the very first chapter – titled 'Something to be done' – so it is worth pausing for a moment to survey the conditions and working conditions of the principal setting, Berande Plantation. The lone white man is suffering an attack of acute dysentery together with many of his Islander labourers and in mortal fear for his life from the more healthy of his workers. The mutual hatred of planter and Islanders is palpable, 'swine' he calls them under his breath and in return 'the well men who obeyed his orders scowled malignantly' (*Adventure* 16). It is equally apparent that the Islanders are only intimidated into submission to his demands by the threat of violence signified by 'the large calibre automatic pistol and several more clips, loaded and ready for quick work' which forms the conclusion of the opening paragraph (*Adventure* 14) and the immediacy with which the white man will resort to physical assault: 'One muttered deep in his chest as he took the corpse by the feet. The white man exploded in speech and action. It cost him a painful effort, but his arm shot out, landing a backhand blow on the black's mouth' (*Adventure* 16). Yet bizarrely, and immediately following on from his muttered insult 'swine' he is joking with his patients to alleviate their suffering.

The next chapter sees the planter, now introduced as David Sheldon, deciding to reassert his control with a more public display of violence to keep the Islanders in line. Calling the healthy men in from the fields he chooses to make an example of a worker who had escaped from the plantation by first forcing Billy, one of the more recalcitrant workers, to publically whip him. When he refuses citing the offender's right to be tried and punished by the Colonial Government, Sheldon calls upon another worker, Astoa, to whip both the original offender and Billy. When Astoa also shows signs of resistance, Sheldon reaches for his gun:

> And Sheldon knew that when he had counted three he would drop him in his tracks. The black knew it, too. That was why Sheldon did not have to do it, for when he had counted one, Astoa reached out his hand and took the whip, angered at his fellows for not supporting him and venting his anger with every stroke. From the veranda Sheldon egged him on to strike with strength till the triced savages screamed and howled while the blood oozed down their backs. The lesson was being well written in red. (*Adventure* 32–3)

The image of Sheldon urging Astoa to take out his own sense of impotence, humiliation and frustration under the diktat of his gun, and the lingering oozing blood is unquestionably unpleasant suggestive, even, of sadistic pleasure as Sheldon sinks down spent and 'half-fainting' onto his couch once the spectacle of the punishment has passed its grisly climax.

Such public displays of corporal punishment conjure disturbing images of plantation slavery both in the pre-abolition British Caribbean as well as in the ante-bellum Southern States. Indeed, this episode almost echoes Frederick Douglass' description of the whipping of his aunt, Hester, from *Narrative of the Life of Frederick Douglass, An American Slave, Written by Himself* (1845), which also has erotic overtones: 'he commenced to lay on the heavy cowskin, and soon, the warm, red blood (amid heart-rending shrieks from her, and horrid oaths from him) came dripping to the floor' (Douglass 52). The 'heavy cowskin' is another signifier of slave punishment which is reproduced in London's novel when Sheldon calls for 'a heavy-handled, heavy-lashed whip' (*Adventure* 29). It would go too far to suggest that London is deliberately echoing Douglass' text, but given what seems to be a calculated use of such powerful images from the cultural legacy of British and US plantation slavery it is justifiable to ask how far it relates to the 'adventure' of the title and, more broadly, what view of colonialism is being projected here. Certainly, the representation of the Islanders does much to stress their physical and cultural difference as well as to undermine their humanity. The first few chapters consistently repeat that they are cannibals (see *Adventure* 15, 20, 23 and 25), that their features are 'asymmetrical, bestial; their bodies were ugly and ape like' (*Adventure* 15), and that their facial piercing and ornamentation repellent and utterly alienating. The 'ape analogy' is pressed to its limit in the description of Seelee chief of the local village who, despite being more intelligent than the average, when 'he talked of listened, he made grimaces like a monkey. He said yes by dropping his eyelids and thrusting his chin forward' (*Adventure* 26). Such images have an ancestry that can be traced back to the earliest representations of plantation slavery in the British Caribbean, such as Edward Long's notorious eighteenth-century *History of Jamaica* where he maintained that 'Negroes' were not properly human and ought not to be treated as such: 'Having thus "proved" that white and black on the island were different species, he divided "genus homo" into three species – Europeans and similar people, Negroes, and "orang-outangs"' (Street 94–5).

The mutual hatred between white planter and black workers is also clearly demarcated in the narrative structure reinforcing the fear ascribed to Sheldon and the resentment of the Islanders. While these early chapters encourage a certain wonder for the power of this one man holding so many under his sway, which might have appealed to London's original readership, his repellent ruthlessness and near-sadistic pleasure echoing images of slavery checks an initial urge to admiration. Stasz, commenting on the difficult romance between Sheldon and Lackland later in the novel, observes that the narrative is largely 'told from [Sheldon's] point of view' (Stasz 133), yet the narrative focalization of the novel is subtler. Booth argues that 'any sustained inside view, of whatever depth, temporarily turns the character whose mind is shown into a narrator' and this is what is occurring in the highly negative representation of the Islanders who are seen through the prism of Sheldon's fear, even if the narrative is not explicitly punctuated to mark out the perspective as his. The narrative perspective can also shift, such as when Seelee reflects on Sheldon's method of gaining ascendancy over him and the village when he is beaten and then kidnapped until assured of his future cooperation. Seelee considers himself 'educated' in the ways of the white men and the reader is given a defamiliarizing demonstration of the colonial use of violence and also an insight into the Islanders' hatred of Sheldon and white colonists, recruiters and traders in general (*Adventure* 26–7). The narrative also lingers over the blood oozing from the fresh wounds of the escapee Billy and the perspective is very much that of the assembled Islanders since Sheldon has already sunk from view onto his couch. It is also important to note that the introduction of explicitly racialist language occurs only in the speech of the white characters, for example, the word 'nigger' is first used by Captain Oleson when the *Jessie* lands at the beginning of Chapter III while the narrative voice has persistently used the less-charged 'black' throughout. There is therefore some distance between the narrator and the views of the planters and the shift in narrative perspective to include the thoughts and feelings of the Islanders to suggest, at least to some extent, a rather more sophisticated commentary on the way of life depicted in the plot. While the narrator is perhaps not overtly critical there are certainly opportunities within the narrative for the reader to be.

Another feature of the narrative voice is its careful reminder of the Islanders' humanity even when the focalization is most closely aligned with Sheldon's perspective. For example, when early in the novel he approaches the crude hospital to review the workers suffering from fever and dysentery we hear 'a wild clamour, as of lost souls wailing and men in torment . . . There were shrieks and screams, some unmistakingly of grief, others unmistakingly of unendurable pain' (*Adventure* 14). After entering the hut he encounters a young man crying out with grief over his rapidly sinking brother (*Adventure* 17–18). This relatively sympathetic account of the workers' suffering and grief contrasts with Sheldon's objectification of them as sub-human and utterly uncivilized. His attempts to help them are motivated only by the productive value of their potential labour: 'Since the blacks were worth thirty dollars apiece, or less according to how much of their time had been worked out, Berande plantation could ill afford the loss . . . the deaths were daily reducing the working capital' (*Adventure* 21). The overall impression left by these first three chapters is of a man with considerable endurance and self-will who conceptually refuses to recognize the humanity of his workers whom he values only to the extent that they represent the working capital of his business. At the same time he is a man living in terror of those very same workers over whom he maintains a tenuous control only by the threat of escalating violence that, in turn, fuels an understandable desire for revenge among the Islanders. Andrew Furer observes of London's early work that 'he finds that under certain harsh conditions (such as those obtaining in the Arctic). The recrudescence of Anglo-Saxon "barbaric" traits is a desirable phenomenon' (Furer 161). Superficially it is possible to map such a fantasy here – the masterful white man returning to his barbaric antecedents to win out against overwhelming odds – although there is a crucial difference. When London wrote of the Klondike, his protagonists were pitted against the landscape, the overwhelming power of nature and the ennoblement through struggle has an almost mythic quality. As Earle Labor argues:

> In the face of this awesome force, only the fittest stand a chance of survival, and the only hope for survival is adaptability. Ostensibly, this theme appears to be purely Darwinian; however, London's Northland Code demands not only physical but also intellectual and ethical adaptability, the 'strength of the strong' (as he would preach later in his socialistic writings) being communal rather than individual, and greatest of all (as he would later assert throughout his works) being the salvational power of *agape*. (Labor xvii)

By contrast, what these opening chapters of *Adventure* demonstrate is coercive violence for personal gain met with an equally violent resistance as a consequence of slave conditions. It is literally the 'strength of the strong' or rather of the most ruthless and better armed and not the 'better' man strengthened by social co-operation as Labor implies. The likely endgame of this struggle is mutual destruction through the lack of common unity in the face of the power of nature represented by disease. It is a fight to the death, for profit on the one hand and revenge on the other. Such a tableau fails miserably to justify or ennoble racial hierarchies and claims to physical and mental superiority.

The violence and racial objectification of the opening chapters of *Adventure* exist within a pointedly masculine space. With the important exception of Joan Lackland who has yet to enter the narrative, women are almost entirely absent from the novel. When Melanesian women are mentioned it is generally no more than a swift glimpse and they are barely articulate, doubly silenced on grounds of race and gender. However, for the reasons already mentioned, this is not a positive masculine space. There is none of the great deeds and heroism typical of more representative examples of the imperial adventure genre such as the African-set adventures of H. Rider Haggard, or Stevenson's *Treasure Island* (1883) and R. M. Ballantyne's South Pacific set *The Coral Island* (1858), all of which were successes in the United States as well as Britain. By contrast, this is about profit and exploitation, of unrelenting daily grind rather than an adventure of self-discovery and racial destiny in exotic or mysterious locales that were the staple fare of the immensely popular British magazine, *The Boy's Own Paper*. Indeed, the title of the novel has a more interrogatory function than has hitherto been recognized, especially in a debate concerning the nature of adventure almost immediately following Joan Lackland's arrival on the plantation. As noted, the cultural space of late nineteenth and early twentieth-century colonial adventure reflects a strong masculine bias that Elaine Showalter has described as 'quest narratives' representing 'a yearning for escape from a confining society, rigidly structured in terms of gender, class and race, to a mythologized place elsewhere where men can be freed from the constraints of Victorian morality' (Showalter 81). Indeed, a novel like Ballantyne's *The Coral Island* simply has no female characters, and novels like Haggard's *She* (1887) and *King Solomon's Mines* (1885) could be quite openly misogynistic; Allan Quartermain the central character from the latter novel asserts 'that there is not a *petticoat* in the whole story' (Haggard 9). Richard Phillips suggest that one reason for the more overt masculinization of boys' adventure fiction was partly a response to the inherent ambivalence of the genre and changing ideas about femininity, which were seen as socially and politically transgressive:

> Although superficially confined to male-dominated regions far from home, adventure occupies ambivalent space in which boundaries between home and away, women and men may be fuzzy and unstable. When writers, protagonists and readers of adventure stories observe or transgress these spatial boundaries, they observe or transgress metaphorical boundaries between masculinity and femininity. The polarisation of home and away in adventure literature, particularly British Victorian boys' literature, conforms to contemporary doctrine on private and public space, the spheres of women and men respectively . . . (R. Phillips 89)

While Sheldon is an adult, there is a strong maturation theme which structures the narrative and intersects with the contested master/slave relationship between him and his workers, the masculine ethos of adventure fiction and the question of Joan's agency and property. Joan's history before her arrival at Berande is particularly intriguing when read as a maturational narrative engaging with both the patriarchal family and colonialism. Her powerful seaman turned Hawaiian rancher father (and his partner, Von, who also has two daughter's Joan's age) is her sole parent. Her mother is strikingly absent from the story she recounts when she observes of both her father and Von that 'they didn't have any wives' leaving it unclear whether this means their wives had died, had left them or they had never been married (*Adventure* 61). When a financial crash drives her father to seek a second fortune among the Pacific Islands he had roved as a young man, he dies leaving Joan determined to carry out his last wish to establish himself once more as a planter. In many respects Sheldon replaces her father whom she must impress within the terms of the masculine ethos to which she had been raised by her father. This is a rather brief overview of Joan's antecedents, but it is important to understand this continuity between life with her father and the prospect offered by the equally masculine space of Sheldon's Berande in relation to both adventure fiction and colonialism. In doing so it is necessary to return to the idea of Sheldon as a patriarchal figure which Joan's arrival actualizes. At its most basic level the economy of violence, control and the constant threat of retribution are circular and non-productive; a matter of maintaining pressure since to ease off would lead to annihilation. The workers' near-slave conditions and their dehumanization within a patriarchal colonial system leave them 'unmanned'; a consequence of which they are not unaware. As George Cunningham argues, 'the master as a figure in discourse reserves to himself the masculine authority to generate meaning', so the Islanders' resistance and threatened violent rebellion are the inevitable consequences of their effective imprisonment under the labour contract and their own loss of patriarchal and racial agency. But the figure of Sheldon as patriarchal and racially superior master figure is troubled by the novels opening scene:

> He was a very sick white man. He rode pick-a-back on a woolly-headed, black-skinned savage, the lobes of whose ears had been pierced and stretched until one had torn out, while the other carried a circular block of carved wood three inches in diameter. The torn ear had been pierced again, but this time not so ambitiously, for the hole accommodated not more than a short clay pipe. The man-horse was greasy and dirty, and naked save for an exceedingly narrow and dirty loin-cloth; but the white man clung to him closely and desperately. At times from his weakness, his head dropped and rested on the woolly pate. (*Adventure* 13)

This striking image is established to draw us into the material and discursive realm of the colonial plantation and is loaded with significance. At one level it reflects ideological constructions of white supremacy that defines racial others as sub-human: a domesticated beast of burden explicitly identified with a horse whose head is covered by 'wool' rather than hair. But, critically, it is emblematic of the exploitative economic relationship between the white man and the colonized labourer/slave. The former is enriched by the other's labour and derives dubious benefit from the relationship. And yet almost the entire passage is concerned with the detail of the Islander's appearance, and that detail reveals more of his lived experience than the sick white man who is at this stage no more than a burden. Certainly, the description of the Islander reveals details that are culturally estranging for the Western reader, but once more the subtle narrative focalization reveals the humanity of the man in small details – the small drama of more wisely placing the new ear piercing to prevent it tearing painfully again; the simple pleasure of smoking conveyed by the clay pipe; even the dirt seems to bring him closer to a living picture. We never get a sense of Sheldon indulging in small pleasures and he remains little more than a two-dimensional bully with a powerful gun. A 'cartoon' as Stasz observes (Stasz 132).

Moreover, the picture of this man tottering under the dead weight of another who is at once physically helpless but clinging fearfully to his gun is grotesque. When he rests his head on the bearer's back the scene is almost nurturing. Dependent and cradled, the white man proceeds to bully and chaff the sick plantation workers and then returns to clutch his bearer for support before sinking into semi-consciousness (*Adventure* 18). Fear of his gun or not, it is hard to comprehend many people being so tolerant of the situation than the sick and mistreated workers. This is a quite different relationship to the homosocial male camaraderie often typical of the colonial adventure story. It is even more striking given that the latter type of relationship is present in the novel but almost immediately dismissed when his partner, Hughie Drummond, arrives back from a recruiting voyage mortally ill with Black-water fever and dying without regaining consciousness just as the storm that washes Joan Lackland up on the shores of Berande breaks. The hackneyed adventure plot is being remodelled from the outset of the novel even if it does not quite reach the literary heights one would like. But this still does not entirely resolve the possibilities of the unsettling opening image of the white owner relying entirely on his Islander bearer. There is a link between this image and the other key relationships in the novel between Hughie and Sheldon, Joan and her father, and ultimately Joan and Sheldon. Each combines an emotional and physical dependency with relationships of property or, perhaps more accurately, of capital. Hughie and Sheldon are business partners, a role to which Joan succeeds when she invests her capital in the plantation. At one end of this continuum stands an economy of slave exploitation and racial supremacy, and at the other Joan's eventual metamorphoses into the ideal submissive wife of that same discourse, which is, moreover, defined by patriarchal power. This structure also mirrors class relationships which are, of course, in both cases relationships to capital. London's ambivalent narrative re-enacts many of the ambivalences to be found in *The People of the Abyss* at the periphery rather than centre of empire. The racially other contract 'slave' is consistently depicted as childlike and inferior from Sheldon's point of view, petulant, mischievous and governed by emotions, demanding the care and discipline of the white father. Equally, Joan's desire for 'boyish' adventure – colonial adventure fiction was largely a male adolescent market, even though girls were often avid readers – must be restrained by the white father also. As Stasz observes it is significant that Sheldon deals with Joan's joy in adventure by thinking of her as a boy, which in turn uncomfortably correlates with the way Joan and he refer to the Islanders as 'boys'. Joan's playing-out of this role is a vestige of her life with her father, but even when she assumes a new role of traditional female to complete the romantic plot cliché, it is again to be infantilized within that same patriarchal discourse when she becomes Sheldon's 'little girl' (*Adventure* 313). This parallel lexicon infers that the government of the domestic sphere is coterminous with the government of the plantation, as Susan Meyer suggests: 'This idea that white women were like, or could be likened to, people of other races, with the corollary that events within the English home had a certain parallel with events in the colonies, recurs frequently in nineteenth-century writing' (Meyer 7). Rather than seeing the conclusion of the novel as simply a clichéd romantic resolution contrived for the popular market, there is an important counter-discourse to be detected here which brings such ideological contrivances into view. What might be viewed as weak writing might in fact be more politically affective than an artistic achievement.

It is the arrival of Joan Lackland that polarizes many of the issues featured in the first three chapters of the narrative. From the first, Joan is very much the innocent abroad from Sheldon's perspective and whose initial shock and frequent anger reveals the rigidity of both patriarchal and colonial discourses that regulate the plantation. Sheldon responds with incredulity both to the fact that Joan commands her male Polynesian employees and that she presumes to feed them on 'white man's' tinned food: '"Your men!" he gasped. "On tinned goods! No, no. Let them go out and eat with my boys"' (*Adventure* 50). The subsequent argument is sparked by his implied mockery her presumption of masculine prerogative by taking control of the plantation and over-seeing colonized others. Her anger is articulated through an attack on the poor conditions at Berande and her suspicion of slavery that is intensified by their respective nationalities:

> 'That I won't; my men are *men*. I've been out to your miserable barracks and watched them eat. Faugh! Potatoes! Nothing but potatoes! No salt! Nothing! Only potatoes! I may have been mistaken, but I thought I understood them to say that was all they ever got to eat. Two meals and every day in the week?'
>
> . . .
>
> My men are not niggers. The sooner you understand that the better for our acquaintance. As for tinned goods, I'll pay for all they can eat. Please don't worry about that. Worry is not good for you in your condition. And I won't stay longer than I have to – just long enough o get you on your feet, and not go away with the feeling of having deserted a white man. (*Adventure* 51)

These two passages are important in a number of aspects. Perhaps the most obvious is the emphasis on the poor facilities provided for the labourers. The narrative to this point has contrasted Sheldon's dehumanizing racial prejudices and the Islanders' alien external appearance while allowing their humanity to be appreciated through their pain, grief, resentment and hints of minor pleasures like smoking and personal decoration. It is telling that while Sheldon's beliefs and prejudices are, in a sense, interrogated from within in the narrative, the Islanders are, perhaps of necessity, comprehensible largely through external detail. By providing the reader with such descriptive detail the narrative establishes the possibility of an alternative interpretation from that determined through Sheldon's racial discourse and colonial/business imperatives. Also of interest is the way Sheldon's 'condition' is acerbated by worry caused by the maintenance of the colour line. When Joan insists that her Polynesian companions be allowed to eat tinned goods, Sheldon is shocked since even on a basic level, their status in Sheldon's mind as 'niggers' – which Joan rightly infers – is confused and threatened. The implication is that the oppression of colonial identity created 'worry' and thence poor health in both colonizer and colonized since both are afflicted by fever. The association of the two recalls Frantz Fanon's study of the psychological scarring of colonial conflict in his study of French attempts to put down the Algerian popular uprising in the 1960s and the chronic psychoso-matic symptoms among the combatants of both sides. London too seems to suggest this insight identifying the extreme stress placed on the individual by colonial power relations, whether the abuser exercising that power or the victim resisting it.

Following the introduction of Joan and her new narrative perspective the possibilities for an alternative interpretation of conditions on the plantation come to the fore. What is presented through this perspective is how only the bare minimum of shelter and sustenance is provided to keep the workers alive on the plantation, and from this evidence Joan concludes that they are slaves only to be immediately corrected by Sheldon: 'Recruits . . . Contract labourers. They serve only three years, and they are free agents when they enter upon their contracts' (*Adventure* 54). The Islanders are 'free' men not slaves but from Joan's insistence on the status of her own Tahitian retainers as 'real men' it is clear how far such recognition has been systematically denied to the workers of Berende. When Sheldon refers to the Islanders as 'niggers' he is not just signalling a racial slur, but asserting their effective slave status in much the same way that an earlier generation of slave owners did. While Sheldon is British, it is as well not to underestimate the impact of this word both within the text and to its primary readership since both Joan and the initial market for the novel is American. Moreover, given the colonial possessions gained a few years before following the Spanish–American war, the branding of racial others as 'niggers' creates a pointed conflation of colonialism and slavery. There is another important subtext here that is concerned directly with the formal regulation of the labour trade and the plantations it served. As discussed above, from as early as 1868 a series of highly publicized laws and regulations were introduced by the government of Queensland, the British imperial government and later the High Commissioner for the Western Pacific, which promised to not only curb some of the recruiting abuses but also to establish minimum conditions for the care of Islanders under contract on the plantations. This included the provision of an adequate diet, access to medical assistance and the right to be tried for any offence by the colonial government, not the planter. Limited enforcement of these regulations led to many abuses such as those depicted at Berende – poor housing, inadequate food, dreadful or non-existent medical provision and summary justice – which amounted to a denial of legal rights meaning in practical terms that workers had a status little better than property. Like the neglect of the poor in metropolitan centres, this created a fertile breeding ground for disease which inevitably spread to the planters as it did to the wealthy of the cities. Much of this is implicit to the well-informed reader and signalled by Joan's reaction; the plantation operates beyond even the settler-biased colonial law of the Solomon Islands as well as being morally and practically corrupting of both master and slave and encouraging the spread of lethal disease.

Yet Joan concludes her angry outburst by referring to racial solidarity, of not wanting to desert 'a white man' (*Adventure* 51) in a way that implies this answers to a higher ethical calling than laws which provide – however inadequately – for the protection of colonial subjects who are also Sheldon's employees. In either capacity, he owes a duty of care. This sense of racial loyalty and the sanctity of the white body emerges consistently in the novel and suggests that while the actions of the white colonist can be criticized as Joan does here, ideological constraints – a discursive 'colour line' almost – operate to prevent her from openly taking the side of the workers. Andrew Furer points to London's coverage of the 1908 world heavyweight bout between the white Tommy Burns and the African-American Jack Johnson to show how this sort of prejudice is not as simple or as absolute as it might first appear. London wrote: 'Because a white man wishes a white man to win, this should not prevent him from giving absolute credit to the best man' (Furer 168). Almost from the outset Joan is struggling between this – albeit still racially tinged – sense of fairness and the starker realities of colonial power and exploitation. Her criticism signals an adherence to an arguably higher set of ethical standards that condemns slavery and the abuse of legal power. What she finds at Berende under the labour contract – racial denigration, despotic violence, petty cruelties, poor food and inadequate housing – clearly appals her. Smarting under this moral judgement, Sheldon explodes with even more violence. Apparently insulted by one of the workers, Joan is forced to shoot to save his life exposing the strain between opposing ethical codes when she bursts out: ' "You brute! You coward!" she cried. "You have made me shoot a man, and I never shot a man in my life before" . . . "Then why in the name of common sense did you shoot?" he demanded. "Be-be-because you were a white man," she sobbed. "And Dad would never have left a white man in the lurch" ' (*Adventure* 85). It is significant that a sense of racial solidarity had been instilled in her by another patriarchal figure, her father who, lest we forget, was a planter on Hawaii and before that a South Pacific adventurer. Her father also seems to have shared much of Sheldon's ethos although significantly Joan's education had been completed in the United States, initially at Mills seminary in California and then two years 'back East' in New York. There is another subtle discursive conflict here on three levels: firstly between the ethical standards of the colonial metropole (California and New York) and the brutal realities of colonization; second, between the racial hierarchies of the colonial frontier and perhaps something of an abolitionist tradition from 'back East' reflected in her initial rejection to the near-slavery conditions at Berande and third, the contrast between the mythologizing of the adventure narrative and the racialism, violence and patriarchal structure it ennobles.

Joan's investment in this mythologizing is initially intense and given the obvious idolization of her father – 'Dear good Dad' (*Adventure* 63) – and later attachment to Sheldon, this intensity suggests a psychological strategy that displaces the repellent aspects of colonialism into the idealization of colonial adventure fiction. A few pages later after her angry denunciation of the conditions in which the Islanders are forced to live, comes the following reinvestment in this ideal and her association of it with Sheldon:

> They are really and truly cannibals! And just to think, this is the twentieth century! And I thought romance and adventure was fossilized! . . . But to be among them, controlling them, directing them, two hundred of them, and to escape being eaten by them – that, at least, if it isn't romantic, is certainly the quintessence of adventure. And adventure and romance are allied, you know. (*Adventure* 56)

This new sentiment for Sheldon's situation and behaviour exists simultaneously with the slave conditions and confrontational brutality he perpetuates on the plantation. Stasz suggests that Joan's capitulation is 'incredible' because her actions show her to be more capable than Sheldon but then mutates from this independent woman of action into the 'traditional female' (Stasz 136). However, the potential for this capitulation is there from the beginning since she has internalized the paternalistic colonial outlook from her father despite the veneer of California and New York. This lies at the heart of both Sheldon's attraction to her and a perspective which subsumes the immediate oppression of colonialism and patriarchy into an 'ethical' abstraction which she identifies with adventure. In some ways Joan represents the American peoples' surprising embrace of Old-World colonialism after 1898 since the anti-colonial movement provoked by the long-term occupation of the Philippines and Cuba did not gain much popular support. Accordingly, day-to-day injustices can condemn but never threaten the abstract ideal, nor do they disturb her consequent idealized reconstruction of her father/Sheldon in heroic terms. By highlighting this internal process a rather astute point is made about the practical contradictions of maintaining the ethical fictions of the imperial metropole amid the brute reality of slavery and colonialism that, to a certain degree, the adventure genre romanticizes for consumption by that metropolitan audience.

Just how far this subsumation can go is apparent from Joan's acceptance of Sheldon's explanation for the necessity of the harsh treatment of the Islanders in response to her contention that greater acquiescence would be gained from them if they were treated as human beings with rights to be respected. Sheldon's response falls into two parts. First he characterizes Melanesian Islanders as thoroughly sub-human, 'a whole lot lower than the African niggers . . . They possess no gratitude, no sympathy, no kindness. If you are kind to them, they think you are a fool. If you are gentle with them they think you are afraid. And when you think you are afraid, watch out, for they will get you' (*Adventure* 86). Second, the workers on his plantation are the worst in the Solomons because the previous owners, two drunken Germans, were slave drivers who could only recruit murderers fleeing justice from their own people. He would, however, like to treat his labourers better but only once the five-year contracts of this hard-bitten crew had expired and others replaced them. The two parts of this argument are, yet again, mutually contradictory. On the one hand, following his first assertion, if the Solomon Islanders are so irredeemably sub-human, good treatment would be pointless regardless of the disposition of the individual workers. Yet, on the other hand, he argues that they would respond to good treatment if the previous owners had not treated them like slaves. The absolute racial condemnation of his first assertion precludes the validity of the second and vice versa. The Islanders are either redeemable or not depending on the charge to which he is called to answer. Whatever the scenario, he is heroically struggling against impossible odds, either at the forefront of the 'civilising mission' bringing 'abject savages' to useful cultivation of the land they so wastefully occupy, or struggling to deal with the depravity created by 'bad' colonizers who are, rather ironically, characterized as slave drivers (and not surprisingly given the geopolitical context, they had to be Germans). It is Joan's romanticization of this practice that obscures the underlying violence and enslavement: ' "By the bitter road the younger son must tread, Ere he win to hearth and saddle of his own," she quoted. "Why if that isn't romantic, then nothing is romantic. Think of all the younger sons out over the world, on a myriad of adventures, winning to those same hearths and saddles" ' (*Adventure* 56–7).

This creates a wider contradiction within the narrative between Joan's sense of romance and what is evident from the awful conditions and practices on the plantation. This is most apparent in the narrative when her character is explicitly trying hardest to displace the reader's shock at what is being represented. The brute economic reality is that the plantation, and by implication all colonialism, simply needs cheap labour to be profitable, which locally is reflected in reluctance to formally recognize the labour trade and system as a form of slavery. William Wawm, a former labour recruiter and later opponent of the practice, was clear that 'a cheap and servile labour [force] was absolutely necessary for the cultivation of sugar-cane under a tropical sun' and 'it was axiomatic that whites themselves could not work without risk to their health' (Scarr 147). The near-slavery system of the South Pacific is therefore based on the economic realities of plantation agriculture and the colonizers' physical limitations (even if this conception of the debilitating tropics was another self-justifying colonial myth). Unsurprisingly, this duel theme of commercial imperatives and what is, in effect, the weakness of the supposedly superior white race is expressed forcibly in the novel as a Dawinian-inspired 'logic' of slavery formulated to excuse what amounts to constructive genocide:

> 'But it will never become a white man's climate in spite of all that,' Joan reiterated.
> 'The white man will always be unable to perform the manual labour.'
>   'That is true.'
>   'It will mean slavery,' she dashed on.
>   'Yes, like all the tropics. The black, the brown and the yellow will have to do the work, managed by the white men. The black labour is too wasteful, however, and in time Chinese or Indian coolies will be imported. The planters are already considering the matter. I, for one, am heartily sick of black labour.'
>   'Then the blacks will die off?'
>   Sheldon shrugged his shoulders and retorted –
>   'Yes, like the North American Indian, who was a far nobler type than the Melanesian. The world is only so large, you know, and it is filling up –'
>   'And the unfit must perish?'
>   'Precisely so. The unfit must perish.' (*Adventure* 98)

This passage is important in the way the brute realities of colonial exploitation are explicitly stated. It also illustrates how the dual consciousness of colonialism does not preclude recognition and understanding of the actuality of colonialism as an economic system and the practices that are required to sustain it. While not great art, it is the novel's very directness that prompts disgust and readings of the novel demonstrate a displacement onto the author to suggest his implied racism rather than an appreciation of its boldness as a myth-busting narrative. There is something of the yellow journalism of the time in its urgency to reveal naked self-interest and economic exploitation, as well as the corruption and brutalization of all who are involved that follows. Colonial discourse and the adventure genre is designed to obscure or reconfigure blunt truths and much like the dichotomy that the early chapters opened up between the image of Sheldon as the strong enduring pioneer and the brutality and inhumanity that defines this role; the narrative is designed to reveal the incommensurability between the ideological obfuscation of such idealization and the actuality of colonial practices.

It is important to recognize that the narrative voice London creates is restricted to conveying Sheldon's and Joan's vehemence and is relatively non-partisan. As a result the excessiveness of this Darwinian discourse is exposed to direct questioning. Further, the situation itself suggest the bankruptcy of the colonial 'idea' as Conrad would call it in *Heart of Darkness* sustained by ideologies of racial superiority and a mythology of adventure. At the risk of belabouring the point, both the United States and Great Britain had cathartic experiences of rejecting slavery embedded in their national mythologies and despite widely held views of the superiority of the white man, the proposition that any form of colonialism was effectively slavery would have been disconcerting to many readers who would be generally approving of colonialism and white supremacy as a matter of course. Thence the public outrage over the South Pacific labour trade and official attempts to ensure that it outwardly resembled earlier forms of slavery as little as possible. Yet as H. C. Brookfield argues such an apparently ethical stance is always subservient to the search for commercial profit:

> Even in its beginnings, the pacific labour trade confronted Victorian colonialism with a dilemma. While convinced of the virtues of permitting private enterprise to operate free of 'miserable regulation,' Victorian Europeans were at the same time almost habituated in the ethical doctrines of a once fiery ant-slavery move-ment. The British especially were convinced over the folly of extending rule where the cost was not counterbalanced by gains in trade, and on such grounds resisted the acquisition of empire in the Pacific Islands for more than fifty years. Yet the ethical motive drew them deeper into the region, and if rivalry with France and Germany precipitated the final scramble, it was concern over protec-tion and evangelisation of the 'savages' which brought Britain to the position of emerging dominant from that scramble. (Brookfield 31)

But in fact the 'ethical' concerns were actually being used to justify the expansion of British colonial power by assuming the writ of law in the region supposedly for the protection of the 'natives' from themselves and the predatory activities of citizens of other countries, particularly France and Germany. Thence strategic and economic interests were enhanced and it is this which underpins the dynamic of the relationship between Joan and Sheldon.

Informing this local portrayal of the purpose and brute realities of colonia-lism is the broader question of the rapid expansion of Western empires – or

Western-styled empires in the case of Japan – in the latter years of the nineteenth and early years of the twentieth centuries exemplified by the 'scramble for Africa' during the 1880s and 1890s, and the colonial expansion of the United States after the 1898 war spurred by specific developments in capitalism during the same period. That Sheldon is British and Joan American has particular resonance within this context, reflecting not only the United States' entry into Old-World imperialism, but a particular belief in rapprochement between Britain and the United States that was characteristic of the period between 1890 and the end of World War I. 'From the outset,' writes Richard Hofstadter in his study *Social Darwinism in American Thought 1860–1915*:

> its devotees had usually recognized a powerful bond with England; the historians of the Anglo-Saxon school, stressing the common political heritage, had written of the American revolution as a temporary misunderstanding in a long history of common political evolution, or as a welcome alliance which came to rapid fruition in the closing years of the nineteenth century. (Hofstadter 157)

Such thought was related to and influenced by notions of national and racial 'manifest destiny' and the 'white man's burden'; notions avidly debated in the wake of the United States' imperial venture and central to British discourses of colonialism. The US already had a colonial history of its own in the settlement of the West as Joan's identification as the daughter of a rancher reminds the reader, although on closer examination her history straddles both British and US traditions of settlement – while Hawaii had become the westernmost outpost of the United States it had, for many years previously, been subject to *ad hoc* colonization more akin to British or French colonies in the same region and throughout the world. As noted above, what is revealed of her father's ideas predisposes Joan to accept many of Sheldon's assertions regarding race and colonialism that would otherwise have seemed alien to an American from the mainland, supplementing Westward expansion with the colonial traditions of American settlement on Hawaii. This led to a settler coup which overthrew the indigenous government in 1893 that initially presented the US government with an embarrassing dilemma only resolved by formal annexation in 1898 when colonialism inexplicably became acceptable to the American public and political classes. Her ambition to acquire 'government land' of her own in the Solomons in order to found a plantation is strongly evocative of an attempt to replicate the frontier ethos and recast herself in the role of a latter-day pioneer hero to be found in some of London's other works such as the *The Valley of the Moon* (1913).

As Stasz argues, Frederick Turner's 'frontier thesis' is important to any reading of *Adventure,* given its importance to American national mythology in the early twentieth century, yet Turner's proposition interprets American development as a drawing away from European traditions and ways of thinking (Stasz 130). Earle Labor draws a similar comparison between the formative experience of survival in the harsh Arctic wastes and the uniqueness of the characters and cooperative society depicted in London's Northland tales. As Turner wrote:

> In short, at the frontier the environment is at first too strong for the man. He must accept the conditions which it furnishes, or perish. Little by little he transforms the wilderness, but the outcome is not the old Europe, not simply the development of Germanic germs . . . The fact is, that there is a new product that is American . . . Thus the advance of the Frontier has meant a steady movement away from the influence of Europe, and steady growth of independence on American lines. (Turner 185)

This position is at odds with the historically coterminous idea of pan-Anglo-Saxonism current at the time of the United States' emergence as an imperial nation as the articulation of a shared racial destiny with Britain, the nation that had provided the benchmark for modern imperialism as it had done so for the industrial state. Indeed, there are similarities between the two discourses since both, most obviously, involve the settling of land occupied by a racially different and denigrated other. Equally, there is a substantial investment in the adventurousness and unique qualities of the individual colonizer/pioneer that enables Joan to overlap the one onto the other in her construction of Sheldon's heroism. However, Joan's character in *Adventure* clearly brings such notions of the uniqueness of the American character into question and, in doing so, raises questions about the implications of the United States' rush into international empire. The narrative engineers a confrontation between an ideal of national character shaped by the process of taming and settling the land – it is of course significant that Joan's family name is 'Lackland' – versus the imposition of a predefined national mythology confined to an elite caste ruling over a subject people, characteristic of British imperialism in Asia and much of Africa. As Ania Loomba argues: 'British colonialism . . . did not allow for easy social or sexual contact with local peoples . . . Thus it often incorporated rather than disturbed native hierarchies.' Further, 'This kind of "shallow penetration" can be seen as a prototype for modern imperialism, which functions largely through remote control' (Loomba 111). Thence having secured his obedience through the threat of retaliatory violence, Sheldon is content to leave Seelee, the local chief at Berende, in power. This is in direct contrast to the American tradition of incorporating new territories into the Union that, significantly, had changed with the acquisition of the Philippines from the Spanish and its status as an unincorporated territory more akin to a British colony. The racialist anxiety that this tradition of incorporation inspired as the Americans moved into colonial shoes of the Spanish was very real and reflected one aspect of American anti-imperialist protest of the time. This is captured in a *New York World* editorial in June 1898 which asked did the United States which 'already had a black elephant' in the South 'really need a white elephant in the Phillippines, a leper elephant in Hawaii, a brown elephant in Port Rico and perhaps a yellow elephant in Cuba' (Beisner 116).

It is in this context that Joan's embodiment of two traditions provides the key to the contradictory discursive structure of *Adventure*. The narrative positioning and unusual upbringing of Joan's on Hawaii suggest that she is already receptive to colonial discourse, indicated by her ready acquiescence to Sheldon's Social Darwinist racial views and lack of concern for the slavery this entail, despite her more liberal beliefs which emerge in her initial resistance to him and this manifestation of colonialism. Yet Joan's apparent accommodation of the contradictions of colonial practices that range from the tawdry to the violent with the heroic ideals of adventure is ideologically crucial in spite of her relatively passive role. Her character undergoes an important transformation from opposition to being physically active in the practice herself, and just as the treatment of recruited Islanders is revealing in relation to Sheldon's character, so it proves with Joan. The turning point comes with her direct participation in labour recruiting. After purchasing from the insurers and recovering the beached ship *Martha* for use by the plantation as a trading and recruiting vessel, she proceeds to recruit Islanders and in the process 'wantonly breaks the recruiting laws' (*Adventure* 206). Not only does she exceed the number of passengers allowed by the recruiting licences applicable to the ships under her charge – Martha does not even have one – but she takes the local chief, Kina Kina, hostage and manipulates him with threats to regain gear stripped from the beached ship and to force 150 Islanders to sign themselves into service since 'Kina Kina's word was law, and he was scared to death' (*Adventure* 213). Joan not only responds to Sheldon's racial theorizing and his implementation of a slave system on the plantation, but actively duplicates his methods of disrupting and manipulating indigenous social structures to compel them to work on behalf of the plantation. The entire episode is directly reminiscent of the worst days of kidnapping and her actions constitute a felony under the Pacific Islanders Act of

1872. Her actions also establish continuity with her father's history in the Pacific as a 'resource raider'; although rather than men and women he had plundered the Pacific Islands for pearls.

Joan's indoctrination also marks a turning point in her relationship with Sheldon who declares his love for her soon after she returns to the plantation. She initially reacts with anger to the declaration and an uneasy truce is declared under which Sheldon promises not to raise the matter again. The terms of Joan's rejection are important: 'I have *my* own way to make in the world, and I came to the Solomons to do it. Getting married is not making *my* way in the world. It may do for some women, but not for me, thank you' (*Adventure* 228). Despite Joan's insistence on retaining her independence, she has already been ideologically drawn into the practice of 'Old World' colonialism to the extent that, while she may be able to claim to make her own way in the world, she is effectively duplicating Sheldon's way which is, moreover, the British way. Rather than building on her own experience of engagement with local conditions and being moulded by that practice – to recall Turner – she is now being shaped by a practice external to both her and the Solomons. This might be extended further to suggest that by entering into a global system dominated by 'Old World' imperialism, the United States is at risk of losing that which the national myth vaunts as part of the uniqueness of the American character defined by Turner. That this episode should also mark the beginning of Joan's metamorphosis into the 'traditional female' is important and traces a similar process of absorption since as well as representing a certain form of colonialism in the novel, he is also the centre of patriarchal authority in the novel who not only lays down the 'natural' order of races (*Adventure* 98), but also the 'natural' order of gender roles: 'You can't help being yourself. You can't help being a very desirable creature so far as I am concerned. You have made me want you. You didn't intend to; you didn't try to. You were so made that is all' (*Adventure* 230). Over the span of the novel Joan's character shapes itself to Sheldon's racial outlook, his manipulation and abuse of the local chief, near-slave treatment of the plantation's workers and punitive violence to maintain control and, ultimately, she bows to her role as the 'traditional' female in this authoritarian order which supplants her investment in the pioneer ideal.

Describing a similar transition in London's later novel, *The Valley of the Moon*, Christopher Gair argues that the pioneer spirit is doomed to perish 'because of the corporate, anti-individualistic nature of urban post [Civil] war America: the perceived self-determination of the pioneer is replaced by the deterministic laws of the market' (Gair 147). It is the 'market' which underlies both Joan's ideological and personal capitulation and Sheldon's and the plantation's need for her. His paternalistic code and racial ideology are initially challenged and revitalized by Joan's American brashness and commercial energy – 'That's the American of it . . . Push, and go, and energy, and independence' (*Adventure* 176) – indeed, the practices which she adopts from Sheldon during her own experience of recruiting are so quickly internalized that she characterizes the entire episode as the consequence of her 'forceful American business methods' (*Adventure* 203). Note how it is no longer the pioneering spirit which defines the American identity of her character, but commercial acumen and energy; just as Sheldon has the land that Joan 'lacks', so Britain has a huge colonial empire while the more vigorous and commercially powerful United States was just emerging as an imperial nation with capital to invest. Whereas Joan's dream of financial and social independence might be said to reflect Turner's frontier ethos, the gradual co-optation of her character through the narrative traces the transformation of that myth into the more commercially shaped ideal of the 'American Dream'. Capital is ultimately the single most important theme underlying the narrative. Even though Sheldon has usurped the land at Berande from the indigenous people and enslaved a captive workforce for his profit, he initially stands to gain little from it because he and his former partner were about to be defeated by a lack of liquid capital. That is exactly how he objectifies his workers – 'the deaths were daily reducing his working capital' (*Adventure* 21) – while he awaits the ship that carries both his former partner and new recruits to replenish the working capital of the plantation. Indeed, the workers are more broadly identified as the circulating capital of empire as his reference to the distribution of Indian and Chinese coolies throughout the colonies infers (*Adventure* 98) and he can afford no more. As Eric Hobsbawm has observed, the British Empire was by this time 'becoming a parasitic rather than a competitive economy, living off the remains of world monopoly' (Hobsbawm 192).

Indeed, Berende is almost bought out by the speculators Morgan and Raff the representatives of a purer, asset-striping, form of capitalism in the novel at a fraction of Sheldon's investment. They are also differentiated in class terms by Joan – 'Nor did they talk like gentlemen . . . Undoubtedly, they were men of affairs' (*Adventure* 131) – establishing an aristocratic distaste for mere trade as opposed to land ownership which is striking coming from a commercially minded American praised for her 'push, and go'. Once Joan adds her capital and the plantation becomes financially viable again, they both take a crucial step towards another form of capitalist accumulation which coexists with that represented by Morgan and Raff, but is socially more acceptable being based on a steady, unearned, parasitic dividend from invested capital and absentee landlordism. Leaving day-to-day management of the plantation to overseers, Sheldon dreams of that day: 'Three more years and the plantation would be a splendid paying investment. They could take yearly trips to Australia, and oftener; and an occasional run home to England – or Hawaii, would come as a matter of course' (*Adventure* 180). The anticipation of this British and American union is of an aristocratic lifestyle that would distance them from the socially undesirable unpleasantness of the day-to-day oppression that is colonialism – including the Darwinist genocide and slavery that Sheldon projects for the benefit of Joan's education – from which their income is derived. The price of that lifestyle is a disregard for the ethical considerations of the means by which that wealth and privilege are secured. Moreover, Joan must comply with the social restrictions placed on her as a woman. Joan's and Sheldon's marriage (and business partnership) seems improbable as a plot development because London's representation of capital, colonialism and the relationship between the United States and Britain in *Adventure* reveals the emptiness and improbabilities behind such 'idea's as the 'civilizing mission' or the influence of the frontier on national character that were important aspects of the national myth of both countries at this time and perhaps since articulated and reaffirmed by adventure and romance. Their union signals the pre-eminence of a discourse predicated on racial, class and gender hierarchies and supported by capital, which hindsight tells us will not bode well for the twentieth century. Frederick Turner was not unaware of this contradiction and attempted an accommodation between the myths of the frontier in a new age of corporate capitalism. In an article for the *Atlantic Monthly* of 1896 he observed: 'The striking and peculiar characteristic of American society is that it is not so much a democracy as a huge commercial company for the discovery, cultivation and capitalization of its enormous territory' (Munslow 183). As Joan reflects echoing Conrad in *Heart of Darkness*: 'We whites have been land robbers and sea robbers from remotest time' (*Adventure* 92). There is not a little irony when Joan the new recruiter and plantation owner is chaffed by one of her captains for the hard work she demands – 'My word, she's a slave driver' (*Adventure* 204). Quite so, London utters under his breath by the conclusion of the novel with a glance towards the future of his own nation.

7

Fragments of Empire, Fractured Identities

The foregoing chapters have explored the development of a complex narrative discourse across the work of Stevenson and London by which racial, class and national identifications are negotiated and confirmed or, more often, questioned. What is striking in both writers' work is not so much the various general ideas that reflect shared assumptions of the culture in which they are embedded, but how that work struggles to take the reader beyond those cosy assumptions to force a reconsideration of the relationship between class categories, colonial ideals and the ideological sanitization of what imperial commerce actually means in the raw. Thus the work of both writers achieves significance beyond the commonplaces of both naturalizing ideas and narrative expectation. As Raymond Williams argues:

> No expression, that is to say – no account, description, depiction, portrait – is 'natural' or 'straightforward'. These are at most socially relative terms. Language is not a pure medium through which the reality of life or the reality of an event or experience or the reality of a society can 'flow'. It is a socially shared and reciprocal activity, already embedded in active relationships, within which every move is an activation of what is already shared and reciprocal or may become so. (Williams 166)

Certainly the 'tradition', literary and otherwise, of representing the South Pacific exerts a powerful influence in Stevenson's and London's writing, which they frequently challenge. In its place Western commerce is represented as the constant. However unique or incomprehensible the event or situation, the commercial imperative is the shared and reciprocal naturalizing force for the character and reader, but the process by which it shapes and distorts the language is brought to the fore rather than allowed to rest. The 'activation of what is shared and reciprocal' is disrupted. Indeed, the generic form deployed in these texts asserts a framework that would be expected to normalize the moment, such as tropes of illness, or familiar presumptions about class, race or commerce, or literary tradition. But what increasingly is at stake in London's and Stevenson's South Pacific writing is the very belief that everything can become 'shared and reciprocal' that lay behind Victorian certainties. This in turn makes them of their moment which saw an assertive imperialism both at its height and on the cusp of decline giving way to a New Imperialism fuelled by global industrial capitalism energizing the flow and influence of capital across the world, and anticipating a concurrent cultural and social insecurity that would come to be recognized as modernism.

This concluding chapter will explore and juxtapose a selection of Stevenson's and London's shorter fiction as exempla of the political, economic and aesthetic transition in which the older idea of a heroic imperial 'frontier' is shown to be in conflict with grubby activities on the ground that lies behind the contradictory anti-imperialism that reinforced the New Imperialism. As Denis Judd argues: 'there emerged a curious equation between anti-imperialism and feelings of resentment towards those indigenous people whose rebellions, resistance and intransigence necessitated the intervention of British forces. In other words, it was "their" fault that there was trouble and expense, not "ours"' (Judd 232). In these stories, Western constructions of the primitive and primitive cultures are brought into contact with international commercial interests. While it might be a stretch to claim that all the stories examined in this chapter are unproblematically modernist in an aesthetic sense (although one might for Stevenson's story *The Ebb Tide*), they do question dominant certainties defining race, empire, class and the purpose of colonialism as less than fixed, as well as demonstrating a new awareness of the complexities of cultural difference along the road to what Steve Clark suggest separates nineteenth-century representations of other cultures from that of the twentieth: 'high imperial travelogues engage in robust heroics whereas twentieth-century texts assert their whimsical exquisiteness' (Clark 9). Such 'whimsical exquisiteness' can be found in Stevenson's and London's South Pacific travel writing, but their fiction dramatically undermines the 'robust heroics' of the nineteenth century and point to something more disturbing, but equally 'twentieth century'. As Bradbury and MacFarlane observe of the period in which Stevenson and London were writing: 'if anything distinguishes these decades and gives them their intellectual and historical character, it is a fascination with evolving consciousness: consciousness aesthetic, psychological and historical'

(Bradbury and MacFarlane 47). The texts examined in this section mark this transition making them, if not entirely modernist, at least the first modern representations of the South Pacific.

'The Beach of Falesā'

In terms of literary accomplishment, Stevenson's 'The Beach of Falesā' and London's 'David Grief' stories appear to have little in common other than a South Pacific setting. 'Falesā' is among the most technically accomplished of Stevenson's stories and represents a conscious attempt to write in a new vein that was only tentatively approached in *The Wrecker*, while London's 'David Grief' stories were intended to appeal to popular taste as adventure stories. Yet even when he is at his most popularist, London is able to boldly pose discomforting questions by articulating and pushing Western ideological assumptions to their logical and disturbing limits as was evident in *Adventure*. 'The Beach of Falesā' represents an unremitting confrontation with the tawdriness of the local transactions of big business, whereas the Grief stories spin a fantasy of an anachronistic, superhuman and morally impeccable Western trader dispensing justice and wisdom while reaping a handsome profit in the process. Both texts interrogate that ambiguous narrative and cultural space between the trading agent of global commercial enterprises and the individualistic and culturally indeterminate beachcomber. Unsurprisingly, perhaps, both texts progressively move away from the Western-centred certainties with which they begin (in both a commercial and cultural sense) into openly hybrid situations. While it is possible to construct an argument for 'Falesā' as a proto-modernist text aesthetically – its controlled technical experimentation and unusual subject matter alone make this a sustainable claim – no such claim on aesthetic grounds is possible for London's Grief stories and, indeed, the stories have no such pretension. But rather than a comparable experimental text, London's Grief stories provide a fascinating fantasy of commercial modernity as a *reductio ad absurdum* of the colonial ideal that surprisingly finds common discursive ground with Stevenson's story.

'The Beach of Falesā' concerns the trials and tribulations of John Wiltshire the representative of a global trading company on the remote fictional Polynesian island of Falesā heralding the end of the dominance of a sinister group of independent beachcombers who have exploited the Islanders' traditional superstitions for their own profit. Wiltshire, however, comes equipped with his own mantra based on the identity of a British subject bent on bringing the benefits of Western civilization through his trade goods. He demands recognition on these terms as he defends himself before the local headman who has mysteriously tabooed him:

> You tell them that I'm a white man, and a British subject, and no end of a big chief at home; and I've come here to do them good, and bring them civilisation; and no sooner have I got my trade sorted out than they go and taboo me, and no one dare come near my place! Tell them I don't mean to fly in the face of anything legal; and if what they want's a present, I'll do what's fair. I don't blame any man for looking out for himself, tell them, for that's human nature; but if they think they're going to come any of their native ideas over me, they'll find themselves mistaken. And tell them plain that I demand the reason of this treatment as a white man and a British subject. ('Falesā' 121–2)

The reduction of Western civilization to trade goods rather than the contribution of the trader is telling, but the flat contradictions of Wiltshire's speech also require attention. The assertion that he does not want to transgress local law – 'anything legal' – is then understood to mean that he accepts an obligation to bribe the chiefs that reveals the purely transactional nature of his outlook to which local and Western civilization are reduced. Local law based on anything more than this – 'native ideas' – are rejected as inapplicable to a British subject. There is also the advancement of a doctrine of selfishness represented by trade and bribery – 'I don't blame any man looking out for himself'. In effect, this whole passage is a rejection of culture, community and human relationships on anything other than a transactional basis. There is not even the hypocrisy of empire's 'civilising mission' to cover over the cultural bankruptcy that Wiltshire represents. His opponent is the shady Case a local beachcomber whose livelihood is threatened by Wiltshire and the company he represents. Case is more subtle, manipulating the Islanders through their culture and it is he who has engineered Wilshire's taboo. In effect, commercial competition has become an exercise in manipulating local people; ostensibly a small-scale travesty of the imperial 'great game' with Wiltshire the representative of British imperial interests in competition with another Western empire. Case is European but distinctly foreign: 'Case would have passed muster in a city. He was yellow and smallish, had a hawk's nose to his face, pale eyes, and his beard trimmed with scissors. No man knew his country, beyond he was of English speech . . .' ('Falesā' 103). His henchman is an African-American called Black Jack, which suggestively covers Britain's commercial competitors. Moreover, they have usurped the station of the derelict Captain Randal pointing to the dangers of a loss of commercial vigour.

The Western civilization on offer to the Islanders lies between Wiltshire's trade goods and Case's subtle knowledge and manipulation of local custom for his own ends. While the latter is hardly a positive alternative, it does acknowledge something more than relationships built purely on transactions. Interestingly this does point the way, if reductively, towards the development of modern anthropology. Bronislaw Malinowski was to base his ground-breaking study *Argonauts of the Western Pacific* (1922) on field work undertaken among the Trobriand Islanders during World War I. This work advanced the idea of 'reciprocity' arguing that primitive society is based on ritualized exchange of people, ideas and technology which Malinowski argued points to the origins of the far more sophisticated social transactions of the developed world. Stevenson's insight is impressive in its anticipation of Malinowski as is his recognition that to reduce such transaction purely to the abstraction of money is to lose the very basis of society. The association between Case and the urban is also significant. One of the technical triumphs of the story is the deftness by which Stevenson maintains the limitations of Wiltshire's first-person narrative especially in the manner by which he identifies his antagonists. Wiltshire is most definitely of working-class origins and yet while he seems intimidated by Case's city-bred sophistication, his suspicions rest on clichés associated with the urban residuum that London recorded in *The People of the Abyss*, particularly through hints at Case's indeterminate ethnicity being 'yellow and smallish' having 'hawk's nose to his face, pale eyes, and a beard trimmed with scissors'. This easily fits contemporary stereotypes of Jewish features the reviled internal racial other of the West, which in turn provides a further association of a none-too-honest money-grabbing outlook. There is something of Fagin in Wiltshire's caricature of Case; Fagin's exploitation of street children being replaced by Case's exploitation of the child-like Islanders. Yet, if this is the filter through which Wiltshire presents Case to the reader, how does he present himself? His representation of Case does not quite succeed in suppressing the fact that he is a small independent trader protecting a precarious livelihood from the encroachment of a large commercial house with whom he would presumably be unable to compete. Indeed, Wiltshire muses over the competitive potential of his commercial rivals: 'If these are my only rivals . . . I should do well in Falesā. Indeed, there was only the one way they could touch me, and that was with guns and drink' ('Falesā' 106). Since this is Wiltshire's narrative, the perspective on Case's manipulation of the Islanders and the rumours of psychological persecution – if not outright poisoning – of the previous representative of the company is given full force.

Striking a more curious initial note, however, is Wiltshire's early attraction to Case and Black Jack despite their potential as commercial competitors:

> When these two came aboard I was pleased with the looks of them at once or, rather, with the looks of both, and the speech of one. I was sick for white neighbours after my four years at the line, which I always counted years of prison; getting tabooed, and going to the Speak House to see and get it taken off; buying gin and going on a break, and then repenting; sitting in the house at night with the lamp for company; or walking on the beach and wondering what kind of fool to call myself for being where I was. There were no other whites on the island, and when I sailed to the next, rough customers made the most of society. Now to see these two when they came aboard was a pleasure. One was a Negro, to be sure; but they were both rigged out smart in striped pyjamas and straw hats . . . ('Falesā' 102–3)

Vanessa Smith summarizes the plot of the 'The Beach of Falesā' as that of 'The trader, John Wiltshire, pit[ting] himself against a defeating his rival, the gentleman beachcomber Case, and in the process affirming his loyalty to the island community he has made his own' (Smith 167). But this is to take Wiltshire's highly deceptive narrative at face value. In fact Wiltshire's initially positive reception of Case is purely selfish reflecting a history of deliberate estrangement from the local communities in which he has previously lived. Why does he spend so much time alone during his previous posting, tabooed or on a 'break' with a gin bottle? And why should the Islanders with whom he traded taboo him on a regular basis. However, Smith is right to identify that that Wiltshire's response to Case is at least partly motivated by class in terms of not only the urban sophistication that initially intimidates him, but also cultural attainments manifested in Wiltshire's faith in Case's 'splendid education' and 'good family' ('Falesā' 103). However, Wiltshire's judgement and his own class limitations are amusingly deflated by the revelation of his equal admiration for Case's ability with the accordion, his ability 'to blaspheme worse than a Yankee boatswain' and his sleight of hand parlour tricks that are 'equal to any professional' ('Falesā' 103). Like Loudon Dodd the first-person narrator of *The Wrecker*, Stevenson quickly undermines the reliability of Wiltshire as narrator. However, unlike his representation of Dodd who as a bourgeois is afforded some gravitas despite his highly questionable and ultimately criminal nature, the attitude encouraged towards Wiltshire has more than a little class-based ridicule and contempt to it.

As to his 'commitment' to the local Polynesian community, this ultimately rests on his commitment to Uma the woman who is tricked into his bed by Case as part of a strategy to remove him as a commercial competitor. While Wiltshire eventually develops a genuine attachment to Uma, she is also an outsider in this community and thence does not represent a local tie. In the final analysis, Wiltshire's attachment to the island and its people rests upon the wishes of the company he represents to retain him there and on the personal debt he acknowledges to the local missionary, Mr Tarleton, which he resents. It is with evident personal and commercial satisfaction when he is able to leave the island and cast off this restraining obligation: 'I was half glad when the firm moved me onto another station, where I was under no kind of pledge and could look my balances in the face' ('Falesá' 169).

The issue of the regular taboo of his last station still lingers and the view taken of it is measured by the reader's attitude towards the custom. On the one hand it will be readily dismissed if the view is adopted that the Pacific system of taboo (*tapu*) is nothing more than primitive capriciousness, which was quite likely among the casual readers of Stevenson's work. A more attentive Stevenson reader would however be aware of his surprise when he found that this presumption was not borne out by his experience of local practice as he recorded it in *In the South Seas*:

> It will be observed with surprise that both these *tapus* are for thoroughly sensible ends. With surprise, I say, because the nature of the institution is much misunderstood in Europe. It is taken usually in the sense of a meaningless or wanton prohibition, such as that which to-day prevents women in some countries from smoking, or yesterday prevented anyone taking a walk on Sunday. The error is no less natural than it is unjust. The Polynesians have not been trained in the bracing, practical thought of ancient Rome; with them the idea of law has not been disengaged from that of morals or propriety; so that *tapu* has to cover the whole field, and implies indifferently that an act is criminal, immoral, against sound public policy, unbecoming or (as we say) 'not in good form'. (*South Seas* 39)

We learn that Wiltshire has become tabooed by his association with Uma which Case has manipulated. Like Western law and custom, the taboo system can be corrupted and Case has inflamed local jealousies to have Uma tabooed to thwart a local chief who sought her marriage contrary to his own desire for her. Moreover, as an outsider she potentially represents a certain threat to local custom. Yet with no jealous beachcombers seeking to protect their livelihood, responsibility for his regular taboo status at his last station can only rest with Wiltshire and the list that concludes the passage above offers intriguing scope for speculation ranging across the 'criminal, immoral, against sound public policy . . . or . . . "not in good form"'. Taken together with a demonstrated tendency for arrogant claims to precedence as a British subject and his reduction of social relations to money and gifts with his admission of frequent 'breaks' with a bottle of gin suggests that his presence was a burden to his previous hosts from which the elders ought to protect their community by the exercise of taboo. His actions on Falesā have, therefore, to be read less as reconciliation with the local Polynesian community as Smith suggests, than an attempt at possible redemption of his status as a trader and as a part of white colonial society.

It is tempting to romanticize Wiltshire for his comparatively honourable actions to the decidedly attractive character of Uma, even though critics have recognized that even this is finely designed to further his own interests and is further limited by an incipient racism that is frequently foregrounded in his narrative and extends beyond just a casual verbal characteristic no doubt common at the colonial frontier. The final jarring note of this motif returns at the end of the narrative when a mature Wiltshire reflects on his marriage to Uma and the children they have brought up together: 'But what bothers me is the girls. They're only half-castes, of course: I know as well as you do, and there's nobody thinks less of half-castes than I do; but they're mine, and about all I've got. I can't reconcile my mind to their taking up with Kanakas, and I'd like to know where I'm to find the whites?' ('Falesā' 169). The racism is perhaps unremarkable as a document of its time, but the manner by which it violates the sanctity of the Victorian family both in terms of Wiltshire's valuation of his own children and also by virtue of the violation of the colour line and sexual conventions which come together in a contemporary horror of miscegenation. Even for Stevenson's original readership this would signal what is all wrong about Wiltshire as a representative of Western culture. This challenge to contemporary mores is asserted early in the story, but was extraordinarily also played out in an extra-textual battle over publication. In his study of the difficult publication history of the story, Barry Menikoff is rightly fascinated by the unusual tone of the narrative and the pruderies of Stevenson's publishers. He recounts how the original text was distorted by literal-minded proof readers anxious to diminish the ambiguities of Stevenson's experiential style, and by nervous publishers unwilling to print that Wiltshire and Uma were fraudulently married before they slept together 'and that Mr John Wiltshire is at liberty to send her to hell the next morning' ('Falesā' 109). Clement Shorter, editor of the *Illustrated London News* where the story first appeared, refused to print the original version insisting on changes to the 'profane' dialogue and the removal of the reference to the fake marriage certificate altogether (Calder 16).

When the story came to be published as a book form it was as part of the collection *Island Night's Entertainments* with the parables 'The Bottle Imp' and 'The Isle of Voices' – despite Stevenson's objections that it should not appear with work of such different tone and intent – the one day was extended to one week. Stevenson acquiesced to this extension with amusement: 'Well, well, if the dears prefer a week, I'll give them ten days, but the real document, from which I have scarcely varied, ran for one night' (*Letters IV* 183–4). Strict fidelity to his own experience is not Stevenson's aim since one week or ten days does nothing to diminish his dramatic purpose or to disguise the sexual exploitation of the colonial frontier. In technical terms the incident also demonstrates the use of multiple narrative implications of a single event that Stevenson developed in *The Wrecker*. While the fraud is knowingly enacted by Wiltshire the colonizer over Uma the colonized, a further level of manipulation exists as Case completes a circle of manipulation as the commercial competitor. It is difficult to overlook the symbolism of how even the most intimate of colonial social relationships are diminished and denigrated by unrestricted struggles over commercial ascendency. Uma is reduced to a commodity/object to be disposed of and manipulated by men seeking sexual and trading advantage. It is difficult to avoid the implication of prostitution that the association of sex with commerce creates as well as the echo of a history of miscegenation within slavery given the widely publicized scandal of the Pacific labour trade (even though Uma is Polynesian and the trade largely involved Melanesian islanders). This further underscores the impact of the debased system of circulation in which Case, Wiltshire *and* the reader are implicated.

In a further elaboration of the systematic dissection of a colonial society which embeds sexual and commercial exploitation, Stevenson adds religion to the interplay of forces at the colonial and commercial frontier. The interplay between sex and religion in the story recalls Havelock Ellis' observation that 'love and religion are the two most volcanic emotions to which the human organism is capable' and a third commercial profit (Crawford 79). As Nigel Thomas argues: 'The wave of evangelical energy paralleled the increasing momentum of contact and commerce in Polynesia. If initially these developments were but loosely linked . . . they would . . . become powerfully intertwined' (Thomas 2010 28). However, while Wilshire may enlist the missionary Mr Tarelton to formalize his marriage to Uma and thence restore them to the moral fold, here and later in the story this brings into focus exactly what Christianity represents to Uma and her fellow Islanders. In particular, there is little to choose between Wiltshire's attempts to forestall Uma's objections to his intention to destroy Case's counterfeit shrine and Case's tricks:

> 'I'll tell you what, then,' said I. 'You fish out your Bible, and I'll take that up along with me. That'll make me right.'
> She swore a Bible was no use.
> 'That's just your Kanaka ignorance,' said I. 'Bring the Bible out.'
> She brought it, and I turned to the title-page, where I thought there would be some English, and so there was. 'There!' said I. 'Look at that! "*London: Printed for the British and Foreign Bible Society, Blackfriars*," and the date, which I can't read, owing to it being in these X's. There's no devil in hell can look near the Bible Society, Blackfriars. Why, you silly,' I said, 'how do you suppose we get along with our own *aitus* at home! All Bible Society.'
> 'I think you no got any,' said she. 'White man, he tell me you no got.'
> 'Sounds likely, don't it?' I asked. 'Why would these islands all be chock of them and none in Europe?'
> 'Well, you no got bread-fruit,' said she. ('Falesā' 158)

Uma's amusing logic is significant. Western culture is translated rather than assimilated into this colonial locale. While Uma and the other Polynesian Christians of the island seem creditably dutiful in relation to their adopted belief, they also adapt it to local conditions and their collective heritage. The Bible as a sacred object is not necessarily recognized in a milieu which is, after all, one based on an oral rather than a written culture. Similarly, Uma is unimpressed by the mention of Blackfriars and London and rejects them as a symbolism for an overarching colonial authority. Stevenson also hints at the mutability of doctrinal belief and temporal power with the choice of Blackfriars for this particular publisher, an area that takes its name from the dissolved and long-buried Dominican – and thence Catholic – monastery. The Catholic tradition is also represented on the island in the person of the French priest Father Galuchet. Indeed, the island is pulled between three national/Christian traditions: French Catholic, British Protestant and the local adaptation of the latter led by the Polynesian preacher Namu. While Wiltshire insists on the immutability of the physical colonial/religious symbolism he holds before Uma, her response not only insists on the priority of local conditions but also questions the presumption of Western superiority. As Thomas observes: 'The argument here is in no sense that empire was other than exploitative, indeed brutal . . . Yet it was also the creation of a cosmopolitan arena, which extended and elaborated upon the deeply inter-social character of Islander society' (Thomas 2010 296). This sense of cultural creativity is an insight that Stevenson clearly anticipates in 'The Beach of Falesá', and it is the Western characters that seem parochial, debased and ignorant. This episode between Wiltshire and Uma also recalls Homi Bhabha's discussion of the colonial reception of the Western book in 'Signs taken for Wonders', but rather than the Subaltern 'hybridising' the 'English book', it is the Western subject articulating this process in an attempt to gain temporary authority over a colonized subject who is asserting her identity in a culturally sophisticated and logical manner. It is the Westerner who seems woefully simplistic in his reasoning and out of touch with the fluidity and complexity of the local culture. Indeed, Wiltshire's strategy replicates that of Case and his shrine in the bush built from Western detritus which, thanks to his greater intelligence and understanding of local culture and how to manipulate it, is far more effective.

If Uma represents one example of a successful assertion of agency which writes her subjectivity into this story – in this respect Uma is one of Stevenson's most effective female characters – her counterpoint is Namu the local Pastor and his increasing assertion of local independence from Tarleton the visiting missionary. In both instances it is Case who is the *agent provocateur* of change; his manipulation of all despite his eventual death at the hands of Wiltshire with the tacit sanction of Tarleton proves to be the creative interference that leads to the genuine relationship between Uma and Wiltshire despite the latter's ingrained racism, and seems to give confidence to Namu to forge a distinct hybrid ministry that translates local and imported belief systems. Indeed, Tarleton's description of how Namu falls under Case's influence is akin to a realist representation of another of Stevenson's Pacific stories, the parable 'The Bottle Imp'. There, as here, the underlying struggle is over Western goods and provides a perceptive insight into the material basis of culture and the performative nature of religion:

> The beginning of it was not corrupt; it began, doubtless, in fear and respect, produced by trickery and pretence; but I was shocked to find that another element had been lately added, that Namu helped himself to the store, and was believed to be deep in Case's debt. Whatever the trader said, that Namu believed with trembling. He was not alone in this; many of the village lived in a similar subjection; but Namu's case was the most influential, it was through Namu that Case had wrought most evil; and with a certain following among the chiefs, and the pastor in his pocket, the man was as good as master of the village. ('Falesá' 138)

The corruption that is so shocking to Tarleton is in effect independence from colonial control. While Case is undoubtedly manipulating the local situation for his own benefit, he is integrated into the local community far more than the colonial religious establishment in the person of Tarleton and the missionary society he represents, and the colonial commercial establishment in the person of Wiltshire and the global company he represents. Their role recalls Jean and John Comaroff's description of the advancement of missionary teaching and capitalism in Africa: 'The goods and techniques they brought with them . . . presupposed the messages and meanings they proclaimed in the pulpit and vice versa. Both were vehicles of a moral economy that celebrated the global spirit of commerce, the commodity, and the imperial marketplace' (Comaroff and Comaroff 12–13). Both missionaries and traders introduced ideas and goods side by side by promoting their necessity for everyday life, be it an awareness of Jesus or alcohol and tobacco. Any distinction between Wiltshire and Tarleton on the one hand and Case and Namu on the other is no better than superficial at this level. Tarleton seeks to terrorize the Polynesians with lakes of hell and everlasting torment and the trader follows in his wake to provide Western clothes and other trappings of Western respectability that the missionary insists are so essential for a moral life. Case also introduces a new superstition by more obviously stimulating the demand for his goods; a profit which is gained with less hypocrisy if no less harm. Ultimately, the distinction between the 'good' Wiltshire and the 'bad' Case comes down to a negative view of the individual, stateless operator versus the national religious and commercial colonial system.

What finally maintains the balance within the narrative is Wiltshire's narrative point of view. His motivations are virtually identical to Case's and he resorts to violence to remove his competitor as Case is supposed to have done with Wilshire's predecessors Vigours, Adams and Underhill, thus suggesting the triumph of corporate colonialism over what might be called pioneer colonialism after a struggle that initially favoured the former. While Case uses Uma it is clear she enters into the arrangement satisfied with a trader husband however fraudulently contracted. Wilshire's knowledge of the fraudulent nature of his marriage is more culpable as he is fully willing to make Uma his sexual dupe when given the opportunity by Case. His later commitment to her is arguably a matter of circumstance driven by a need to cement alliances in a life-threatening struggle. This oddly parallels Case's domestic arrangements which are alluded to early in Wiltshire's frame narrative: 'I know but one good point to the man – that he was good to his wife, and kind to her. She was a Samoa woman, and dyed her hair red – Samoa style; and when he came to die (as I have to tell of) they found that one strange thing – that he had made a will, like a Christian, and the widow got the lot' ('Falesá' 103). That Wilshire's domestic arrangements come to mimic Case's is reinforced by the open admiration he initially felt for him before the nature of their commercial rivalry became fully known. While it is clear from the frame narrative that Wiltshire has children with Uma, it is not made clear whether he draws up a will in her favour. By virtue of the finely calculated subjectivity of the first-person narrative it is hard not to accept him as the moral force in the story; even though Wiltshire is no middle-class paragon, he does present himself as the representative of Western trade, civilization and, if reluctantly, the reassertion of missionary influence. As a result the narrative shines a strong light on the affect and operation of the secondary institutions of empire often obscured, in political terms, by the symbolism of the 'civilising mission' and, in narrative terms, by the conventions of adventure. The drama of the story is a microcosm of what J. A. Hobson in his 1900 study *Imperialism* would condemn as the 'essentially illicit nature of this use of public resources of the nation to safeguard and improve private investments' (Hobson 20). Of course a missionary society and a trading company are hardly 'public resources' in the grand sense, and Hobson's target were the machinations of Rhodes and others in South Africa at the turn of the century, but in the South Pacific the missionary societies and trading companies did represent the colonial establishment much of the time. The moral approval sought by Wiltshire's narrative rests upon these shaky foundations and goes to the heart of the intense criticism of colonialism represented by this tale.

One overt signal of that criticism is the absence of any dignity among the Western characters. Ruthlessness there is, however, aplenty. Uma is the obvious example of the contrast, but so too is the village council to whom Wiltshire takes his case of taboo. They respond to his condescending, ignorant rant in a manner that even he recognizes as 'easy and genteel' but 'stern underneath' at odds with his opinion 'that they haven't real government or real law, that's what you've got to knock into their heads; and even if they had, it would be a good joke if it was to apply to a white man. It would be a strange thing if we came all this way and couldn't do what we pleased' ('Falesá' 122). It is, of course, the white men whom have no real government in this story, thence the rather tawdry *ad hoc* violence to protect commercial and religious advantages. As noted, Tarleton lends tacit support to Wiltshire's violent confrontation with Case with evident satisfaction and is quick to capitalize on the murder despite administering burial rites for him: 'Mr Tarleton prayed, which I thought tomfoolery, but I abound to say that he gave a pretty sick view of the dear departed's prospects' ('Falesá' 167).

Namu too is far from cowed by Tarleton's admonishments over the influence of Case. While he comes materially under Case's thrall and accepts his word on supernatural powers, this is, as noted, little different from the ground on which Tarleton wields influence from an Islander perspective which this narrative brings to the fore so well. Though Namu is recognized as a gifted individual by both Tarleton – 'no one could hear him preach and not be persuaded he was a man of extraordinary parts' ('Falesã' 136) – and Wiltshire – 'he was a gun at his business' ('Falesã' 119) – he also shares Uma's ability of logical deduction and discernment when he challenges Tarleton over his use of the Catholic practice of signing the cross as a protection against the 'Evil Eye', a superstition that Case has taught him. If, he reasons, such a practice is present in Europe and he has been taught that all things European are superior; his adoption of the practice is fully justified ('Falesã' 136–7). It is telling that his logic brings him to the opposite conclusion to Uma who rejects the symbolism of the Bible in the context of the island, whereas Namu justifies the adoption of a symbolic practice which exposes the inconsistency of the colonial message. Both Uma and Namu see through the use of such arguments to justify the expediency of the moment rather than any true enlightenment or moral superiority.

As noted in the introduction, there is a long tradition of reading Polynesians as noble savages which perhaps lies at the back of Uma's and Namu's characterization as they are both attractive individuals. This is certainly true of Stevenson's most immediate literary precursor in the Pacific Herman Melville whose *Typee* twins this paradisal image with cannibalism. Here, as in earlier factual and fictional accounts of the Pacific, there is an unusual admixture of the realistic and the idyllic which provided a remarkably resilient literary model extending well into the twentieth century if not to the present. For Stevenson, perhaps in recognition that his desire for the ethnographic and scientific in *In the South Seas* is discursively unsustainable given the weight of this tradition, he finally seeks truth in his increasingly realistic if not naturalistic fiction rather than ethnographic travel writing to bring out the implications of the colonialism that followed and hid behind that tradition. As he wrote to Sidney Colvin: ['The Beach of Falesã'] is the first realistic South Sea story; I mean with real South Sea characters and details of life; everybody else who has tried, that I have seen, got carried away by the romance and ended in a kind of sugar candied sham epic, and the whole effect was lost – there was no etching, no human grin, consequently no conviction' *Letters VII* 161). However, Stevenson owes rather more to that tradition that his letter might suggest. For all their quiet dignity and relative logic, the Islanders perform the function of providing a foil for an analysis of Western behaviour and institutions. Yet this reverse is not unlike the introversion of a modernist sensibility focused on the savage within. Certainly the 'ethnographic and scientific' gaze of Stevenson's narrative is turned wholly upon the Western residents of Falesā through a narrative point of view that creates a division along racial and class line ironically exposing the Western characters as barbaric. Indeed, it is that outlook which is the subject of the narrative, not the life and manners of the Islanders. Indeed, all the Western characters in this story are variously ethically, morally or physically wanting, often all three. Case and Wiltshire viciously compete with each other for control of the local trade, a microcosm of the competitive principle of capitalism; Tarleton is a hypocrite willing to encourage and profit from Wiltshire's violent struggle with Case while preaching peace and forgiveness to the Islanders. Galuchet the local Catholic missionary is 'so dirty you could have written with him on a piece of paper' ('Falesā' 115), and then there is Captain Randall:

In the back room was old Captain Randall, squatting on the floor in native fashion, fat and pale, naked to the waist, grey as a badger, and his eyes set with drink. His body was covered with grey hair and crawled over by flies; one was in the corner of his eye – he never heeded; and the mosquitoes hummed about the man like bees. Any clean-minded man would have had the creature out and once and buried him; and to see him, and think he was seventy, and remember he had once commanded a ship, and come ashore in smart togs, and talked big in bars and consulates, and sat in club verandas, turned me sick and sober. ('Falesā' 106)

This description not only points to the end point of the dissolute life Wilshire has been living in his previous posting amid bouts of drinking, but also Western authority utterly debased. As a former merchant captain he is also directly associated with colonial institutions and the trade which is its *raison d'être*.

Previous chapters have explored the interconnection between images of degeneration, illness, empire, trade and class that are focused on Captain Randall. Taken as the reworking of an older tradition of representing the South Pacific as simultaneously savage and noble, Stevenson is reaching towards an essentially modernist aesthetic. As Rod Edmond argues:

The 'empty cisterns and exhausted wells' of Europe needed replenishment, but what flowed in from outside was unsettling, untreated and possible contaminating. The disturbing implications of suspect relief were registered and analysed in representations of the metropolitan city, which came to be seen in terms of the kind of physical, moral and social collapse typical of the representation of colonial environments. Common to both was the threat to hierarchy, whether from visible forms of ethnic and class-based challenge in colonised territories and cities of Europe, or the more secret against of degeneration ... One of the threatened hierarchies was that of European culture itself, whose terminal condition modernism diagnosed and mourned. In this was the culture of modernism became entwined with the politics of imperialism. (Edmond 2000 59–60)

'The Beach of Falesā' shows us not the threat of degeneration, but a degeneration that is already internalized by the Western characters whose links to the metropole – Case's urban suavity, Wilshire's representation of the Blackfriars published Bible as a product of metropolitan authority – are clearly marked as a contamination of a relatively civilized colonial other. Unlike Conrad's *Heart of Darkness* where it is an exposure to the primitive psyche and primal bush that awakens Kurtz's savage subconscious, Stevenson's vision resembles what T. S. Eliot would later say of the achievement of Baudelaire's dark vision: 'the possibility of fusion between the sordidly realistic and the phatasmagoric, the possibility of the juxtaposition of the matter-of-fact and the fantastic fully realised at the periphery of Western Civilisation as well as at its dark heart' (Eliot 126).

Captain David Grief

While utterly different in their outward tone and literary aspirations, London's cycle of stories about Captain David Grief published as *A Son of the Sun* (1912) dwells upon very similar themes to 'The Beach of Falesā' but from a different perspective. The disparity between Western ideals of bringing civilization and prosperity to the world at large and faith in the white man's racial superiority is severely exposed, not by an episode of violent and ultimate petty trading dispute, but by a grand sweep of commercial interest embodied in an improbable trader-superman, David Grief. On the face of it, Grief might be superficially read as a triumph of the Western imperial and racial myth in the South Pacific; fantastically successful and wealthy, yet governed by ethics and valuing the region and people through an open admiration for at least some of their traditions and integrity:

> As the golden tint burned into his face it poured molten out of the ends of his fingers. His was the golden touch, but he played the game, not for the gold, but for the game's sake. It was a man's game, the rough contacts and fierce give and take of adventurers of his own blood and half the bloods of Europe and the rest of the world, and it was a good game; but over and beyond was his love of all

the things that go to make up a South Seas rover's life – the smell of the reef; the infinite exquisiteness of the shoals of living coral in the mirror-surfaced lagoons; the crashing sunrises of raw colours spread with lawless cunning; the palm-tufted islets set in turquoise deeps; the tonic of the trade winds; the heave and send of the orderly, crested seas; the moving deck beneath his feet, the straining canvas overhead; the flower-garlanded, golden-glowing men and maids of Polynesia, half-children and half-gods; and even the howling savages of Melanesia, head-hunters and man-eaters, half devil and all beast. (*Grief* 29)

This passage is a remarkable assemblage of references to a web of contemporary discourses suggesting that London was reaching beyond the popular fiction in which these stories have generally be read or, more accurately, ignored. One critic who has not is Jeanne Campbell Reesman and as she observes, alongside the crudities demanded of the popular yarn of the time, the stories have the capacity to surprise with 'some highly complex, highly ironic insights into race and power on the "stage" of the South Pacific' which rightly suggests that at their best, this collection deserves a close reading (Reesman 1999 151).

To begin with, the mention of Grief's love of the game of commerce, colonialism and crime in the South Pacific recalls both the 'romance' of Loudon Dodd's adventures in the *The Wrecker*, but more broadly Kipling's 'Great Game' from *Kim* in which, as here, participants like Kim and Grief gain much adventure and excitement from 'playing the game' but always underpinned by the serious business of maintaining constant vigilance to maintain colonial power. The 'white man's burden' is just that for Kim and his compatriots demanding high sacrifices and high risk as well as excitement. The allusion is more literal in London's stories: Grief 'plays' at being a colonial adventurer when his great wealth and extended business interests mark him out as a magnate. The extended metaphor in the passage of his 'golden touch', wealth (gold) being attracted to him reinforced by his pigmentation the 'golden tint burned into his face'. He is both idol and playboy. His adventures, then, have a manufactured, fantastic, artificial quality to them cut from the very same mould and cultural stirrings of the comic book superheroes that would emerge some 20 years later. This is an artificiality that exists within the narrative and which is brought to the fore by design. In the title story to the collection, a trader who has swindled from Grief a relatively small sum complains he is 'worth millions and millions, and Shylocking me for what he wouldn't light his pipe with' (*Grief* 9). If the money is inconsequential to Grief why is he still willing to risk his life and take life to recover it? Indeed, the petty sum recalls 'The Beach of Falesá', but whereas to the chaff of empire a small sum reveals the pathetic ruthlessness of the colonial frontier, to Grief it is a game while the 'straightness' that is given as the cause for this persistence emerges as ambivalent. If the violence created for such little gain is robbed of necessity (however tawdry and destructive such necessity may be in practice), what of the spectacle of such tawdriness and violence reduced to a rich man's entertainment. The adventures soon begin to have a self-consciously mapped out quality to them. In an unusual narrative gambit, it is Grief who is the self-conscious author of his own performance of which the contrived quality of game hunting or safari would be the nearest equivalent. It is his choice to play the role of squabbling petty trader, to potentially take life in competition over petty sums for his own experience and entertainment. The self-indulgence of this act is not heroism, but an amoral hubris that covers a joy in the humiliation of his victim and his desperate situation with a superficial ethical heroism. He does not go unchallenged in the stories. The purposeless and ultimately unedifying risk is frowned upon by the captain of Grief's vessel in this story who stands in as a level-headed father figure whom Grief enjoys teasing while eliciting admiration for his daring. His prowess, then, requires an audience which evokes a different sense of masculinity than he intends. As Richard Phillips observes: 'School playgrounds and sports fields, like the settings of adventure stories, were spaces of male pleasure, while they were also spaces in which masculinities and imperialisms were actively constructed' (R. Phillips 83).

In addition to the ruthless adolescence of this behaviour, there is a further echo of Kipling. The 'men and maids of Polynesia, half-children and half-gods' directly echoes the first stanza of 'The White Man's Burden' – 'Your new caught, sullen peoples,/Half devil and half child' (Kipling 323–4). Significantly, however, the 'half devil' has been allocated along racial lines; the darker-skinned Melanesian islanders having this epitaph to themselves with the Polynesian islanders elevated to half-gods. This racial hierarchy is as old as the advent of a significant European presence in the South Pacific in the eighteenth century, as the anthropologist Nicholas Thomas observes: 'Polynesians were upheld by nineteenth-century writers because they had made a step or two closer to our own exalted state of civilisation, and because they displayed some readiness to adopt a variety of Western goods and practices, which Melanesians conservatively and intransigently resisted' (Thomas 1989 31). Of course one might also interpret the conservatism and intransigence as a robust resistance to colonialism and the relative amenability of the Polynesians to the decimation of their cultures and population on many major island groups. Thanks to the tropical sun – to which he has all the 'natural' resistance that London lacked on his *Snark* voyage – Grief's own complexion approaches that of the Polynesians rendering his blond hair and moustache rather incongruous. The point of this passage is to reveal him to be something of a hybrid figure that staves of the horror of going native like Conrad's Kurtz thanks to his association with the noble Polynesian rather than the black, savage Melanesian who is 'all beast', but at the same time is naturalized in this setting to neutralize the reality of colonist as land thief. Kipling's poem is addressed specifically to the advent of post-1898 U.S. imperialism and is a reminder of the significance of this sea change in perceptions of America's international standing. The poem by a British author closely associated with empire provides the link between a well-developed tradition of European colonial discourse that is, it must not be forgotten, new to American letters. Indeed, London is the only significant writer during this period dealing with the issue of American imperialism even obliquely and in a way that reveals its borrowed clothes. The description of Grief as 'English . . . in blood, yet those who thought they knew contended he was at least American born' (*Grief* 28) is ambiguous at best. Is he American or not? With authorities as reliable as 'those who thought they knew', the question is impossible to resolve within the narrative. The United States had no developed Public School tradition that fostered a direct class-based link between the construction of masculinities and imperialism in quite this way, so the connection to an English tradition both textually by the direct references to Kipling's poem, and in Grief's person through his English antecedents is needed to sustain the type of generic colonial adventurer that Grief in outward appearance represents. A similar narrative and discursive process is explored in Stevenson's *The Wrecker* and London's *Adventure*, but the interchange between an American commercial outlook and a public-school imperial masculinity is split between two people – in the former Loudon Dodd and Norris Carthew and in the latter David Sheldon and Joan Lackland.

Yet the deep-rooted need to somehow belong both physically and by convic-tion to a place as the legitimized successor to land that has in fact been usurped is, I would argue, an aspect of settler colonialism which characterizes American history. As noted earlier, the frontier, according to Turner, was both an actual and imaginative place and space that was key in shaping the American national consciousness. While Wiltshire in 'The Beach of Falesä' becomes a reluctant settler in the Pacific, the locale remains an alien place; his customer adversaries to be cheated. Grief is not only the Western trader *par excellance*, but also someone who belongs to the South Pacific both genetically and by temperament: 'Unlike other white men in the tropics, he was there because he liked it. His protective skin pigmentation was excellent. He had been born to the sun . . . David Grief was a true son of the sun, and he flourished in all its ways' (*Grief* 27). Here is a white man who is both the 'natural' successor to the Pacific Islander and their 'natural' superior and, as such, the moral questions of imperialism which had left many an American politician uneasy after 1898 are discursively assuaged. Yet Grief also differs from the Old World colonial adventurer in his ostentatious success and devotion to commerce. British adventurers might quest for treasure and save distressed maidens like the heroes of Rider Haggard's full-blooded novels, or work selflessly in the service of an imperial ideal like Kipling's Kim, but the immensely successful colonial businessman is not the stuff of the British colonial adventure novel. Indeed, E. M. Forster's near-contemporary novel *Howards End* (1910) finds the British business-type rather wanting, and also points to the essential difference of approach. The British imperial businessman rules his commercial empire from afar; London's American variant plays on the ground. Certainly, the graphic, invariably masculine, violence is a basic characteristic of the genre, but Grief's business activities recall the contemporary American robber baron rather than the imperial servant of a colonial order:

> How many millions David Grief was worth no man in the Solomons knew, for his holdings and ventures were everywhere in the great South Pacific. From Samoa to New Guinea and even to north of the Line his plantations were scattered. He possessed pearling concessions in the Paumotus. Though his name did not appear, he was in truth the German company that traded in the French Marquesas. His trading stations were in strings in all the groups, and his vessels that operated them were many. He owned atolls so remote and tiny that his smallest schooners and ketches visited the solitary agents but once a year.
>
> In Sydney, on Castlereagh Street, his offices occupied three floors. But he was rarely in those offices. He preferred always to be on the go amongst the islands, nosing out new investments, inspecting and shaking up old ones, and rubbing shoulders with fun and adventure in a thousand strange guises. (*Grief* 25–6)

This concentration on material success and the care with which Grief is shown to belong in the South Pacific both arise out of concerns specific to the United States as London adapts the colonial adventure genre to the newly imperial nation. Yet his playboy self-consciousness recalls the leisure activities of the American super rich spoofed by Thorstein Veblen in his 1899 *Theory of the Leisure Class*: 'As seen from the economic point of view, leisure, considered as employment, is closely allied in kind with the life of exploit; and the achievements which characterise a life of leisure, and which remain as its decorous criteria, have much in common with the trophies of exploit' (Veblen 44). As was apparent from London's South

Pacific novel, *Adventure*, he sketches a rather ambivalent identity for Americans in this new age of Old World imperialism. The ambivalence is all the more marked by vesting them in a figure so obviously modelled on British adventure fiction, and yet distinguished by specifically American symbols of commercial drive and frontier spirit.

Indeed, several stories largely re-work situations from stories and literary themes by Kipling, Conrad and Stevenson. The result is, as Reesman argues, profoundly ironic, not least because of clear contradictions such as Grief's straightness and the commercial subterfuge by which he hides his trading activities behind a German company in the Marquesas (tensions between Germany, Britain and the United States were marked in the South Pacific). While this may be read as a sign of decline in London's creative ability, the result contributes to the process of adaptation that familiarizes the American reading public with a discursive identity by which an American tradition can inform and inhabit a novel imperial context. For example, the story 'The Devils of Fautino' (*Grief* 82–136) shares a similar general outline with the denouement of Conrad's *Lord Jim* (1900), where a band of murderous, white-led pirates invade and extract a terrible price from a Pacific island which is, in turn, under the protection and implicit leadership of a white man. Reesman reads this story positively as representative of London's 'shifting allegiances in the Pacific [since] Grief is clearly on the side of the natives' (Reesman 1999 156). It is instructive to refer to London's model and map how his adaptation differs and to what end. Conrad's Jim is a tragic figure whose flawed nature, his 'crime' and the legacy of guilt that exiles him from white colonial society leads him to pursue an ideal of the 'civilising mission' paternalistically protecting the weak indigenous population from local 'oriental despots' and their own factionalism bringing stability to an 'undeveloped' society as defined by his own standards. The South Pacific link in Conrad's story is pronounced since the leader of the cutthroats Brown is compared directly with the real South Pacific desperado, 'buccaneer and blackbirder, barrater and bigamist' Bully Hayes. He is representative of a particularly South Pacific tradition of lawlessness which Conrad exploits, much as the beachcomber Case represents an older tradition of exploitation compared with Wiltshire, the representative of a global trading concern. The same tradition lies behind London's story where the villain, Raoul Van Asveld, who represents the equivalent role to Brown, is also a kind of historical throwback: 'I've handled your kind before. We've pretty much cleaned it out of the South Seas. But you are – how shall I say it? – a sort of anachronism. You're a throwback, and we've got to get rid of you' (*Grief* 129). Whereas in *Lord Jim* a morally idealistic but flawed white man attempts to impose order and social justice on a sophisticated multi-ethnic East Pacific island that is rudely interrupted and challenged by the advent of a piratical cutthroat. London's story features the ostensibly untroubled morals of Grief with a homogeneous and admirably courageous Polynesian community – superficially a popular simplification of the complexities of Conrad's plot. The corruption of the pirate interlopers and the test they represent are pronounced in both stories, although in Van Asveld London has created something of a super villain to Grief's super hero who respects his protagonists cunning and ability: 'I am ashamed to say that I under-rated you . . . I took you for a thieving beachcomber, and not for a really intelligent pirate and murderer' (*Grief* 126).

This simplification of the moral and legal implications has the effect of rendering Grief's advent not only as the harbinger of order, but also the advancement of a paternalistic care for the Islanders. In short, the weakness and lack of leadership among the Islanders and the existence of Van Asveld validates Grief's intervention in a single gesture pointing towards the future of imperial intervention by the 'developed' into the 'underdeveloped' world. There is something elegiac in the exchange between Van Asveld and Grief before the final struggle that defines what their roles would have been in the past and the discursive shift that has occurred:

> 'We are both strong men,' Raoul said with a bow. 'We might have been fighting for empires a hundred years ago'
>
> It was Grief's turn to bow.
>
> 'As it is, we are squalidly scrapping over the enforcement of the colonial laws of those empires whose destinies we might possibly have determined a hundred years ago.'
>
> 'It all comes to dust,' Raoul remarked sententiously, sitting down.
> (*Grief* 126–7)

Given that the reader is being presented with the selflessness and grandeur of Grief's physical and moral heroism matched by the equally grand villainy of Van Asveld, the exchange casts them both as anachronisms in the maintenance of international law. The implication of this passage is twofold and undermines the premise of Grief as a concept. The first concerns the exact nature of Grief's – and by implications, Van Asveld's – apparent superiority resting in part of what appears to be a crude appropriation and misreading of Nietzsche's 'overman', the *Übermensch* who fits in well with the frontiersman of American myth and reflects different moralities for 'masters' and 'slaves'. Yet here is a 'master' apparently enforcing the colonial laws that are not his own and serve in equal measure to restrict his freedom of action as well. In fact his moral code seems to be based upon them. Here he is not the superman, but a businessman. Nietzsche argued that the 'great man' was always undermined by mediocrity and the 'virtue of the herd' an idea that became an important idea within the Modernist movement (see Cassuto and Reesman 3). This is contradicted by Grief's character whose power is derived from his commercial acumen and his wealth, a wealth that thrives on and is contingent upon the international order that is the legacy of imperialism. While one might feel relief that the road to fascism is dodged, the road to twentieth-century corporate commerce is opened up – the 'American century' no less. Yet this also undermines any easy identification of Grief as a hero in the superhuman mould that London has cast for him – deliberately so. Grief embodies another Nietzschean aphorism that foregrounds such contradictions: 'We moderns, we half barbarians. We are in the midst of our bliss only when in the most danger' (Childs 57), which seems to anticipate the systemic crises of capitalism. A portent perhaps of the modern Pacific – a battleground, peppered with military bases, and nuclear test site still constructed as a 'holidaymakers' paradise for the Western consumer.

The Ebb-Tide

The Ebb-Tide is Stevenson's last South Pacific fiction completed in June 1893 and must stand as his final word on the colonial South Pacific thanks to his untimely death at the end of 1894. More than any other story by Stevenson *The Ebb-Tide* demonstrates qualities of Modernism, particularly through a focus on turning within in an attempt to create a psychological realism, although both stories equally draw on 'reversions to the "beast" of naturalistic fiction' (Guerard 245). In a perceptive study of the Modernist features of *The Ebb-Tide*, Alan Sandison points to Malcolm Bradbury's elaboration of the psychological realism of early Modernism:

> One of the consequences was a psychological realism, an intensified impress-ionism, a novel of Paterian 'quickened, multiplied consciousnesses'. Another was a heightened concern with authorial consciousness as such, both as a form of apprehension or an artistic awareness, and as a managing instrument, demanding enormous precision of presentation and point of view, increased formalism. These two kinds of novel – the psychological, and the experimental or fictive – both desubstantiated material reality, and they often tend to merge. (Bradbury 123)

While the central protagonists of *The Wrecker*, *Adventure*, 'The Beach of Falesā' and the 'David Grief' stories all share a common focus on the white man in the Pacific, they lack the degree to which the psychological interiority of this late story 'desubstantiates' the generic realism of the narrative in the search for a greater psychological truth. But Sandison's otherwise excellent analysis tends to understate the interplay of class and the forces of capitalism that underpin both Stevenson's and London's colonial South Pacific. Indeed the emergence of global capital charted in their South Pacific writing is a significant driver of the aesthetic developments and crisis of representation evident from Modernism. As Jean-Jospeh Goux argues: 'Was it purely by chance that the crisis of realism in the novel and in painting coincided with the end of gold money? Or that the birth of "abstract" art coincided with the shocking invention of inconvertible money signs? Can we not see in this double crisis of money and language the collapse of guarantees and frames of reference, a rupture between sign and thing, undermining representation and ushering in the age of the floating signifier' (Goux 3). While the abandonment of the gold standard in the West would not occur until World War I thence post-dating Stevenson – and Goux's causality is a rather crude – his point is difficult to dismiss entirely and an intimation of the relationship between the increasingly abstract nature of global capital and representation precipitating a crisis of moral relativism is evident from the symbolism of the mock stock market of Muskeghon Commercial Academy in *The Wrecker*. It is no coincidence therefore that *The Ebb-Tide* features characters adrift in a sea of moral and material relativity in which the subject is agonizingly stripped back to a state approaching 'savage' superstition.

While a very long short story, if not novella, the short story form allows a greater degree of focus and thematic intensification compared with the looser, digressive form of the novel. The story introduces us to three characters in Part One – a Trio – and adds a fourth in Part Two – a Quartette. The three initial characters are all 'on the beach' – to all intents and purposes destitute tramps – in Papeete, Tahiti, French Polynesia. While they are passing themselves off under assumed names even to each other, the narrative introduces them by their actual names – Robert Herrick, John Davis and Huish. The former is a well-educated scion of the English commercial upper-middle class family, attending the University of Oxford before the crash came to his father's commercial interests forcing the family into relative poverty. Davis is a disgraced American merchant captain whose drunken neglect led to the sinking of his ship and several deaths.

Both have washed up on the beach in the South Pacific fleeing the social shame of their incapacities recreating the multiple tensions between Loudon and his father, Loudon and Pinkerton, and Loudon and Carthew. Both express this social stigma in relation to their families. Herrick cannot face the shame of his inability to get and hold onto a job as a clerk to help support the family; a sacrifice his father does make but that his son seems unable to rise to through class-based pride. Davis equally continually returns to the shame he feels for the family he has abandoned following his disgrace, particularly his children though one, his daughter, whom he talks of as if alive is in fact dead, pointing to an incapacity to face reality. Like Loudon Dodd, Herrick has developed a decidedly 'aristocratic' outlook of his expectations and it is possible to discern in his inability to hold down the job of a common clerk, a refusal to come to terms with this collapse in class status rather than simple incapacity. While not exactly covering himself in academic glory at Oxford, he does take a degree pointing to at least a minimal level of application. Yet he differs from Loudon by ensuing the self-justifying criticism of his father's capacity implicitly acknowledging the latter's nobility in putting the family's need before class pride to which he fails to rise. Davis offers both the possibility of a father figure to Herrick and also foregrounds his total lack of credentials for such a role, failing directly as a father to his own family and as in the paternalistic role of ship's captain. As his disgrace in the latter role stems from drink, such a flaw is unlikely to be confined to one role and the implication is that he was a drunken father as well. It is difficult not to think of Captain Randall from 'The Beach of Falesá' as a possible future for Davis given their shared propensity for drink and the latter's downward trajectory. Herrick and Davis are of course also emblematic in the manner of Stevenson's earlier story, with Herrick representative both of British commercial culture and Carthew-like aristocratic capital, while Davis is a commentary on American commercial enterprise.

The 'trio' is completed by Huish, a disgraced cockney clerk which sharply defines the overt class-stratification of the narrative. Everything in the narrative is built to encourage the reader to despise Huish from his ignorance, uncouthness, common accent to the propensity for a particular kind of underhand violence at the climax of the story. He is irredeemable, it seems. Likewise at the beginning of the tale, it is on him that another powerful symbol – disease – falls which is the opening motif of the narrative: 'Throughout the island world of the Pacific, scattered men of many European races and from almost every grade of society carry activity and disseminate disease' (*Ebb-Tide* 1). Of the three, only Huish shares the illness that has become an epidemic among the islanders, the influenza brought to the island on a ship from Peru:

> The disgust attendant on so ugly a sickness magnified this dislike [of the clerk]; at the same time, and with more than compensating strength, shame for a sentiment so inhuman bound them the more straitly to his service; and even the evil they knew of him swelled their solicitude, for the thought of death is always the least supportable when it draws near to the merely sensual and selfish. . . . There is no one but has some virtue: that of the clerk was courage; and he would make haste to reassure them in a pleasantry not always decent. (*Ebb-Tide* 17)

The equation of Western colonial activity and disease was explored in Chapter 4 in relation to Stevenson's and London's South Pacific non-fiction and there, as here, disease breaks down both class and racial boundaries although it is significant that it is only the lower-class Huish who shares in the local epidemic. He also carries the stigma of degeneration that is marked not only by his propensity for disease, but also his stature and complexion having the 'dwarfish person, the pale eyes and toothless smile [of a] bad-hearted cockney clerk' (*Ebb-Tide* 16). Indeed, it is hard not to read in him the product of what John Hollingshead, a staff member of Dickens's *Household Words*, would describe among the slum courts of London: 'The faces that peer out of the narrow windows are yellow and repulsive; some are the faces of Jews, some of Irishwomen, and some of sickly-looking infants' (Hollingshead 44 (Marriott 123)). There is more than the hint of an amalgam of stock literary stereotypes of urban Jewishness and Irishness in Huish's characterization, and he is arguably the outcome of the 'totally different race of men' that Jack London found among the East End slums (*Abyss* 63), and of course the purveyor of Stevenson's 'truly Cockney baseness' (*Emigrant* 141). The confused hatred and sympathy that Herrick and Davis feel for Huish echo the confused sympathies of paternalistic social reformers for both the poor and the colonized that parallels Judd's reading of the New Imperialism quoted above: 'it was "their" fault that there was trouble and expense, not "ours"' (Judd 232). Yet Huish is also the product of such reforms as presumably the beneficiary of the Board Schools established in the 1870s to which he owes his education and thence subsequent employment as a clerk. In fact, despite his characterization and regardless of his origins, Huish is a representative of a new phenomenon at the turn of the nineteenth century, the lower middle-class clerical worker; a progenitor of Forster's Leonard Bast in *Howards End* (1910) and T. S. Eliot's hapless clerk from *The Waste Land* (1922): 'He, the young man carbuncular, arrives,/A small house-agent's clerk . . ./One of the low on whom assurance sits/As a silk hat on a Bradford millionaire' (lines 231–4). He is, therefore, not strictly working class at all which identifies the source of the dislike felt by Herrick who supplies the prevailing point of view of the narrative; he is close enough to him in terms of occupation to foreground both his origins – his father is 'an intelligent, active, and ambitious man' who had risen (*Ebb-Tide* 12) – and to what he returns when he and his father are reduced to a clerical occupation that they share with the likes of Huish. The comparison is emphasized in the text since they occasionally share the same alias, Hay. Herrick's debility throughout the story is not a particular lack of application which is how he excuses his state, but an unwillingness to acknowledge his fall in class status. This is not unlike Loudon Dodd's refusal to give up his belief in the artistic life through which he can sustain class consciousness in relative poverty. Herrick arguably chooses poverty claiming an inability of application as the means to retain his class distinctiveness rather than acknowledge his fall through work. It is no narrative accident that Herrick carries a well-thumbed copy of Virgil's *Aeneid* and scrawls musical phrases from Beethoven's Fifth symphony on the walls of the abandoned calaboose in which the trio shelter, 'So . . . they will know that I loved music and had classical tastes' (*Ebb-Tide* 40). Equally, his name, Robert Herrick, is identical to the author of Hesperides (1648) which raises the question as to whether he has revealed his true name at all. He has to revile Huish as a symbol of his fall. Yet there is a redeeming characteristic to Huish, his courage which, in the highly adapted adventure narrative from which *The Ebb-Tide* is derived, is the attribute to be valued above all others.

There is also a particularly urban frame to the opening of the narrative focused on Huish and which recalls the urban associations centred on Case from 'The Beach of Falesā' who would 'have passed muster in a city' ('Falesā' 103), and also Wiltshire's attempt to demonstrate his legitimacy to Uma by mention of Blackfriars in London in order to assert his textual power over Case's localized physical symbolism. The opening chapter features a series of fabulous tales which the trio relate in an attempt to distract Huish from his flu symptoms. Herrick begins a tale resonant of the *Arabian Nights* involving an instantaneous transference from the South Pacific to London by means of a magical carpet. His fairy-tale narrative then switches to an extended descriptive pause strong on atmospheric detail:

> The one minute I was here on the beach at three in the morning, the next I was in front of the Golden Cross at midday. At first I was dazzled and covered my eyes, and there didn't seem the slightest change; the roar of the Strand and the roar of

the reef were like the same: hark to it now, and you can hear the cabs and busses rolling and the streets resound! And then at last I could look about and there was the old place, and no mistake! With the statues in the square, and St Martin's-in the Fields, and the bobbies and the sparrows, and the hacks; and I can't tell you want I felt like. (*Ebb-Tide* 21–2)

This is of course ground to which both Herrick and Hay can lay claim. To Huish's disgust, the story quickly leads to the door of Herrick's father which he cannot enter leading to the clerk's outburst 'Well, I think you are about the poorest 'and at a yarn . . . Crikey, it's like Ministering Children!' (*Ebb-Tide* 23). Huish's alternative fantasy consists of a sampling of all the pleasures the metropolis offers to one of his background. Herrick's dose of personal realism is at odds with the form of such tales and the occasion of its telling. After all, the tale telling began with the idea of taking Huish's mind off his illness, but instead becomes a vehicle for Herrick to self-indulgently reproduce the topic of his own despair. A further version of this episode is repeated in Chapter Two when Davis returns from a consultation with the American Consul with pencils and writing paper for them to compose letters home. The divergence between Herrick and Huish follows the same trajectory when Herrick, unable to address his parents directly, writes to his former fiancée asking her to convey his apologies and regret; while Huish writes to a barmaid he met in Northampton boasting of how he is living the high life among the 'hislands' of the South Seas (*Ebb-Tide* 38). Both Herrick and Davis round on Huish in disgust, but who is in the right here? If sent the self-indulgent expressions of regret by Herrick and Davis must do little to console those whom they have abandoned, while Huish at least provides himself and the others with distraction. They are all lying but one does so self-consciously and harms no one. Yet as Vanessa Smith observes: 'His pronunciation slurs the Pacific islands with the Scottish Highlands that were the setting of Stevenson's own romances. . . . However, in the era of Pacific colonialism romance is figured as degenerate' (Smith 158). Indeed, this discursive merging of the colonial motherland with the colonial periphery mirrors the passage above, where the distinction between the sounds of the Pacific and the bustle of the city is descriptively slurred as 'the roar of the Strand and the roar of the reef'. Figuratively, both 'slurs' collapse the discursive distance between the colonial and colonized, between centre and margin, between capital and the practicalities of trade and commerce to which they are all linked.

Romance of course is Loudon Dodd's particular preoccupation and a discursive mode that *The Wrecker* does much to undermine. It is a mode from which

Stevenson's later work consistently moved away in tone and import even as its framework remained in his writing. In *In the South Seas* he was to reflect on an encounter with the despotic chief of a closed island from whom he was soliciting access (the chief rightly surmising that letting in traders and missionaries would ultimately undermine his own authority), his conclusion resonates in this, his final South Pacific fiction. The chief agrees to admit Stevenson and his party on the grounds, 'I look your eye. You good man. You no lie' on which Stevenson comments: 'a doubtful compliment to a writer of romance' (*South Seas* 218). So, if romance is little more than lying, then this is exactly the sense that Huish uses it but as Smith notes, this is a degenerate form in the hands of a character that has been invested by implication with all the turn-of-the-century anxieties of racial, class and cultural degeneration. But other than this demonization by class signifiers, how is Huish any worse than Herrick? It is Herrick that Davis deliberately tries to bring on board with his schemes often leaving Huish in the dark on the assumption that he will follow. This creates the impression in the narrative that Herrick alone has scruples to be overcome, but he always capitulates. When Davis is offered the command of a disease-ridden schooner – the captain and first mate have died of smallpox ironically contracted on an unknown island which they had visited in a drunken rampage (echoes of Wiltshire's 'drunks' here, perhaps), the spreaders of disease become its victims – he soon falls in line with his plan to steal it and the cargo of Californian wine. Later discovering that the cargo is itself an insurance fraud being mostly bottles of water, he again falls in line when Davis proposes blackmail in echo of Loudon's relationship with Carthew. Finally, when they make landfall on a mysterious pearling atoll, he agrees to try and persuade the owner to surrender his pearls under Davis' threat of violent robbery otherwise. It is this threat of murder and the equivocal attraction of the planned victim that finally persuades Herrick to switch sides. While Huish falls in with all these plans he is a follower; Davis is the active element as he has been throughout Part One of the story and Herrick the knowing collaborator. Huish's role, excluded and diminished by the others, is relatively passive beyond his search for pleasure until the conclusion.

The encounter with Attwater, the fourth character making up the Quartette of Part II, represents a further amalgam of character types already encountered in Stevenson's and London's writing and is a further intensification of the underlying themes of class and colonial commerce:

> He was a huge fellow, six feet four in height, and of a build proportionately strong, but his sinews seemed to be dissolved in a listlessness that was more than

languor. It is only the eye that corrected this impression; an eye of an unusual mingled brilliancy and softness, sombre as coal and with lights that outshone the topaz; an eye of unimpaired health and virility; an eye that bid you beware of the man's devastating anger. A complexion, naturally dark, had been tanned in the island to a hue hardly distinguishable from that of a Tahitian; only his manners and movements, and the living force that dwelt in him, like fire in flint, betrayed the European. He was dressed in white drill, exquisitely made; his scarf and tie were of tender-coloured silks; on the thwart beside him there leaned a Winchester rifle. (*Ebb-Tide* 113–14)

Attwater's physical presence and complexion recalls directly London's David Grief which there as here is a colonial fantasy of naturalized Western power. Yet where in the David Grief stories the adventure motif remains upper hand and, however unconvincingly, ameliorates the brute force and rapaciousness of the global capital he personifies, there is something far more sinister in the force that Attwater represents. There is the hardness of his gaze and the threat of 'devastating anger', and as Alan Sandison notes there is something of Conrad's company clerk from *Heart of Darkness* in his maintenance of immaculate Western dress. In Conrad's narrative the clerk is an incongruous projection of Western commercial administration in the jungle of the Congo; indifferent to the crisis of the suffering and dying Africans around him of which his immaculate dress is symbolic of the indifference of commerce to the human cost of profit, he is still a clerk. Here, as with David Grief, a symbol of Western commercial administration is wed to the superman from the colonial adventure genre, joining a no less pronounced indifference to suffering with oppressive power. The gun of course further symbolizes this oppression in a similar manner to the maintenance of Sheldon's power over his plantation workers in London's *Adventure*. Not surprisingly we learn later that Attwater never misses, or rather always expects to hit his target. Yet unlike Sheldon and his susceptibility to illness, Attwater is distinguished by 'unimpaired health and virility' even though his islander workforce has been devastated by smallpox. Attwater ostensibly represents authority and power, but how successfully? Hannah Arendt argues that authority is derived from respect and power is derived from the group (Arendt 44–5). Attwater is, without question, an extreme individualist so his power is not collective but derives from the threat of violence represented by the gun. If violence is the lynchpin of his authority, that authority is not based on respect, but fear.

Yet what is missing is an ideology so it comes as no surprise to learn that he is also a fanatical missionary who has ruled his island with all the ruthlessness of a vengeful god. Indeed, Sandison argues that 'A hierarchical structured reality and the assumption of a necessary connection between word and thing come with Attwater's creed and they suggest an analogy with the claims of realism in fiction to represent reality' (Sandison 342–3). This is certainly the case insofar as he galvanizes the force of authority and power to socially polarize the trio by class. Within minutes of boarding the ship, Huish self-identifies his humble origins and Herrick betrays that he attended university: 'The presence of the gentleman lighted up like a candle the vulgarity of the clerk; and Herrick instinctively, as one shields himself from pain, made haste to interrupt . . . Attwater leaned to him swiftly. "University man?" . . . "Yes, Merton," said Herrick' (*Ebb-Tide* 115). Of course, Herrick's 'pain' is a class-based embarrassment over the company he is keeping and is highly suggestive of why he shuns his own kind in his avoidance of work. It is also an early indication of why he is bound to betray Davis and Huish for Attwater: 'Herrick was embarrassed; the silken brutality of their visitor made him blush; that he should be accepted as an equal, and the others thus pointedly ignored, pleased him in spite of himself, and then ran through his veins in a recoil of anger' (*Ebb-Tide* 116). He is also the only one of the trio to fully comprehend the insult that Attwater is handing out wreathed in the subtleties British social codes and is both flattered and angered as a result. Given subsequent events, the anger is less than genuine and is more likely indicative of the guilt for the betrayal that he subconsciously anticipates. The subsequent dinner replicates the dynamics of this initial encounter. Huish is blind to the social codes by which he is denigrated and mocked, Davis perceives the slights but is more or less incapable of countering them, while Herrick conceives a horror for all that Attwater reflects back to him of his class. A class status that he is unwilling to forego symbolized by the musical phrase and Latin he scrawls on the calaboose wall in Part I, but is unwilling to unsentimentally act directly to maintain that status and the violence and oppression it necessitates. Much as Huish represents a parvenu lower middle class still driven by working-class desires, Herrick not Attwater represents the vast majority of upper-middle class and upper-class beneficiaries of empire at several removes unwilling to recognize the violence and exploitation by which their position is sustained. Davis and Attwater in their different ways represent this active side of empire: one, the trading captain is persistently revealed to be a crook despite his manly, open facade, while the other is a megalomaniac behind the poise of a gentleman and moral rectitude of a missionary. The usually subsumed elements of both identities are pointedly and uncomfortably exposed in this narrative. Action for both is first and foremost informed by commercial gain and violence of which David Grief was the fairy tale to their direct ruthlessness. It is by narrative design that Davis is the only one of the trio to openly admire Attwater's ability to control an islander workforce of over thirty with the ideology of religion and the absolute force of his gun and it is he who ultimately becomes Attwater's convert.

While Herrick manages to maintain his pretence of diffidence throughout the story – the conclusion finds him ready to drift on without being caught by or growing as a consequence of what he has experienced, perhaps like many contemporary readers of the story – it is the fate of Huish that has the greater significance. When Davis explains to him how Attwater has systematically insulted him, he is spurred to violent retribution and demonstrates for the first time an agency that his courage has promised throughout the narrative. While substantively dismissed through an encoded class perspective dominated by Herrick's point of view throughout the narrative, his is the role of the hero of romance spurred to active violence not for gain, but by the insult to his self-respect which is conspicuously lacking in the other members of the trio. The fine calculation that Davis makes in turning to Huish is revealing: 'Rage, shame, and the love of life, all pointed the one way; and only invention halted: how to reach him? Had he strength enough? Was there any help in that misbegotten packet of bones against the house?' (*Ebb-Tide* 176). Davis consciously manipulates Huish to provide the means to carry out his design to try and murder Attwater for his pearls without directly exposing himself prompted by 'love of life'; a parable of manipulative commercial competition in the South Pacific as the lower-class Huish is goaded into carrying out the dirty work. It is also hard not to perceive the national colonial struggle that has run through many of London's and Stevenson's South Pacific texts as Davis is of course American and Attwater British. Their particular moral failings are caricatures of their respective national commercial styles. Moreover, there is an overwhelming hypocrisy in Davis' horror at the means that Huish proposes to gain this end – to blind Attwater by casting vitriol into his face – 'it's too damned hateful' (*Ebb-Tide* 183). Unable to compete with Attwater's physical strength or his firepower, Huish resorts to guile. Yet while the narrator describes his strength – 'the villainous courage and readiness of the creature shone out of him like a candle from a lantern' (*Ebb-Tide* 184) – that courage is still 'villainous' and Huish is not a man but a creature, a characterization that reeks of class prejudice. The narrative voice, often associated with Herrick's point of view, does not operate as such in this scene since Herrick is now absent from the trio and aligned with Attwater. The expression of this moral horror, therefore, has an authority that is at odds with the conclusion of the narrative. Huish is sacrificed, Herrick drifts onwards more or less unchanged and Attwater triumphs over Davis. The narrative voice of the story has no platform on which to sustain an authoritative moral stratification and this demands a reading against the grain of its false presumptions about Huish. This is where the moral resolution expected of realism collapses to become something else. Indeed, the sacrifice of Huish's character is a moral and narrative fudge which brings crisis but little resolution of the questions raised by the story, and is no less than a trope of class and colonial struggle. As Arendt argues: 'In a contest of violence against violence the superiority of the government has always been absolute; but this superiority lasts only as long as the power structure of the government is intact . . . When this is no longer the case, the situation changes abruptly' (Arendt 48) – Huish is a failed image of resistance to the authority invested in Attwater and his form of government which remains intact subsuming Davis and approving of Herrick's self-neutering. That by no means makes Huish a saint and he is a peculiar sacrificial lamb, but that is the particular insight of this story: it is the suppression of the newly educated masses at home and throughout the empire that hinges emblematically on his death and the failure of that resistance. It is a fitting prophecy for the conflicts of the twentieth century suggesting the representational crisis associated by Goux above with the abandonment of the gold standard and therefore absolute value which is shown to have a much earlier origin on the front line of empire.

Afterword

The South Pacific in the Twentieth Century

By contrast to the dense literary construction of the nineteenth-century colonial South Pacific that is the focus of Stevenson's and London's writing, twentieth-century Western perspectives on the region are curiously ephemeral. It is ephemeral in the sense that the Pacific becomes an arena in which certain experiences are staged, or a bowl to be traversed to another point on the bustling 'rim'. In the former construction, the modern Pacific is variously a space in which to realize a holiday in paradise, or to wage a quasi-colonial war, to test nuclear weapons, or to provide an exotic backdrop for movies. It is the Pacific as theatre, from a theatre of war to Rodger and Hammerstein's *South Pacific* and Elvis Presley's gyrations, or the cinematic space for the numerous adaptations of the *Bounty* mutiny to unfold on the big and small screen. Of course it is only the 'centre' that evokes this performative space in contrast to the economic frission of the Pacific Rim economies that rage and burn despite the temporary setbacks of recessions and collapses. This Pacific is the descendant of America's open-door policy towards China, a place to traverse to reach the teeming markets of the tiger economies of the East – a 'bowl' with a gilded rim but a curiously empty container (excepting the 'hard' economic outpost of America in the Pacific – Hawaii). But a container for what – the predominantly white settler nations? They are certainly *in* the Pacific, but hardly *of* the Pacific unless one refers their displaced indigenous inhabitants. They prefer to see themselves as part of the 'rim' rather than belonging to the voided, fantasized, fought-over, exploded centre.

So what is this 'space'? A cultural signifier, certainly, but not a *post*-colonial signifier. It is a space no longer filled-up by indeterminable Western words. The eighteenth-, nineteenth-, and twentieth-century discursive Pacific – of which Stevenson and London were arguably the high point – no longer exists. The Hollywood blockbuster or throbbing Technicolour musical, the exceptional holiday experience or the underground rumbling that still echoes from Mororou Atoll are poor substitutes. So what is this 'empty' Pacific we are left with? It is a space of sights rather than sites. As Jack London observed in *The Cruise of the Snark*:

> There are hosts of people who journey like restless spirits round and about this earth in search of seascapes and landscapes and the wonders and beauties of nature. They overrun Europe in armies; they can be met in droves and herds in Florida and the West Indies, at the pyramids and on the slopes and summits of the Canadian and America Rockies . . . Honolulu is six steaming hours from San Francisco; Maui is a night's run on the steamer from Honolulu . . . Yet the tourist comes not, and Haleakala sleeps on in lonely and unseen grandeur. (*Snark* 112)

Surprisingly little has changed of the movements of 'restless spirits' other than they come in ever-increasing numbers to the South Pacific. The tourist guide and the navigational map have become the signifiers of the South Pacific. Even the abstraction of international boundaries or the hard truths of military bases fail to fill the conceptual gap between this and the commercial fantasies of a commodified Pacific. Henri Lefebvre argues: 'When codes worked up from literary texts are applied to spaces . . . we remain, as may easily be shown, on the purely descriptive level. Any attempt to use such codes as a means of deciphering social space must surely reduce that space itself to the status of a *message*, and the inhabiting of it to the status of a *reading*' (Lefebvre 7). The Pacific of the nineteenth and early twentieth centuries was a literary text, a text that was at its most complex in Stevenson's and London's writing. In their hands it was a form that demanded ever deeper, ever more detailed readings until the economic and cultural exploitation of the South Pacific which had been occluded come ever more to the fore. Yet later in the twentieth century the South Pacific 'text' becomes a code, no longer self-interrogating, never willing to give way to the lived experiences of those who inhabit this space – the message and reading is not theirs. I am not suggesting that Stevenson's and London's writing allow the inhabitants of the Pacific Islands top speak for themselves, far from it. Both writers believed that they must be spoken for, yet their writing allowed for the possibility of lived experiences even if contained, bowdlerized and written out, an after-image in a manner that a sunny vacation or nuclear test are assuredly not.

Stevenson's and London's South Pacific writing is significant not only in revealing the process of how 'we' – the Westernized reader – got from the 'there' of the colonial Pacific to the 'here' of a commodified simulacrum of the modern South Pacific, but a pertinent reminder of those who become ever more elided in the 'post' of our thought. Both authors start from conventional contemporary assumptions about colonialism, commerce, race and class which their texts ultimately reveal to be untenable. The Pacific that enters 'our' so-called post-colonial temporality lacks even an unconscious self-scrutiny since it is constructed according to the events that are 'staged' within it – war, weapons testing and shipping times, despite the statistics of the *Journal of Pacific History*, the anthropologists, and the regional development studies of the United Nations. As Anne McClintock observes:

> The word 'post', moreover, reduces the cultures of peoples beyond colonialism to *prepositional* time. The term confers on colonialism the prestige of history proper; colonialism is the determining marker of history. Other cultures share only a chronological, prepositional relation to a Euro-centred epoch that is over (*post-*), or not yet begun (pre-). In other words, the world's multitudinous cultures are marked, not positively by what distinguishes them, but by a subordinate, retrospective relation to linear, European time. (McClintock 293)

Where is the post/past of the modern Pacific? Colonial history and culture in writing such as Stevenson's and London's still constitute its 'past' while its 'post' exists beyond dry statistics, re-enacting the earlier *la Nouvelle-Cythère* of Bourgainville. How many holiday advertisements echo this preposition: '*C'est la veritable Eutopie?*' (Rennie 89). The 'prepositional time' of the Pacific, the condition on which it enters the *post*-colonial is its pre-history; the colonial period then and now defining a past that is also present. It is a sad truth, I feel, that contemporary representations of what should be the *post*-colonial Pacific (the films, the bomb testing, the vacations) should appear more ephemeral or terrible that the 'solid' history of Stevenson's and London's colonial Pacific.

Bibliography

Achebe, Chinua (1975), 'An Image of Africa: Racism in Conrad's *Heart of Darkness*', *Massachusetts Review*, 18.4, winter, 782–94.

Ahmed, Aijaz (1992), *In Theory: Classes, Nations, Literatures*, London: Verso.

— (1995), 'The Politics of Literary Postcoloniality', *Race & Class*, 36.3, 1–20.

Anderson, Benedict (1991), *Imagined Communities*, London: Verso.

Anderson, Charles (1939), *Melville in the South Seas*, New York: Columbia University Press.

Arendt, Hannah (1970), *On Violence*, Orlando, FL: Harcourt.

Arnold, Matthew (1869), *Culture and Anarchy*, London: Smith, Elder & Company.

Auerbach, Jonathan (1996), *Male Call: Becoming Jack London*, Durham and London: Duke University Press.

Ballantyne, R. M. (1858), *The Coral Island*, London: W. & R. Chambers.

Banks, Joseph (2006) [1773], *The 'Endeavour' Journal of Joseph Banks*, Fairford, AL: The Echo Library.

Barltrop, Robert (1976), *Jack London: The Man, the Writer, the Rebel*, London: Pluto Press.

Beames, Thomas (1850), *The Rookeries of London: Past, Present, and Prospective*, London: Thomas Bosworth.

Becke, Louis (n.d.), *Tom Wallis: A Tale of the South Seas*, London: The Religious Tract Society.

— (1901), *By Rock and Pool: On an Austral Shore and Other Stories*, London: T. Fisher Unwin.

— (1902), *The Strange Adventure of James Shervinton and Other Stories*, London: T. Fisher Unwin.

Beckson, Karl (1992), *London in the 1890s: A Cultural History*, New York and London: W. W. Norton.

Beisner, Robert L. (1992), 'The Imperialists' Case and Failure', in Thomas G. Paterson and Stephen G. Rabe (eds), *Imperial Surge: The United States Abroad, The Early 1890s–Early 1900s*, Lexington and Toronto: D. C. Heath.

Bennett, Frederick D. (1840), *Narrative of a Whaling Voyage Round the Globe, from the Year 1833 to 1836. Comprising Sketches of Polynesia, California, the Indian Archipelago, etc. With an Account of Southern Wales, the Sperm Whale fishery, and the Natural History of the Climates Visited*, London: Richard Bentley.

Berridge, Virginia and Griffith Edwards (1981), *Opium and the People: Opiate Use in Nineteenth-Century England*, London and New York: Allen Lane/St Martin's Press.

Bhabha, Homi (1986), 'Remembering Fanon: Self, Psyche and the Colonial Condition', forward to Frantz Fanon, *Black Skin, White Masks*, London: Pluto Press, vii-xxvi.

— (1994), *The Location of Culture*, London: Routledge.

Booth, Bradford A. and Ernest Mehew (eds) (1995), *The Letters of Robert Louis Stevenson*, 8 vols, New Haven and London: Yale University Press.

Booth, Martin (1997), *Opium: A History*, London: Simon & Schuster.

Booth, William (1890), *Darkest England and the Way Out*, London: The Salvation Army.

de Bougainville, L.-A., (1772), *A Voyage Around the World*, London: J. Nourse and T. Davies.

Bradbury, Malcolm (1991), 'London 1890–1920', in Malcolm Bradbury and James McFarlane (eds), *Modernism A Guide to European Literature 1890–1930*, Harmondsworth: Penguin.

Bradbury, Malcolm and James McFarlane (eds) (1991), *Modernism: A Guide to European Literature, 1890–1930*, Harmondsworth: Penguin.

Bradley, Patricia (2009), *Making American Culture: A Social History, 1900–20*, New York: Palgrave Macmillan.

Brantlinger, Patrick (1988), *Rule of Darkness: British Literature and Imperialism, 1830–1914*, Ithaca and London: Cornell University Press.

— (2009), *Victorian Literature and Postcolonial Studies*, Edinburgh: Edinburgh University Press.

British Parliamentary Papers (1869a), Belmore to Granville, 26th February, Parliamentary Papers 1868–9, XLIII, 408.

— (1869b), Sir Alfred Stephen to Earl Belmore, Sub-enclosure No. 2, Parliamentary Paper 6.

— (1872a), *NSW Correspondence between the governor of NSW and the Earl of Kimberley respecting certain statements made by Capt. Palmer, RN in his book entitled 'Kidnapping in the South Seas'*, House of Commons Paper 43.

— (1872b), *Correspondence respecting the deportation of South Sea Islanders*, House of Commons Paper 43.

— (1872c), *Further Correspondence respecting the deportation of South Sea Islanders, February 1872*, House of Commons Paper 43.

— (1873), L, 244.

Brogan, Hugh (1985), *The Pelican History of the United States of America*, Harmondsworth: Penguin.

Brookfield, H. C. (1972), *Colonialism, Development and Independence: The Case of the Melanesian Islands in the South Pacific*, Cambridge: Cambridge University Press.

Brooks, Peter (1984), 'An Unreadable Report: Conrad's *Heart of Darkness*', in *Reading for the Plot*, Cambridge, MA: Harvard University Press.

Browne, Sir Thomas (1658), *Hydriotaphia, Urn Burial, or a Discourse of the Sepulchral Urns lately found in Norfolk*, London.

Bullock, Alan (1991), 'The Double Image', in Malcolm Bradbury and James McFarlane (eds), *Modernism: A Guide to European Literature, 1890–1930*, Harmondsworth: Penguin.

Calder, Jenni (1979), 'Introduction', *Dr Jekyll and Mr Hyde and Other Stories*, Harmondsworth: Penguin.

Cantile, James (1885), *Degeneration Amongst Londoners*, London: Field & Tuer.

Carr, Helen (1996), *Inventing the American Primitive: Politics, Gender and the Representation of Native American Literary Traditions 1789–1936*, New York: New York University Press.

Cassuto, Leonard and Jeanne Campbell Ressman (1996), *Rereading Jack London*, Stanford, CA: Stanford University Press.

Césaire, Amié (1972), *Discourse on Colonialism*, trans. Joan Pinkham, New York: Monthly Review Press.

Childs, Peter (2000), *Modernism*, London and New York: Routledge.

Chrisman, Laura (1993), 'The Imperial Unconscious? Representations of Imperial Discourse', in Patrick Williams and Laura Chrisman (eds), *Colonial Discourse and Postcolonial Theory: A Reader*, London: Harvester Wheatsheaf.

Clark, Steve (ed.) (1999), *Travel Writing and Empire: Postcolonial Theory in Transit*, London and New York: Zed Books.

Colvin, Sidney (ed.) (1911), *The Letters of Robert Louis Stevenson*, 3 vols, London: Methuen.

Comeroff, Jean and John Comaroff (1991), *Of Revelation and Revolution: Christianity. Colonialism and Consciousness in South Africa*, Chicago, IL: Chicago University Press.

Conrad, Joseph (1989) [1897], *The Nigger of the 'Narcissus'*, Harmondsworth: Penguin.

— (1995) [1899], *Heart of Darkness*, Harmondsworth: Penguin.

— (2007) [1900], *Lord Jim*, Harmondsworth: Penguin.

Cook, James (1968), in J. C. Beaglehole (ed.), *The Journals of Captain Cook on His Voyages of Discovery: The Voyage of the Endeavour 1768–71*, Cambridge: Cambridge University Press.

Crawford, Robert (1987), *The Savage and the City in the Work of T. S. Eliot*, Oxford: Clarendon Press.

Cumpston, Mary, *Indians Overseas in British Territories, 1834–54*, London: Dawsons.

Darwin, Charles (1859), *The Origin of Species by Means of Natural Selection*, London: J. Murray.

Day, Gary (2001), *Class*, London and New York: Routledge.

Dean, Tim (1998), 'The Germs of Empire: *Heart of Darkness*, Colonial Trauma, and the Historiography of AIDS', in Christopher Lane (ed.), *The Psychoanalysis of Race*, New York: Columbia University Press.

Dening, Greg (1980), *Islands and Beaches*, Honolulu: University of Hawaii Press.

Denning, Michael (1987), *Mechanic Accents: Dime Novels and Working-Class Culture in America*, London and New York: Verso.

Denoon, Donald, *et al.* (eds) (1997), *The Cambridge History of the Pacific Islands*, Cambridge: Cambridge University Press.

Dinnerstein, Leonard, Roger L. Nichols and David M. Reimers (1990), *Natives and Strangers: Blacks, Indians and Immigrants in America*, New York and Oxford: Oxford University Press.

Docker, Edward W. (1970), *The Blackbirders: The Recruitment of South Seas Labour for Queensland, 1863–1907*, Sydney: Angus and Robertson.

Dodge, Ernest S. (1965), *New England and the South Seas*, Cambridge, MA: Harvard University Press.

Douglass, Frederick (1845), *Narrative of the Life of Frederick Douglass, An American Slave, Written by Himself*, Boston: Anti-Slavery Office.

Drayton, Richard (1995), *Nature's Government: Science, Imperial Britain, and the 'Improvement' of the World*, New Haven and London: Yale University Press.

Du Bois, W. E. B. (1899), *The Souls of Black Folk*, Chicago: A. C. McLurg & Co.

Easthorpe, Anthony (1996), 'The Two Narratives of the Western', in Gavin Cologne-Brooks, Neil S., and David Times (eds), *Writing and America*, London and New York: Longman.

Edmond, Rod (1997a), *Representing the South Pacific: Colonial Discourse from Cook to Gauguin*, Cambridge: Cambridge University Press.

— (1997b), 'Leprosy and Colonial Discourse: Jack London and Hawaii', *Wasafiri*, 25, Spring 1997, 78–82.

— (2000), 'Degeneration in Imperialist and Modernist Discourse', in Howard J. Booth and Nigel Rigby (eds), *Modernism and Empire*, Manchester and New York: Manchester University Press.

Eliot, T. S. (1922), *The Waste Land*, New York: Boni and Liveright.

Ellis, William (1831), *A Vindication of the South Sea Missions from the Misrepresentations of Otto von Kotzebue*, London: F. Westley and A. H. Davis.

Engels, Friedrich (1999) [1844], *The Condition of the Working Class in England*, Oxford: Oxford University Press.

Faber, Richard (1966), *The Vision and the Need: Late Victorian Imperialist Aims*, London: Faber & Faber.

Forster, E. M. (1910), *Howards End*, Edward Arnold & Co.

Fothergill, John M. (1889), *The Town Dweller*, London: H. K. Lewis.

Foucault, Michel (1977), *Language, Counter-Memory, Practice: Selected Essays and Interviews*, trans. Donald F. Bouchard and Sherry Simon, Ithaca: Cornell University Press.

Furer, Andrew (1997), '"Zone Conquerors" and "White Devils": The Contradictions of Race in the Works of Jack London', in Leonard Cassuto and Jeanne Campbell Reesman (eds), *Rereading Jack London*, Stanford, CA: Stanford University Press.

Furnas, Joseph C. (1950), *Anatomy of Paradise: Hawaii and the Islands of the South Seas*, London: Victor Gollancz.

— (1951), *Voyage to Windward: The Life of Robert Louis Stevenson*, New York: William Sloane.

Gair, Christopher H. (1996), ' "The Way our People Came": Citizenship, Capitalism, and Racial Difference in *The Valley of the Moon*', in Leonard Cassuto and Jeanne Campbell Reesman (eds), *Rereading Jack London*, Stanford, CA: Stanford University Press.

Galsworthy, John (1978) [1921], *To Let*, in *The Forsyte Saga*, London: Penguin.

Giddings, Franklin H. (1900), *Democracy and Empire, with Studies of their Psychological, Economic, and Moral Foundations*, New York: Macmillan & Co.

Gilman, Sander L. (1985), *Difference and Pathology: Stereotypes of Sexuality, Race and Madness*, Ithaca and London: Cornell University Press.

— (1988), *Disease and Representation: Images of Illness from Madness to AIDS*, Ithaca and London: Cornell University Press.

— (1995), *Health and Illness: Images of Difference*, London: Reaktion Books.

Gilmore, Peter (1985), 'Robert Louis Stevenson: Forms of Evasion', in Andrew Noble (ed.), *Robert Louis Stevenson*, London: Barnes & Noble.

Gladstone, William E. (1999) [1855], 'Our Colonies', in Barbara Harlow and Mia Carter (eds), *Imperialism and Orientalism: A Documentary Sourcebook*, Oxford: Blackwell.

Gossett, Thomas F. (1973), *Race: The History of an Idea in America*, New York: Schocken Books.

Grattan, Clinton H. (1963), *The Southwest Pacific to 1900: A Modern History*, Ann Arbor, MI: The University of Michigan Press.

Green, Martin (1979), *Dreams of Adventure, Deeds of Empire*, New York: Basic Books.

— (1991), *Seven Types of Adventure Tales: An Etiology of a Major Genre*, Pennsylvania: The Pennsylvania State University Press.

Gunson, Neil (1978), *Messengers of Grace: Evangelical Missionaries in the South Seas 1797–1860*, Melbourne: Oxford University Press.

Haggard, H. Rider (1989) [1885], *King Solomon's Mines*, Oxford and New York: Oxford University Press.

— (1994) [1887], *She*, Harmondsworth: Penguin.

Hamilton, David M. (1986), '*The Tools of My Trade*': The Annotated Books in Jack London's Library, Seattle, WA: University of Washington Press.

Harlow, Barbara and Mia Carter (eds) (1999), *Imperialism and Orientalism: A Documentary Sourcebook*, Oxford: Blackwell.

Harman, Claire (2005), *Robert Louis Stevenson: A Biography*, London: Harper Collins.

Hart, James (1966), 'Introduction', *From Scotland to Silverado* (including *The Amateur Emigrant* and *The Silverado Squatters*), Cambridge, MA: The Belknap Press of Harvard University Press.

Hawkins, Mike (1997), *Social Darwinism in European and American Thought, 1860–1945: Nature as Model and Nature as Threat*, Cambridge: Cambridge University Press.

Heindel, Richard H. (1968), *The American Impact on Great Britain, 1898–1914: A Study of The United States in World History*, New York: Octagon Books.

Hendrick, King and Irving Shepard (eds) (1966), *Letters from Jack London*, London: MacGibbon & Kee.

— (1970), *Jack London Reports: War Correspondence, Sports Articles, and Miscellaneous Writings*, New York: Doubleday.

Herbert Jr, Tome W. (1980), *Marquesan Encounters: Melville and the Meaning of Civilisation*, Cambridge, MA and London: Harvard University Press.

Herrick, Robert (1648), *Hesperides*, London.

Hillier, Robert I. (1989), *The South Seas Fiction of Robert Louis Stevenson*, New York: Peter Lang.

Hobsbawm, Eric J. (1979), *Industry and Empire: From 1750 to the Present Day*, Harmondsworth: Penguin.

Hobson, Jhon A. (1985) [1902], *Imperialism: A Study*, Ann Arbor, MI: The University of Michigan Press.

Hofstrafter, Richard (1945), *Social Darwinism in American Thought, 1860–1915*, Philadelphia: University of Pennsylvania Press.

Holthouse, Hector (1969), *Cannibal Cargoes*, London: Angus & Robertson.

Hutchinson, John (1994), 'Cultural Nationalism and Moral Regeneration' in John Hutchinson and Anthony D. Smith (eds), *Nationalism*, Oxford and New York: Oxford University Press.

Jackson, Holbrook (1913), *The Eighteen Nineties*, London: Grant Richards.

Jolly, Roslyn (1996), 'Introduction', Robert Louis Stevenson, *South Sea Tales*, Oxford: Oxford University Press.

— (2009), *Robert Louis Stevenson in the Pacific: Travel, Empire, and the Author's Profession*, Farnham: Ashgate.

Jones, Gareth S. (1971), *Outcast London: A Study in the Relationship between Classes in Victorian Society*, Oxford: Clarendon Press.

Judd, Dennis (1996), *Empire: The British Imperial Experience, from 1765 to the Present*, London: Harper Collins.

Karl, Frederick and Laurence Davies (eds) (1986), *The Collected Letters of Joseph Conrad*, Cambridge, MA: Harvard University Press.

Kern, Stephen (1983), *The Culture of Time and Space, 1880–1918*, London: Weidenfeld and Nicholson.

Kershaw, Alex (1997), *Jack London: A Life*, London: Harper Collins.

Kiely, Robert (1965), *Robert Louis Stevenson and the Fiction of Adventure*, Cambridge, MA: Harvard University Press.

Kiernan, Victor G. (1978), *America: The New Imperialism – From White Settlement to WorldHegemony*, London: Zed Books.

Kipling, Rudyard (1994) [1901], *Kim*, Harmondsworth: Penguin.

— (1995), *The Works of Rudyard Kipling*, Ware: Wordsworth.

Knight, Alanna (1986), *R.L.S. in the South Seas: An Intimate Photographic Record*, Edinburgh: Mainstream Publishing.

Kotzebue, Otto von (1830), *A New Voyage Round the World in the Years 1823, 24, 25 and 26*, London: H. Colburn & R. Bentley.

Labor, Earle (1974), *Jack London*, New York: Twayne.

— (1994), 'Introduction', *The Portable Jack London*, Harmondsworth: Penguin.

Ladurie, Emmanuel L. R. (1981), *The Mind and Method of the Historian*, trans. Siân and Ben Reynolds, Brighton: The Harvester Press.

Lee, Ying S. (2007), *Masculinity and the English Working Class: Studies in Victorian Autobiography and Fiction*, New York and London: Routledge.

Linehan, Katharine B. (1990), 'Taking up with Kanakas: Stevenson's Complex Social Criticism in "The Beach of Falesā"', *English Literature in Transition*, 33.4, 406–22.

London, Charmian K. (n.d.), *A Woman Among the Headhunters: A Narrative of the Voyage of the 'Snark' in the Years 1908–9*, London: Mills & Boon.

— (1918), *Jack London and Hawaii*, London: Mills & Boon.

— (1921), *Jack London*, New York: The Century Co.

London, Jack (n.d.), *Captain David Grief*, Honolulu: Mutual Publishing.

— (1977) [1903], *The People of the Abyss*, London: The Journeyman Press.

— (1994) [1903], *The Call of the Wild*, Harmondsworth: Penguin.

— (1970) [1904], 'The Yellow Peril', in King Hendricks and Irving Shepard (eds), *Jack London Reports: War Correspondence, Sports Articles, and Miscellaneous Writings*, New York: Doubleday.

— (1994) [1906], *White Fang*, Harmondsworth: Penguin.

— (1967) [1907], *The Road*, London: Arco Publications.

— (1961) [1908], *Martin Eden*, New York: Holt, Rinehart and Winston.

— (1971) [1911], *The Cruise of* The Snark, London: Seafarer Books.

— (1924) [1911], *Adventure*, London: Mills & Boon.

— (1946) [1911], *South Sea Tales*, Cleveland and New York: World Publishing.

— (1913) [1912], *A Son of the Sun*, Leipzig: Bernard Tauchnitz.

— (1914) [1912], *The House of Pride and Other Tales of Hawaii*, London: Mills and Boon.

— (1915) [1914], *Mutiny of the Elsinore*, London: Mills and Boon.

— (1927) [1914], *The Valley of the Moon*, London: Mills and Boon.

— (1916), *Turtles of Tasman and Other Stories*, London: Mills and Boon.

— (1917), *Jerry of the Islands*, London: Mills and Boon.

— (1949) [1917], *Michael, Brother of Jerry*, London: Werner Laurie.

— (1968), *Jack London and His Times: An Unconventional Biography*, Seattle and London: University of Washington Press.

Loomba, Ania (1998), *Colonialism/Postcolonialism*, London and New York: Routledge.

Lubbock, Basil (1931), *Bully Hayes*, London: Hopkinson.

Lunquist, James (1987), *Jack London: Adventures, Ideas and Fiction*, New York: Unger.

Macaulay, Thomas B. (1999) [1835], 'Minute on Indian Education', in Barbara Harlow and Mia Carter (eds), *Imperialism and Orientalism: A Documentary Sourcebook*, Oxford: Blackwell.

Mackay, Margaret (1968), *The Violent Friend: The Story of Mrs Robert Louis Stevenson 1840–1914*, London: J.M. Dent.

Malinowski, Bronislaw (1922), *The Argonauts of the Western Pacific*, London: Routledge and Kegan Paul.

— (1967), *A Diary in the Strict Sense of the Term*, Harcourt, Brace & World.

Marcus, Laura (1994), *Auto/Biographical Discourses: Theory, Criticism, Practice*, Manchester and New York: Manchester University Press.

Marriott, John (2003), *The Other Empire: Metropolis, India and Progress in the Colonial Imagination*, Manchester and New York: Manchester University Press.

Maude, Henry E. (1981), *Slavers in Paradise: The Peruvian Labour Trade in Polynesia*, Suva, Fiji: Institute of Pacific Studies.

Maugham, William S. (1993), *South Sea Tales*, London: Madarin.

May, Earnest R. (1991), *American Imperialism: A Speculative Essay*, Chicago, IL: Imprint Publications.

Mayhew, Henry (1985) [1851–2], *London Labour and London Poor*, Harmondsworth: Penguin.

McClintock, Anne (1992), 'The Angel of Progress: Pitfalls of the Term "Post-colonialism"', *Social Text*, 31/32, Spring, 1–15.

McClintock, James I. (1976), *White Logic: Jack London's Short Stories*, Cedar Springs, MI: Wolf House Books.

McClure, Samuel S. (1963) [1914], *My Autobiography*, New York: Unger.

McLynn, Frank (1993), *Robert Louis Stevenson: A Biography*, London: Hutchinson.

Mellor, G. R. (1951), *British Imperial Trusteeship 1783–1850*, London: Faber.

Melville, Herman (1950) [1846], *Typee: A real Romance of the South Seas*, Boston, MA: L.C. Page.

— (1969) [1847], *Omoo: A Narrative of Adventures in the South Seas*, New York: Hendricks House.

Menikoff, Barry (1984), *Robert Louis Stevenson and 'The Beach of Falesā': A Study in Victorian Publishing*, Edinburgh: Edinburgh University Press.

Meyer, Susan (1996), *Imperialism at Home: Race and Victorian Women's Fiction*, Ithaca and London: Cornell University Press.

Millar, Richard H. (ed.) (1970), *American Imperialism in 1898: The Quest for National Fulfilment*, New York: John Wiley.

Moore-Gilbert, Bart (1997), *Postcolonial Theory: Contexts, Practices, Politics*, London and New York: Verso.

Morrell, William P. (1960), *Britain in the Pacific Islands*, Oxford: Clarendon Press.

Morris, James (1992), *Heaven's Command: An Imperial Progress*, London: Folio.

Morrison, Arthur (1895), *Tales of Mean Streets*, London: Methuen & Co.

Munslow, Alan (1996), 'Writing History: Frederick Jackson Turner and the Deconstruction of American History', in Gavin Cologne-Brookes, Neil Sammells, and David Timms (eds), *Writing and America*, London and New York: Longman.

Nietzsche, Friedrich (1887), *The Genealogy of Morals*, New York: Boni and Liveright.

Nobles, Gregory H. (1997), *American Frontiers: Cultural Encounters and Continental Conquest*, Harmondsworth: Penguin.

North, Michael (1994), *The Dialect of Modernism: Race, Language, and Twentieth-Century Literature*, New York and Oxford: Oxford University Press.

Oliver, Douglas L. (1962), *The Pacific Islands*, Cambridge, MA: Harvard University Press.

Pakenham, Thomas (1992), *The Scramble for Africa 1876–1912*, London: Abacas.

Palmer, Captain George, R. N. (1971) [1871], *Kidnapping in the South Seas*, Folkstone and London: Dawsons.

Parnaby, Owen W. (1964), *Britain and the Labor Trade in the Southwest Pacific*, Durham, NC: Duke University Press.

Paterson, Thomas G. and Stephen G. Rabe (eds) (1992), *Imperial Surge: The United States Abroad, the Early 1890s–Early 1900s*, Lexington, MA: D.C. Heath.

Pearson, Bill (1984), *Rifled Sanctuaries: Some Views of the Pacific Islands in Western Literature to 1900*, Auckland: Auckland University Press and Oxford University Press.

Peluso, Robert (1996), 'Gazing at Royalty: Jack London's *The People of the Abyss* and the Emergence of American Imperialism' in Leonard Cassuto and Jeanne Campbell Reesman (eds), *Rereading Jack London*, Stanford, CA: Stanford University Press.

Perry, John (1981), *Jack London: An American Myth*, Chicago, IL: Nelson-Hall.

Phillips, Lawrence (1999), 'The Indignity of Labour: Jack London's *Adventure* and Plantation Labour in the Solomon Islands', *Jack London Journal,* No. 6, 175–205.

— (2000a), 'The Canker of Empire: Colonialism, Autobiography and the Representation of Illness—Jack London and Robert Louis Stevenson in the Marquesas', in Laura Chrisman and Benita Parry (eds), *English Association Annual Series of Essays & Studies, 1999: Postcolonial Criticism and Theory*, Cambridge: Brewer, 115–32.

— (2000b), 'British Slavery after Abolition: The Pacific Labour Trade and the Case of the *Daphne*', *Race & Class*, 41.3 (January–March), 13–27.

— (2005), 'The Bourgeois Artist as Social Critic: Discourses of Class, 'Race' and Colonialism in Robert Louis Stevenson's *The Amateur Emigrant*', *Race & Class*, 46.3 (January–March), 39–54.

— (2007a), 'Jack London and the East End: Socialism, Imperialism, and the Bourgeois Ethnographer', in Lawrence Phillips (ed.) *A Mighty Mass of Brick and Smoke: Victorian and Edwardian Representations of London*, Amsterdam and New York: Rodopi, 213–34.

— (2007b), 'Colonial Culture in the Pacific in Robert Louis Stevenson and Jack London', *Race & Class*, 48.3 (January–March), 63–82.

Phillips, Richard (1997), *Mapping Men and Empire: A Geography of Adventure*, London and New York: Routledge.

Pick, Daniel (1989), *Faces of Degeneration: A European Disorder c. 1848-c. 1918*, Cambridge: Cambridge University Press.

Pleseur, Milton (1971), *America's Outward Thrust: Approaches to Foreign Affairs, 1865–90*, DeKalb, IL: Northern Illinois University Press.

Porter, Bernard (1975), *The Lion's Share: A Short History of British Imperialism 1850–1970*, London and New York: Longman.

Pratt, Julius W. (1936), *Expansionists of 1898: The Acquisition of Hawaii and the Spanish Islands*, Baltimore, MD: The Johns Hopkins Press.

Pratt, Mary L. (1992), *Imperial Eyes: Travel Writing and Transculturalism*, London and New York: Routledge.

Ralston, Caroline (1977), *Grass Huts and Warehouses: Pacific Beach Communities of the Nineteenth Century*, Canberra: Australian National University Press.

Reesman, Jeanne C. (1999), *Jack London: A Study of the Shorter Fiction*, New York: Twayne.

— (2009), *Jack London's Racial Lives: A Critical Biography*, Athens and London: The University of Georgia Press.

Reid, Julia (2006), *Robert Louis Stevenson, Science, and the* Fin de Siècle, London and Basingstoke: Palgrave Macmillan.

Reissman, Leonard (1960), *Class in American Society*, London: Routledge & Kegan Paul.

Rennie, Neil (1995), *Far-Fetched facts: The Literature of Travel and the Idea of the South Seas*, Oxford: Clarendon Press.

Richards, David (1994), *Masks of Difference: Cultural Representations in Literature, Anthropology and Art*, Cambridge: Cambridge University Press.

Riis, Jacob (1890), *How the Other Half Live*, New York: Charles Scribner's Sons.

Rimmon-Kenan, Shlomith (1993), *Narrative Fiction: Contemporary Poetics*, London and New York: Routledge.

Romilly, Hugh H. (1886), *The Western Pacific and New Guinea: Notes on Natives, Christian and Cannibal with some Account of the Old Labour Trade*, London: J. Murray.

Ruskin, John (1865), *Sesame and Lilies: Two Lectures, Delivered at Manchester in 1864*, London: Smith, Elder & Co.

Sandison, Alan (1996), *Robert Louis Stevenson and the Appearance of Modernism: A Future Feeling*, London: Macmillan.

Scarr, Deryck (1967), *Fragments of the Pacific: A History of the Western Pacific High Commission, 1877–1914*, Canberra: Australian national University Press.

Schwendinger, Robert J. (1988), *Ocean of Bitter Dreams: Maritime Relations between China and the United States, 1850–1915*, Tucson, AZ: Westernlore Press.

Scott, Walter (1820), *Ivanhoe*, Archibald Constable & Co.

Slagel, James (1996), 'Political Leprosy: Jack London the *Kama'āina* and Loolau the Hawaiian' in Leonard Cassuto and Jeanne Campbell Reesman (eds), *Rereading Jack London*, Stanford, CA: Stanford University Press.

Smith, Howard M. (1975), 'The Introduction of Venereal Disease into Tahiti: A Re-examination', *Journal of Pacific History*, 10, 38–45.

Smith, Vanessa (1998), *Literary Culture and the Pacific: Nineteenth-Century Textual Encounters*, Cambridge: Cambridge University Press.

Snow, Philip A. (1971), 'Introduction' to Captain George palmer R.N., *Kidnapping in the South Seas*, Folkestone and London: Dawsons.

Sontag, Susan (1983), *Illness as Metaphor*, Harmondsworth: Penguin.

Stanley, Henry (1878), *Through the Dark Continent*, London: Harper.

— (1890), *In Darkest Africa*, New York: Charles Scribner's Sons.

Stasz, Clarice (1996), 'Social Darwinism, Gender and humor in *Adventure*', in Leonard Cassuto and Jeanne Campbell Reesman (eds), *Rereading Jack London*, Stanford, CA: Stanford University Press.

Stevenson, Fanny Van de G. (1915), *The Cruise of the* Janet Nichol *among the South Sea Islands*, London: Chatto and Windus.

— (1924), 'Prefatory Note to Robert Louis Stevenson, *The Wrecker*, London: William Heineman.

Stevenson, Fanny and Robert Louis Stevenson (1956), *Our Samoan Adventure*, London: Weidenfeld & Nicolson.

Stevenson, M. L. (1903), *From Saranac to the Marquesas and Beyond*, London: Methuen & Co.

Stevenson, Robert L. (1994) [1883], *Treasure Island*, Harmondsworth: Penguin.

— (1966) [1883], *The Silverado Squatters*, in *From Scotland to Silverado*, Cambridge, MA: The Belknap Press of Harvard University Press.

— (1994) [1886], *Kidnapped*, Harmondsworth: Penguin.

— (1979) [1886], *Dr Jekyll and Mr Hyde*, Harmondsworth: Penguin.

— (1979) [1891], 'The Bottle Imp', in *Dr Jekyll and Mr Hyde*, Harmondsworth: Penguin.

— (1966) [1892], *Across the Plains in From Scotland to Silverado*, Cambridge, MA: The Belknap Press of Harvard University Press.

— (1979) [1892], 'The Beach of Falesà' in *Dr Jekyll and Mr Hyde*, Harmondsworth: Penguin.

— (1924) [1893], *The Wrecker*, London: William Heinemen.

— (1987) [1893], *Island Night's Entertainments*, London: The Hogarth Press.

— (1893), *The Ebb-Tide*, Chicago, IL: Stone & Kimball.

— (1998) [1896], *In the South Seas*, Harmondsworth: Penguin.

— (1926), *Vailima Letters: Being Correspondence from R.L. Stevenson to Sidney Colvin, November 1890 to October 1894*, London: Methuen.

— (1966), *The Amateur Emigrant*, in *From Scotland to Silverado*, Cambridge, MA: The Belknap Press of Harvard University Press.

Stoddard, Martin (1983), *California Writers: Jack London, John Steinbeck, The Tough Guys*, London and Basingstoke: Macmillan.

Stone, Irving (1938), *Sailor on Horseback: The Biography of Jack London*, London: Collins.

Street, Brian (1975), *The Savage in Literature: Representations of 'Primitive' Society in English Fiction, 1858–1920*, London and Boston: Routledge & Kegan Paul.

Streetby, Shelley (2002), *American Sensations: Class, Empire, and the Production of Popular Culture*, Berkeley and London: University of California Press.

Sutton, Martin (1995), *Strangers in Paradise: Adventurers and Dreamers in the South Seas*, Sydney: Angus & Robertson.

Thomas, Nicholas (1989), 'The Force of Ethnography: Origins and Significance of the Melanesia/Polynesia Division', *Current Anthropology*, 30.1 (1989), 27–41.

— (1994), *Colonialism's Culture: Anthropology, Travel and Government*, Cambridge: Polity Press.

— (2010), *Islanders: The Pacific in the Age of Empire*, New Haven and London: Yale University Press.

Trocki, Carl A. (1999), *Opium, Empire and the Global Political Economy: A Study of the Asian Opium Trade 1750–1950*, London and New York: Routledge.

Trotter, David (2001), 'Mummies Boys', *Times Literary Supplement*, 19 January 2001, 12.

Turner, Frederick J. (1996) [1893], 'The Significance of the Frontier in American History', in Gavin Cologne-Brookes, Neil Sammells, and David Timms (eds), *Writing and America*, London and New York: Longman.

Twain, Mark (1923), *Europe and Elsewhere*, New York and London: Harper Brothers.

Veblen, Thorstein (1899), *Theory of the Leisure Class: An Economic Study of Institutions*, New York: The Macmillan Company.

Walvin, James (1993), *Black Ivory: A History of British Slavery*, London: Fontana Press.

Wawn, William T. (1893), *The South Seas Islanders and the Queensland Labour Trade, 1875–91*, London: S. Sonnenschein & Co.

Weisberger, Bernard A. (1987), *Many People, One Nation*, Boston, MA: Houghton Mifflin.

Wells, H. G. (1895), *The Time Machine*, London: William Heinemann.

Wilde, Oscar (1891), *The Picture of Dorian Gray*, London: Ward, Lock & Co.

Williams, Patrick and Laura Chrisman (eds) (1994), *Colonial Discourse and Post-Colonial Theory: A Reader*, Hemel Hampstead: Harvester Wheatsheaf.

Williams, Raymond (1977), *Marxism and Literature*, Oxford: Oxford University Press.

Young, Robert (1995), *Colonial Desire: Hybridity in Theory, Culture and Race*, London: Routledge.

Youngs, Tim (ed.) (1997), *Writing and Race*, London and New York: Longman

Index

Aboriginal Protection Society   135
Aborigines, Australia   130
adventure narrative   47–50, 53–4, 93–8,
        104–5, 115, 121, 123, 134–5,
        141–4, 149, 151, 154, 158, 161,
        171, 179, 185, 188
aestheticism   98, 102–4, 107, 120
Afghanistan   34
Africa   36, 90, 153
African-Americans   162–3
African slave trade *see* slavery
American Civil War 1860–5   42
American dream   114, 157
American Federation of Labor   64
American imperialism   1, 56, 87–8
American Press Association   20
American Revolution   9
Anderson, Benedict   98
Anglo-American War of 1812–15   9, 41
Anglo-Saxonism   3, 8–10, 43–4, 64–5, 96,
        103–4, 106, 108–10, 112, 141,
        153–4
anthropology   13, 48–9, 70–1, 163
anti-Chinese agitation   114, 122
    see also Kearney, Denis
anti-slavery campaign *see* slavery
Antoninus, Wall of   110 *see also* Roman
        Empire
Arabian Nights   185
Arendt, Hannah   123, 188, 191
aristocracy   37, 59, 96, 127–30, 157, 183
Arnold, Matthew, *Culture and
        Anarchy*   37–8
Aryan   9
Asian   90
Atlantic Monthly   158
Auerbach, Jonathan   21–2, 28, 47–8, 51, 61
Augustine, *Confessions*   81
autobiography   76, 81, 84

Balboa, Vasco Núñez de   49
Ballantyne, R. M., *The Coral Island*   141–2

Balzac, Honoré de, *Comédie
        Humaine*   107–8
Banks, Joseph   10–11
Baudelaire, Charles   174
Baxter, Charles   96
Beames, Thomas, *The Rookeries of
        London*   9
Becke, Louis   135
Beckson, Karl   105–6
Beethoven, Ludwig van   185
Beisner, Robert L.   155
Bennett, Frederick   13–14
Berkeley, George, 'On the Prospect of
        Planting Arts and Learning in
        America'   8
Bhabha, Homi   14–15, 89, 169
    'Signs Taken for Wonders'   169
Blackbirding *see* labour trade
Boer War   9, 20, 61–2
Booth, Charles   27
Booth, General William   26–7
        Darkest England and the Way Out   26
Booth, Martin   117
Booth, Wayne C.   139
Bougainville, Louis Antoine de   10–12,
        83, 195
bourgeois   1, 20–1, 23, 30, 46–7, 53–4, 57,
        107, 124–6, 128–9, 164
Boy's Own Paper   142
Bradbury, Malcolm   27, 160–1, 181
Brantlinger, Patrick   115
Brett, George   60
British Empire   9, 56, 87–8, 106, 129, 157
    see also Great Britain
British and Foreign Antislavery Society   135
British and Foreign Bible Society   168
Broadwood, General Robert George   59
Brogan, Hugh   103, 106, 112
Brookefield, H. C.   152
Browne, Sir Thomas, *Hydriotaphia,
        Urn Burial*   125
Bryan, W. J.   62

Bunyan, John, *The Pilgrim's Progress* 81
Burlingame, Edward 76, 93, 95–6
Burns, Tommy 148
Burton, Richartd 52–3

Calder, Jenni 167
California 19, 25, 48, 58, 63, 73, 98, 110, 148, 187
California Gold Rush 1849 110
cannibalism 79, 90, 139, 149, 172
Cantile, James, *Degeneration Amongst Londoners* 59
capitalism 56–7, 173, 182
Carr, Helen 4, 6, 48
Cassuto, Leonard 181
Catholicism 168, 172–3 *see also* Christianity
Celtic 9
Césaire, Amié 131
Charlesworth, Maria Louisa, *Ministering Children* 186
Chicago 5, 7, 101
China 16, 88, 112–13, 116–22, 151, 157, 193 *see also* opium trade
Christianity 13, 168, 171–2 *see also* missionaries
civilising mission 26, 96, 103, 107–8, 114–15, 120, 130, 150, 158, 162, 171, 179
Clark, Steve 74, 160
Cockney 43–5
Colbrook, Claire 134–5
Coleman, William Tell 113
Colvin, Sidney 20, 22–3, 26, 28, 75, 99, 172
Comaroff, Jean and John 170
commerce *see* trade
Common Sense 57–8
Conrad, Joseph 1, 7, 15, 40–1, 43, 46, 48, 69, 75, 79–80, 94–6, 111–12, 118, 131, 133, 151, 158, 174, 177, 179, 188
    Heart of Darkness 1, 7, 15, 46, 69, 75, 79–80, 94–5, 111, 118, 131, 133, 151, 158, 174, 177, 188
    Lord Jim 75, 94, 179
contact zone *see* Pratt, Mary Louise
Cook, Captain James 10–12, 67
Cornhill Magazine 25

Cortés, Hernán de Monroy y Pizarro 49
Cosmopolitan Magazine 60, 72–3
Crawford, Robert 167
Cuba 105, 149
Cunningham, George 143

Daily News 61
Dante, *The Divine Comedy* 81
Darwin, Charles, *On the Origins of Species by means of Natural Selection* 8–9, 88–9, 141, 151–2, 158 *see also* Social Darwinism
Day, Gary 16–17, 21
Dean, Tim 79
decadence 2, 59, 98, 100, 118
degeneration 15–16, 30, 45–6, 61–4, 68, 79, 96, 111–12, 120, 125, 173, 186–7
Derrida, Jacques 69
detective narrative 93–4, 104–5, 121
determinism 88, 91, 156 *see also* naturalism
Dickens, Charles 27, 46, 68, 163
    Bleak House 68
    Oliver Twist 163
disease and colonialism 13, 16, 67–91, 141, 160, 173, 183–4
Docker, Edward, *The Blackbirders* 52, 135–6
Douglass, Frederick, *Narrative of the Life of Frederick Douglass* 138–9

East End (of London) 3, 5, 20–1, 28, 35, 44–65, 79, 184
Edinburgh 27
Edmond, Rod 67, 69, 79–80, 93–4, 173–4
Edward VII 55
Eliot, T. S. 81, 184–5
    Four Quartets 81
    The Waste Land 184–5
Ellis, Havelock 167
Ellis, William 13
ethics 94, 100–2, 107–8, 114–15, 121, 126, 128–9, 131, 148–9, 152, 158, 173–4
ethnography 21, 26, 40, 47, 49, 54, 172–3
eugenics 68
evangelism 167 *see also* missionaries
evolution 125 *see also* Darwin, Charles

Fabian, Johannes, *Time and the Other* 113–14
Fanon, Frantz 36, 146
fascism 181
feudalism 39, 58
Fiji 136
fin de siècle 1–2, 112
First World War 2–3, 9, 16, 163, 182
flâneur 21
Forster, E. M., *Howards End* 178, 184
Fothergill, J. Millar, *The Town Dweller* 59
Foucault, Michel 69, 110
France 3, 118, 152
French Polynesia 118
Freud, Sigmund 33
frontier 6, 87, 89, 112–13, 153–4, 158, 160, 177 *see also* Turner, F. J.
Frye, Northrop 69
Furer, Andrew 140–1, 148

Gair, Christopher 156
Galapagos Islands 77
Galsworthy, John, *To Let* 57–8
Gasalee, Sir Henry 59
Gautier, Pierre Jules Théophile, *Mademoiselle de Maupin* 106–7
genocide 158
Germany 3, 106, 150, 152, 179
Gilman, Sander 5, 68–9
Gissing, George 27
gold standard 182–3
Gompers, Samuel 64
Goux, Jean-Joseph 182, 191
Great Britain 2, 26, 47, 134, 152
great game 162, 175 *see also* Kipling, Rudyard
Greeley, Horace 7
Green, Martin 93
Greenblatt, Stephen 85–6

Hadrian's Wall 111 *see also* Roman Empire
Hakluyt, Richard 74
Hawaiian Islands 11, 77, 80, 105, 122–3, 125, 142, 148, 153, 155
Hawkins, Mike 9
Heart, James 32
Heindel, Richard, *The American Impact on Great Britain, 1898–1914* 7–8

Herrick, Robert, *Hesperides* 185
High Commissioner for the Western Pacific 147
Hobsbawm, Eric 57–8, 117, 127, 129, 157
Hobson, J. A., *Imperialism* 42, 121, 171
Hofstadter, Richard, *Social Dawinism in American Thought 1860–1915* 153
Hollingshead, John 184
Hollywood 12, 193
homosexuality 104
homosocial 144
Hoover, Herbert 27
House of Commons 135
Household Words 184
Hutchinson, John 98
Huxley, T. H. 111–12
hybridity 14–15, 89–90, 112–14, 130–1, 169 *see also* Bhabha, Homi

illness *see* disease
Illustrated London News 166–7
immigration 6
India 38, 117–19 *see also* opium trade
Indian indentured labourer scheme 137, 157 *see also* labour trade
Indian Mutiny 63
Industrial Revolution 5
Irish identity 130–1

James, Henry 78, 94–5
James, William 62
Jameson, Dr Leander Starr 57
Japan 153
Jewishness 163
Johns, Cloudesley 9, 20, 53, 56
Johnson, Jack 148
Jolly, Roslyn 96
Jones, Gareth Stedman 61–2
Journal of Pacific History 195
Judd, Denis 160, 184

Kearney, Denis 113
Kershaw, Alex 58, 74
Kew Gardens 10
Kiely, Robert 40–1
Kiernan, Victor G. 62, 64

Kipling, Rudyard　2, 24, 48, 53, 69, 88, 96,
　　　175–7, 179
　　Kim　53, 69, 175
　　'White Mans' Burden'　2, 4, 88, 153,
　　　175–7
Kitchener, Field Marshall Horatio
　　　Herbert　59
Klondike　60–1, 141 *see also* Yukon
　　　Gold Rush
Kotzebue, Otto von　12–13

Labor, Earle　141
labour trade　16, 73–4, 120, 135–58,
　　　167, 179
Ladurie, Emmanuel Le Roy　90
Lang, Andrew　49
Latin Quarter, Paris　107, 114
Lawrence, Karen　33–4
Lefebvre, Henri　194
leprosy　76–7
Liverpool　5
Lloyd's Insurance Market　115–16, 129
London, Charmian　74–5, 86
　　Jack London　73
London Daily News　60
London, Jack,
　　Adventure　16, 120, 133–58,
　　　177, 179
　　The Call of the Wild　48
　　The Cruise of the Snark　15, 67–91, 72,
　　　133, 176–7, 194
　　'The Devils of Fautino'　179–81
　　Jerry of the Islands　134
　　The People of the Abyss　15, 19, 21–4,
　　　45–65, 72–4, 87, 115, 145, 163
　　A Son of the Sun　174–81
　　The Valley of the Moon　153–4, 156
London, Joan　5, 20
London Missionary Society　13
　　see also missionaries
Long, Edward, *History of Jamaica*　139
Loomba, Ania　12–13, 23–4, 33, 154
Loti, Pierre　85
Lunquist, James　78

Macauley, Thomas Babington, 'Minute on
　　　Indian Education'　38
MacKay, Margaret　32
Macmillan　73

Malay Peninsula　119
Malinowski, Bronislaw　71, 163
　　Argonauts of the Western Pacific
　　　71, 163
　　*A Diary in the Strict Sense of the
　　　Term*　71
Mandeville, John　74
manifest destiny　8, 96, 105, 125, 153
Marquesas Islands　16, 67–91, 118, 125,
　　　130, 178–9
Marriott, John　6–7
Marx, Karl　63
masculinity　104, 123–5, 141, 176–8
Masterman, C. F. G.　60
Mathias, Henry Harding　59
Maudsley, Henry　125
Maui　10 *see also* Hawaiian Islands
Maurice, General John Frederick　61–2
May, Earnest R.　62
McClintock, Anne　195
McClure, Samuel　70
McClure's Magazine　72
McFarlane, James　160–1
McKinley, President William　62
McLynn, Frank　22, 27, 76, 78, 81
Mecca　52
medieval *see* feudalism
Melanesia　79–80, 141, 150, 167, 175–6
melting pot　110 *see also* migration
Melville, Herman　67, 70–1, 76, 79, 85–6,
　　　89–90, 172
　　Omoo,　70–1, 76
　　Typee　67, 70–1, 76, 79, 85–6, 90, 172
Menikoff, Barry　166
Meyer, Susan　145
Michener, James A.　12
　　*Tales of the South
　　　Pacific*　12
Micronesian Islands　110
Midway Island　110, 121, 126, 130
migration　34–44, 67, 88–9, 113, 119–20
Miles, R.　23–4
Millard, Bailey　60, 72
Milton, John　11
mimicry　14 *see also* Bhabha, Homi
miscegenation　89, 166–7
misogyny　142
missionaries　12–13, 16, 67, 71, 135, 165,
　　　169–71, 173, 188–9

modernism 1–2, 5, 15, 17, 31, 95, 160–1, 173, 181–2
Monroe Doctrine 88
Montaigne, Michel de 12
Morris, James 111
multiculturalism 111 *see also* hybridity

nationalism 2, 6, 15–16, 33, 35, 47, 50, 53, 58, 63, 96–7, 105, 129, 146, 154, 156, 159, 190
Native Americans 43–4, 48, 151
naturalism 47–8, 88–9, 95, 172, 181
Nelson, Claudia 104
New Guinea 178
New Hebrides (Vanuatu) 137
New Imperialism 17, 160, 184
New Woman 133, 135
New York 5, 19–20, 42, 47, 63–4, 101, 148–9
New York Tribune 7
New York World 155
Nietzsche, Friedrich 69, 180–1
   The Genealogy of Morals 69
Nobles, Gregory H. 6, 64
Norris, Frank 88
North, Michael 15

O'Sullivan, John 105
Oakland, California 20, 22
Old Testament 55
opium trade 98, 115–25, 130
Orientalism 120, 179
Osbourne, Lloyd 77
Osbourne, Samuel 19
Outing Magazine 72

Pacific Islanders Act 1872 155–6
Parnaby, O. W. 137
Pater, Walter 181
patriarchy 33–4, 38, 84–5, 87, 105, 142–3, 145, 148–9, 156–7, 179–80, 183
Paumotus Islands 178
Peluso, Robert 46–7, 53, 56, 61–3
Philippine Islands 4, 88, 105, 149, 155
Phillips, Richard 32, 48–9, 104, 135, 176
picaresque 96
plantation labour system 134–58
Plesuer, Milton 4
Plummer, Herbert 1st Viscount 59

Polynesia 10, 12, 14–15, 70–1, 79–80, 96, 145–5, 161, 165–8, 170, 172, 175–6
postcolonial 193, 195
Pound, Ezra 4
poverty 7, 46–7, 108, 147
Pratt, Mary Louise 23, 30, 48, 85, 109–10, 113
proselytization *see* missionaries
prostitution 167
Puerto Rico 105
Purchas, Samuel 85–6

Queen Victoria 56
Queensland 136, 147

racism 113, 131, 133–58, 166, 169
realism 41, 96, 108, 172, 181–2, 186, 189, 191
Reesman, Jeanne 59–60, 133, 175, 179, 181
Reissman, Leonard 4, 6
Rennie, Neil 10–11, 71, 80–1, 83, 195
Rhodes, Cecil 57, 171
Rider Haggard, Henry 48, 69, 141–2, 178
   King Solomon's Mines 69, 142
   She 142
Riis, Jacob, *How the Other Half Lives* 28
Rimmon-Kenan, Schlomith 95, 100, 134
Roberts, Lord Frederick 59
Rodgers and Hammerstein, *South Pacific* 12, 193
Roman Empire 110–12, 165
Rousseau, Jean-Jacques 12
The Royal Society 10
Ruskin, John 33, 105–6

Said, Edward 52–3, 88, 105
Salvation Army 26 *see also* Booth, General William
Samoan Islands 78, 130, 170–1, 178
San Francisco 16, 22, 63, 77, 109–16, 120
   Chinatown 120
   earthquake 73
Sandison, Alan 95, 181–2, 188–9
Scarr, Deryck 151
Schwendinger, Robert 42, 119
Scotland 25, 110–11, 186
Scott, Sir Walter, *Ivanhoe* 39
Scribiner's Magazine 76
Second World War 8, 12

Seymour, Admiral Sir Edward Hobart   59
Shorter, Clement   166
Showalter, Elaine   93–4, 142
Sinclair, Upton, *The Jungle*   7
Slagel, James   88
slavery   7, 16, 64–5, 73–4, 89, 135–58, 167
Smith, Vanessa   83, 99, 164, 186–7
Social Dawinism   2, 6, 38, 73, 153, 155,
      158 *see also* Darwin, Charles
socialism   22, 47, 49, 52, 56, 60, 64
sociology   33, 47, 54
Solomon Islands   73–4, 133–58, 178
South Africa   62
Spanish-American War of 1898   2, 4, 6,
      62, 88, 147, 149, 153, 155, 177–8
Spencer, Herbert   125 *see also* Social
      Dawinism
Stanley, Henry   26–7
   In Darkest Africa   26, 45–6
   Through the Dark Continent   26
Stasz, Clarice   133–4, 139, 144–5, 149, 154
Stevenson, Robert Louis,
   The Amateur Immigrant   15, 19–44, 65,
      70, 72, 74, 88
   The Beach of Falesā   75, 161–75, 177
   The Black Arrow   39
   'The Bottle Imp'   167, 169
   The Ebb Tide   75, 81, 86, 91, 95, 160,
      181–91
   From Scotland to Silverado   3, 8,
      19–44, 106
   In the South Seas   15, 67–91, 108,
      117–18, 125, 165, 172, 187
   An Inland Voyage   70
   Island Night's Entertainments   167
   'The Isle of Voices'   167
   Kidnapped   41
   New Arabian Nights   22
   'A Note on Realism'   41
   *The Strange Case of Dr Jekyll and
      Mr Hyde*   51
   Travels with a Donkey   19, 22, 70, 81
   Treasure Island   41, 75, 141
   The Wrecker   16, 93–131, 133, 161,
      177, 186–7
Stoddard, Charles Warren   76–7
   The Lepers of Molokai   77
Street, Brian   139–40
Strunsky, Anna   5, 47

Subaltern   169
Suffragettes   2
Swindells, Julia   76
Sydney   114, 129, 178
syphilis   11

taboo (*tapu*)   164–6, 171
Tahiti   10–13, 83, 182–3, 188
Thomas, Nicholas   74, 176
Thomas, Nigel   167–9
Thomas Cook & Son   45–6, 115
The Times   95
trade   36, 93–131, 173, 187–8
Transatlantic Slave Trade *see* slavery
travel writing   74–91
Trobriand Islands   163
Trocki, Carl A.   117–20
Trotter, David   2
Turner, F. J., 'The Significance of the
      Frontier in American History'
      7–8, 64, 154, 156–8, 177
Twain, Mark   56, 62

United Nations   195
United States   2–5, 24, 26, 39, 50, 62, 64,
      105–6, 122, 127, 134, 148, 152–3
   and class   6–7, 39, 50–1, 62–3, 127

Veblen, Thorstein, *Theory of the Leisure
      Class*   178–9
violence   49, 59, 64, 69, 88, 93–4, 96,
      104–5, 107, 113, 123–4, 129,
      130–1, 136, 138, 140–1, 143, 148,
      150, 155–6, 170–1, 173, 178, 183,
      187, 189–91
Virgil, *Aeneid*   185

Wall Street   101
Wallis, Samuel   83
Washington, George   10
Waugh, Evelyn   96
Wawm, William   150–1
Weisberger, Bernard A.   64
Wells, H. G., *The Time Machine*   59
Whitechapel   50–1
Whitehall   58
Whitman, Walt   102
Wilde, Oscar, *The Picture of Dorian
      Gray*   107

Williams, Raymond   3, 31, 159
Wordsworth, William, *The Prelude*   81

yellow journalism   151
'yellow peril' *see* anti-Chinese
         agitation

Youngs, Tim   75
Yukon Gold Rush   1, 20, 22, 48

Zola, Émile   25, 95
    L'Assommoir   25
Zululand   34